WHAT EVER HAPPENED TO THE AMERICAN DREAM

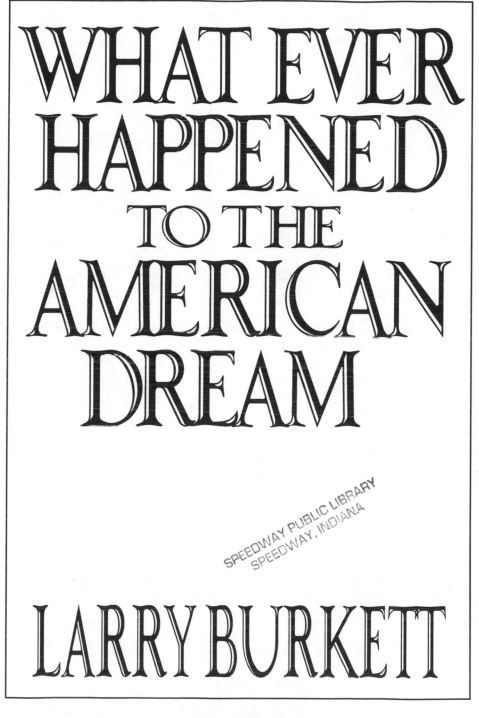

WHAT EVER HAPPENED TO THE AMERICAN DREAM

LARRY BURKETT

MOODY PRESS
CHICAGO

Contents

Acknowledgments 7
Introduction 9
1. Where Are We? 15
2. Defining the American Dream 27
3. Our Heritage 39
4. What's Killing Our Economy 51
5. Trends in Government 65
6. OSHA: The Inside Indicator 77
7. EPA: The Outside Regulator 91
8. The Global Warming Myth 105
9. The Hole in the Ozone Myth 113
10. The War Against the World's Hungry 127
11. Blueprint for Disaster 139
12. Regulation by Litigation 155
13. The Litigation Lottery 169
14. The Aging of America 181
15. Defining the Problem 197
16. How Bad Can It Get? 207
17. A View of the Future 221
18. National Solutions 237
19. Local Solutions 255
20. Preparing for the Worst 265
Notes 279
Appendix: Resources 285
Index 293

Acknowledgments

This was one of the most difficult books I have ever written. As I got into the research I realized it would most certainly be the most controversial book I've written because of the environmental issues. I would sincerely like to thank several people, without whose help this task would have been virtually impossible.

Adeline Griffith, my editor, who spent countless hours editing and re-editing the manuscript, while working on at least four other projects simultaneously.

Joseph Slife, my researcher, who checked and rechecked the facts presented in this work.

Congressman Dan Burton (R–IN), who helped with contacts within the government.

Congressman Tom Delay (R–TX), who leads the battle against abusive regulation in Washington.

And I especially appreciate the courageous cadre of scientists referenced in this book, who risk their reputations and their jobs to deliver the truth to the American people.

Thanks to the great people at Moody Press, who are willing to take the flack that a book like this is sure to generate. I have never worked with a more committed and cooperative group of people.

And special thanks to my wife Judy, my family, and the staff of Christian Financial Concepts, who put up with my irritability as I found myself confronted with the reality of what is being done to our country. It was only in the last edit of this book that I finally calmed down enough to change the words stupid, dumb, and corrupt to misguided, misinformed, and blind.

It is my prayer that the readers of this book will sense the danger that is confronting our economy, our society, and especially our children—and then do something about it!

Introduction

When I completed *The Coming Economic Earthquake* in 1991, I assumed I would not be writing anything further on our economy. I am, after all, a teacher on personal finances—not an economist. The first time I realized I had to write something further was after I had been asked to address a group of representatives from Congress in 1992 on how the economy affects the average family. This is one area I understand very well since those are the people I speak to and teach on a daily basis.

One of the real shocks came after my presentation when a well-seasoned congressman commented, "If what you have shared with us is really true, why aren't more people upset?"

That's a very good question. Why *aren't* more people upset? Obviously the 1992 elections demonstrated that a lot of people are concerned about the economy but, in reality, the majority were upset about the short-term economic problems they were experiencing. In other words, they were concerned about their *jobs* but not necessarily about the state of the U.S. economy in general.

Ross Perot helped to focus on the bigger issue of the national debt and the growing deficits, but even that stimulus has proved to be relatively short-lived. Most of our politicians *say* they are concerned about the debt and deficits but, when faced with the harsh choices necessary to bring the deficits under control, they aren't willing to pay the price.

Let me share something that demonstrates just how pervasive this problem really is. In February of 1993 I was asked to speak to a group of first-term members of Congress, along with a group including Senator Warren Rudman (retired); Les Lenkowsky, president of the Hudson Institute; John White, director of the Kennedy School of Government; and other leaders in the fight for responsible spending in the government.

Each of us presented a different side of the deficit issue, but the commonality was that all of the speakers recognized the need for immediate action to reduce spending at the federal level and start a realistic plan to reduce the overall debt.

After nearly two hours of presenting facts and figures, the chairman of this meeting, Congressman Dan Burton of Indiana, asked for comments or questions from the floor. One of the new members stood up and said, "I hear what you say, and I agree with most of it; but it won't make any difference. There are too many special interest groups in America who feed at the 'federal trough' to expect any real change."

He then went on to explain that he had been appointed to the House Appropriations Committee, which allocates the funds necessary to run the House functions. He had been a congressman only thirteen days at that point and was already disillusioned by what he had seen.

"We can't even agree to cut our own internal budget," he said. "When I first arrived I was excited to hear that the appropriations committee had already agreed to cut congressional spending. That is until I understood what the term 'cut spending' really means up here.

"Last year the Congress spent nearly $2 billion on its internal functions. So I logically assumed that a cut meant we would spend less than last year. Not so. This year the committee allocated an extra $200 million for operating the House. They then decided to reduce that amount to $100 million, thus effecting a budget cut of $100 million.

"In other words, we will spend an additional $100 million over last year, but save $100 million in the process. And the members actually believe that is a cut!"

His comments pinpoint the problem with bringing the federal budget process under control. In Washington its called "smoke and mirrors" economics. Allocate an increase, shave some of it off, and call it a budget cut.

But before we indict those in Washington we must first face the fact that, other than the amount spent to operate the Washington offices and the federal facilities around the world, the majority of the spending takes place to the benefit of the American public. We are the recipients of their federal largess. Until we stop demanding more benefits from the federal Treasury, the problems will persist and expand.

The more information I gather on the depth and breadth of our problems, the more I have come to realize that there are many other things that *can* be done, but nothing of any consequence that *will* be done to avert what appears to be an inevitable economic collapse in America.

There are things that each of us can do to help ourselves, and certainly there are things that we can do together, such as vote out the "big spenders." But time is of the essence, and unless some real changes are made quickly we'd better be planning *now* how we can help each other when this house of debt collapses around us. In the latter part of this book I'll provide a plan of action for what we can do, individually and collectively.

In preparing for this book, initially I focused my attention on deficits and debt, but I quickly realized the problems we face are not just related to the debt and deficits. In fact, the debt is merely a *symptom* of a much greater issue.

I came to realize that even if we were able to balance the budget tomorrow and eliminate the entire federal debt in the next five years, we couldn't halt the slide of our country. America is under siege by a committed group of extremists who probably don't even realize they are destroying our economic system. Our way of life is under the greatest moral, social, and economic assault in history, and it probably began in earnest shortly after World War I.

During World War I, millions of American GIs were exposed to the amoral values of the European communities and, upon returning home, the "doughboys" spread these values like a virus throughout our nation.

We can see the effects of immorality on the generation of the twenties, then later that of the thirties, when Americans surrendered much of their freedoms (and ours) to the growing federal government. World War II only served to strengthen the role of the federal government and to spread the amoral values of the European community to millions more American soldiers.

The apparent resurgence of family values after World War II was merely a spiritual interlude that began to fade rapidly as more and more Americans were disciplined in humanism through our public universities. The teachings of Dewey, Nietzche, Marx, and Lenin became the dominant theme on the campuses. We can see this clearly in the "me" generation of the sixties and seventies.

All this time the church and the Christian community were "asleep at the switch." The growth of church attendance duped both pastors and laypeople into thinking that Christianity was a growing influence. All the while, Christian influence was steadily being eroded, both in the educational system and in the government.

Even the resurgence of "values" during the Reagan era was little more than a brief interlude at the White House. Virtually all the gains made in the area of morality and deregulation of the government were cosmetic and are being dismantled quickly under the liberal influence that is back in control of Washington. Those who were forced back into the academic world while Reagan held office have returned to Washington and are stepping up their agenda with a vengeance.

Christian values will come under assault in the next few years as never before in the history of our nation. The platform for this assault has been prepared well in the public schools and universities of America.

Even a casual observer of American history has to be shocked at how far the American concept of right and wrong has degraded in just one generation. Abortion is legal, "safe sex" is taught as being normal in our schools, drugs now dominate life in the cities (and the suburbs), adultery is no longer an issue in national politics, homosexuality is rapidly becoming an acceptable lifestyle, and Christianity is a forbidden doctrine in nearly all areas of government—even on the public streets in some areas.

The American Dream has definitely changed since I was growing up in the fifties. The change has been more than just economic and it affects more than just jobs and material things. Unless we get out of our complacency, the American Dream for our grandchildren will be a nightmare. They will lose their right to worship in public, attend Christian schools—perhaps even hold down jobs. I guess I've always believed that Christians could be persecuted in America. I didn't realize until I assimilated all this information just how *imminent* that possibility is.

What is bringing the church into direct conflict with the secular humanists today is not how we worship—or even how we live our lives. They would tolerate our having one wife or husband, attending our private church services, even speaking out against sin; after all, they now control the public schools and have more direct contact with American youth than most of us do. What they will not tolerate is Christians interfering in their plans to "enlighten" our society on social issues and their goal of returning the Earth to its "natural" state. This involves their ultimate objective: population control.

Population control is the stated (not implied) objective of the Planned Parenthood abortion movement, the environmental movement (at least the radical side), and the rapidly growing New Age movement. Ultimately population control comes down to economics. The more people there are, the more ways the pie must be divided. According to the activist theory, the way to keep the population down is to keep much of the Earth in its natural (undeveloped) state.

If the rest of the world were as productive as the U.S. is in growing food, our planet could support several times the existing population. Such an idea terrorizes those who hold human life as less important than returning the planet to its "natural" state. The radicals have launched an all out assault on modern technology and industry, which is a large part of why the American Dream is fading.

Some of the facts I discovered in the process of preparing for this book are so incredible they were difficult for me to believe; yet they are easily verifiable.

Lest you think that I've slipped over into the conspiracy movement mentality, I have not. I still believe the people who are planning and funding these efforts are selfish, greedy people who, having had their basic needs (and a lot more) met, would now like to close the door on more people, particularly the impoverished of the world, and stop them from spoiling their landscapes.

The programs these extremists groups promote will have the effect of lowering the living standards for all of us, but especially our children. If we don't wake up *now*, we'll find ourselves living in the Dark Ages again.

The battle we are fighting is spiritual as well as material. Those who would destroy our way of life are totally dedicated to their agenda. Unless we are equally dedicated to God's agenda, *we will lose*.

The platform for a government-controlled society is being prepared with each new government regulation. Once the American people have been convinced that the government should manage their lives, the rest of the world will follow.

It is difficult to write about environmentalism because the very idea that someone might disagree with the environmental movement labels him or her a "radical rightwinger" in the media. But this is not a book about environmentalism. It is a look at what has happened to the American Dream; and our growing debt, declining morals, increasing crime, low quality schools, and abusive environmental regulations are simply a part of that story.

I know that most Americans would rather believe everything is well. But, everything is *not* well. And the longer we wait to get organized and involved, the more entrenched the enemy becomes. Individually, we can easily be defeated; collectively, we cannot.

Also we must remember always that the *Lord* is our strength! *"Thus says the Lord, cursed is the man who trusts in mankind and makes flesh his strength, and whose heart turns away from the Lord"* (Jeremiah 17:5).

CHAPTER ONE

Where Are We?

Over the last several years the term "American Dream" has become more and more commonplace in the media. Often it is used to describe the vanishing opportunities for the current generation of younger workers. For instance, one television anchorman commented, "Young people today are facing an economy in which their lifestyles will be lower than that of their parents for the first time in our history. The American Dream is fading."

He went on to say that a typical high school graduate in 1972 had more job offers than a college graduate in 1992, and the prospects for the next ten years looked even dimmer.

What this commentator said is generally true: There are fewer jobs, or at least fewer good-paying jobs per capita, than there were in 1972. But what he didn't address is why. Much of the media today focus on the failure of the government to provide these jobs through some type of federal works program. Of course they also attack the politicians for failing to allocate enough tax dollars to solve this problem.

What most people fail to understand is that the problems of the diminished American Dream go much deeper than just jobs, and no amount of government spending can resolve the real problems. In fact, government spending is a part of the problem. America is not losing just jobs; our nation is losing its heritage—both moral and social.

We, as a people, are facing some enormous challenges and problems of our own making. In reality, the short-term economic problems we face are not more severe than those faced by previous generations of Americans. In fact, in many ways they are actually less severe. A brief study of the eighteenth century reveals our country was destitute and on the brink of collapse. The nineteenth century saw more Americans die in the Civil War than in all the external wars of the twentieth century, and the post-Civil War period plunged millions of Americans into total poverty for nearly a decade.

Even the Great Depression of the thirties saw a virtual collapse of the world's economies. Millions of Americans slept in tents, begged for their food daily, and owned nothing but the clothes on their backs.

The difference between those generations and ours is a basic attitude called "hope." The people of past eras had confidence (hope) that things would get better and faith that God was still with them. On the other hand, we live in a generation that has been subjected to so much media brainwashing that government, not God, is our resource. And hope is waning.

If we really believe that the federal government is our last great hope, we should be discouraged. I can assure you, based on the testimonies of those who for many years have seen the inner workings of our government, if that's where our hope lies, we're in real trouble.

We are facing some severe economic challenges in the next decade that will test the very ability of our republic to survive. If the country is plunged into depression and then hyperinflation (as the government attempts to print its way out of debt), I believe we can easily have anarchy in the streets of our cities.

We, the people, have been led down a very dangerous path by the media and by our political leaders, who apparently believe federal control is the best policy. At the same time, the media have consistently belittled and undermined the ability of the government to govern. More government is apparently acceptable only if a politically correct social agenda is promoted. If not, then violence is presented as an acceptable alternative to majority rule. We are perilously close to a situation in which violence will dictate policy. If and when the economic situation gets bad enough, the biggest danger is that even the normal, law-abiding citizens may take to the streets—first to protest, then to riot.

It is entirely possible that a severe economic disaster will further undermine our government. After all, any government rules by consent. A quick review of history reveals that those in authority who forgot this lesson learned the hard way. I pray we will not repeat the mistakes of the past.

In truth, there are many able politicians who understand the problems, have a good grasp of what needs to be done to resolve them, and are diligently working to make the necessary changes; but they are clearly in the minority at this time.

Virtually every elected official who is not either senile or senseless understands the basic problems facing our nation, and most understand what it would take to fix them. The difficulty comes in them finding a way to deal with the problems without losing their jobs in the process. For instance, most Americans say they want a balanced budget until a politician talks about reducing Social Security growth or shutting down the military bases in their towns; then they roar in anger and threaten to fire the scoundrel.

Politicians also know that when they go back home to run for reelection, the debate with their opponents won't center around how fiscally responsible their actions were for the country as a whole. They will center around what "bacon" they brought home to their district.

The true cost of continuing our huge government deficits is not reflected in just the annual interest paid. The real cost is much more subtle: less economic growth and fewer jobs.

There is a simple truth known throughout financial circles: Government and industry are competitors in the credit markets. Each dollar consumed by the government is a dollar not available to start or expand a business. This is especially true since the government has the ability to create laws that restrict lending to businesses (while expanding their own ability to borrow), as well as raise taxes, which further drains private resources.

The federal debt and the resultant annual deficits are like the two-fold problems of barnacles and rust on a ship's hull. The barnacles (debt) slow the ship down and create more drag. The rust (deficits) eats away at the structure and weakens it.

If allowed to run their course, the barnacles will eventually create so much drag that the engines will burn out; and the ship will stop. Then the rust eventually eats through the hull; and the ship sinks. All of this can be avoided by regular cycles of dry docking (economic recession), scraping the hull (paying off old debt), and repainting (buffering the economy from the government).

Our problem is that most Americans really don't want to pay the price that debt repayment will cost. Nor do they want to get the government out of managing the economy since 70 percent of all government expenditures go directly to them. The fortunate few who are reaping the majority of the benefits apparently would prefer to see the whole economy die rather than give up their largess. For them the American Dream is college loans, FHA loans, farm subsidies, welfare, aid to dependent children, Social Security, Medicare, Medicaid, and a host of other "entitlement" programs.

I am reminded of how natives in the Philippines catch monkeys. They build a wooden box with a hole in it just large enough for a monkey to reach inside. Then they tie the box securely to a tree and place an orange inside. When the monkey sticks his hand in and grasps the orange, he cannot withdraw his clenched fist while holding the orange. His natural greed (once he has the orange) keeps him trapped until a native comes to collect him. Many Americans similarly have their fists clenched around government money.

There are several basic factors working against the American Dream today. Some can be altered through good, logical planning; others are cast in stone and cannot be altered by anyone—except God. The following diagram shows some of these converging factors that are changing the structure of our economy and, ultimately, our lives.

Five factors are theoretically alterable (political considerations notwithstanding). We can (1) reduce the debt, (2) increase industry, (3) increase national savings, (4) reduce the regulations, and (5) reduce the number of lawsuits (in theory at least). But what can be done about our aging population? Or the lack of younger workers to pay taxes? Or the increasing cost of health care for the aged and for AIDS? In reality, not very much.

I could have added several more factors that will converge before the end of this decade, but I trust you see the problem: The American Dream is going to turn into the American nightmare—and then some—if immediate actions are not taken!

The problems we face are not without solution. An educated public is the best defense against a wasteful, over-regulating government.

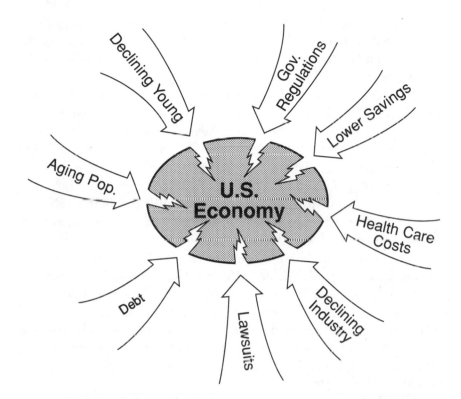

But if no real changes are made to correct our economic problems, I would suggest you adopt an aggressive economic "bomb-shelter" mentality. When you construct a bomb shelter you pray that it will never be needed. Building a bomb shelter that is never used is a waste of money, but needing a bomb shelter that was never built is a lot worse.

We should all work to correct as many of the problems as possible but also work diligently to develop plans to ride out the storm that now appears inevitable.

God's Word clearly tells us that our strength lies in unity. *"Two are better than one because they have a good return for their labor"* (Ecclesiastes 4:9). The plans I will outline require individual effort, but group *application*, for them to succeed.

Every writer uses a different technique in outlining a book. I work from only a brief outline of the topics or chapters I want to cover. Then I gather articles from a wide variety of sources and file them in individual folders. These articles usually become the foundation for the contents of the book.

This particular book was difficult only from the standpoint that I had too much material available. My problem was condensing the available information into a few general topics that could be discussed intelligently. Allow me to share a "for instance."

I believe the real problem America is facing is *spiritual*, not *financial*. It is directly related to our turning away from God as a nation. This began shortly after World War I but became public policy with an ill-conceived notion from the Supreme Court in 1962 that the Constitution mandates a separation of church and state. Historical evidence demonstrates that nothing is further from the truth. The framers of the Constitution intended only that the federal government not be allowed to establish an official "state" religion, such as had been established in England.

Obviously a whole book could be written on this one aspect of our lost dream and still not do it justice. However, since my primary purpose is to evaluate the economic decline of America, I elected to omit much of the data dealing with our spiritual, moral, and political decay. However, all three absolutely are interrelated, and when our nation strayed away from God's path morally, the government and the economy, burdened by the myriad of self-interest programs, merely tracked along the same path.

Clearly there was no one wise enough in the founding of this nation to have blueprinted our economic success. Even after nearly four decades of irresponsible spending at every level, we still have the largest economy and one of the highest standards of living in the world. It seems clear to me, however, that if we continue down this path, God's blessings will be withdrawn from our country. And why not? We kill millions of unborn children primarily for economic reasons.

We teach our children that nothing is immoral; then we spend billions to control the diseases they contract.

We use welfare to promote illegitimate births; then we wonder why the family structure is breaking down in the inner cities.

Our kids see murder, sex, and violence glorified in virtually every Hollywood movie; then we wonder why so many of them take guns to school, use drugs, and commit suicide.

Thomas Jefferson warned the generations to come that they should never take the largess offered by their government. And he specifically warned that the government should never be viewed as the provider, lest it also become the policymaker. Jefferson once wrote: "I place economy among the first and most important virtues and public debt as the greatest of dangers. . . . We must make our choice between economy and liberty, or profusion and servitude. If we can prevent the government from wasting the labors of the people under pretense of caring for them, they will be happy."

Presidents from George Washington to Calvin Coolidge warned about the dangers of taking public monies to support private citizens. Congressman Davy Crockett stood on the floor of the House and shouted down those who would have taken American tax dollars to support a Revolutionary War veteran's widow. Instead, he proposed that members of the Congress agree to help her from their own resources but not rob the public coffers— no matter how just the cause.

President Grover Cleveland forfeited a second term in office rather than sign a bill that would have taken tax dollars to facilitate an orphanage in New York.

These men knew what we are just now beginning to prove: Once the Treasury is opened to the public, there are no limits to the "needs."

Only a nation as wealthy as ours can afford to squander its resources—material and human—as we do. Americans spend billions of dollars a year on pornography, vile movies, drugs, sex, and violence. These pleasures come with a high price: more prisons, more welfare, barred windows, assault weapons to defend our homes, teen suicides, divorce, higher taxes, and a constant demand for more and better tranquilizers to endure the pressures of daily life.

The American Dream has always been that each generation could, if they worked hard, live better than the generation that preceded them.

Is there hope? Absolutely! But the hope doesn't lie in Washington, D.C. The rise of Ross Perot as a presidential candidate in 1992 was evidence that many Americans are looking for strong leadership to rescue them. But we need to be careful, lest we get it! Remember the lesson of the Jews who demanded a king. God warned that a king would rob them, enslave them, and make servants of their sons and daughters. Still they cried out for a king, so God gave them one: Saul.

Americans tried the route of a strong leader who promised to get them out of the depression that gripped the country in 1932. Franklin Roosevelt campaigned under the banner of more government intervention in the economy. When he was elected he did exactly what he promised: to put the government in charge of the finances of America.

With the best of intentions the groundwork was laid for virtually the only way anyone could take away the basic freedoms of the American people: from the inside. Just look around at almost any area where the federal government has assumed authority, from welfare to Social Security, and it can be traced back to the New Deal administration. Some people would obviously say that the average American is better off as a result of this government intervention but, in reality, no one is better off by allowing someone else to provide for them what they can, and should, provide for themselves.

Once the federal government assumed the role of protector and provider for the general public, the role of the church diminished proportionately until, today, few Americans see the church (and God) as their financial resource in times of need.

Lyndon Johnson's Great Society thrust the federal government into the role of total provider, even of the most basic needs: food and shelter. But without the tempering influence of God's Word at the heart of the program, the Great Society quickly broke down the basic structure of the family and morality.

What started out to be a government program to eliminate poverty quickly became a multi-billion-dollar boondoggle promoting slothfulness, immorality, and political greed. Almost every government welfare housing project in the country became a magnet for the lazy and irresponsible, as well as the truly needy. Instead of helping the needy, the welfare programs simply trapped them at the bottom of the economic ladder—in public housing units controlled by pimps and drug dealers.

The black family unit that had survived 150 years of slavery was decimated in less than 30 years by welfare payments that stopped if the family structure remained intact.

Based on that "sterling" success, the government then launched out into the private business sector, surrounding it with federal agencies and regulations designed to "protect" the American workers and, more recently, our environment. I am convinced that the failure of the welfare program has been duplicated in virtually every area where the federal government has assumed authority. Until, and unless, we Americans decide to wrest control over our daily lives away from the government, the problems we face are not solvable.

In a human sense, it is necessary for free people to accept the responsibility for their own decisions, both good and bad. The free enterprise system, which created most of the wealth we now enjoy, rewards ability, thrift, and risk-taking (in balance). But it also punishes slothfulness, greed, and poor decisions. In other words, those who take the risks necessary to save, invest, and create new companies prosper; but those who abuse the system fail.

Today we treat successful businesspeople like criminals who should be shunned by society. In a government-run economy the success factor is eroded to the lowest common denominator. In other words, it is better for everybody to have virtually nothing than it is for a few to have too much.

This mentality is directly contradictory to the American Dream. The American Dream has always been that each generation could, if they worked hard, live better than the generation that preceded them. That's only possible if the previous generation has invested in their children's futures, instead of having consumed their inheritance, as we are doing today.

Even the inheritance laws of our present society are designed to prohibit parents from passing on the majority of their assets to their children. As the "now" mentality grows, so does the desire to keep everything for immediate consumption. In the not too distant future we will certainly see more legislation aimed at keeping virtually any wealth from passing from one generation to the next. This attitude, along with the current anti-business environment in Washington, just puts one more nail in the coffin of American free enterprise.

The struggle today seems to be between the forces of bigger government and those of private industry. As the size of government expands and reaches into every nook and cranny of our society, it crowds out those who need flexibility and freedom in order to succeed in business. Big government makes it harder and harder for the small businesses to succeed in a global economy. Lawsuits and government regulations can wipe out virtually any private enterprise in America today, as you will see.

But most Americans aren't even aware of the fact that the regulations and lawsuits spread like a virus, infecting and weakening our economy. They have bought into the idea that more government is better, and those in authority are working toward the common good of the country.

More and more Americans are turning to their government to solve their problems. In spite of all the evidence to the contrary, Americans naively believe they can trust the government to meet their needs.

Our hope lies in turning back to God, not in a flawed political system. But until God's people turn to God there is no hope that the unbelievers will. Our society needs a model of what can be done with less government, not more.

We need to grasp the problems, not focus on the symptoms. In order to do this we must first be confronted with the truth about where we are—and why. As I worked on this book I found myself getting angry about what is happening and how it will affect my children and grandchildren. I sincerely pray you will get angry too, and then you'll help do something about it.

Unless we wake up to the danger of passivity, we will not be able to alter the direction of our economy and our nation. The last president who had the opportunity to correct the moral and economic direction of our country was Ronald Reagan. He came into office with an overwhelming mandate from the American people. But even President Reagan was blocked by an intractable political system. Certainly Bill Clinton does not have such a mandate, since he actually received a minority of the popular vote.

Such details are not lost on the politicians in Washington. Making the necessary changes without the support of the voters is political suicide in a town that lives and breathes the latest popularity ratings.

We simply don't have the luxury of waiting until the next presidential election. By the time another president is elected, the problems will be so acute that real changes will be impossible in our political climate.

Perhaps they are already too difficult to be dealt with through our political system. With so many Americans eating at the public trough now, it will require sacrifice on the part of everyone to salvage our economy. This means sacrifices on the part of the young and the old.

Without fundamental changes to health care, welfare, and Medicare, the problems can't be solved. Recently I tried a personal survey on just one issue: Are the current retirees willing to sacrifice a portion

of their "entitlements" for the next generation even if it means paying a larger portion of their own medical expenses, taking less cost of
living increases, or even taking less actual income?

After having suggested these ideas to many retired people, I
found that the response was not encouraging. The normal reaction
was, "I paid my dues. I have it coming."

Perhaps they are right. I know the government made many
promises to a lot of people in the past. But what if everyone takes the
same position; what then? College students need government loans
to go to school. Welfare recipients need what they are receiving (and
more). New home buyers need FHA and VA loans to be able to get
into their first homes. Depositors need government protection for
their savings deposits; and so it goes.

At some point we must make the hard choices that require placing the interests of the next generation ahead of our own, or one day
they will look back on us with contempt. God's people are supposed
to pass along an inheritance to their children's children. I don't think
the Lord intended that inheritance to be debt!

*"A good man leaves an inheritance to his children's children, and the
wealth of the sinner is stored up for the righteous"* (Proverbs 13:22).

CHAPTER TWO
Defining the American Dream

When I grew up in the fifties, the American Dream could be defined rather simply: If you work hard and get an education, realistically you can expect to live better than your parents did.

This dream was expanded in the sixties to include a nice home, a nice car, a good education for the children, and retirement at 65, with a reasonable degree of comfort.

In the seventies the American Dream expanded to include a bigger home, two cars, longer vacations, guaranteed employment, and government aid in everything from housing to health care.

By the eighties the Dream had begun to fade, as the side effects of welfare, drugs, and the "me" generation surfaced. But rather than allow the dream to die, Americans borrowed their way back into prosperity. But, I'm getting ahead of myself. I need to back up and take a look at what my generation called the American Dream.

THE SPIRITUAL SIDE OF THE DREAM

I was born in 1939 and, therefore, was a teenager in the fifties, at the height of America's supremacy—both economically and militarily. I also believe it was the height of America's spirituality in this century. This nation had just been through a battle for its very survival. Our spiritual heritage may have been declining in Washington, D.C. during World War II, but our military leaders were still crying out to God for deliverance. As Winston Churchill once said: "God forbid that the world should fall into Hitler's hands."

I was a non-Christian in the fifties so I didn't see the spiritual side of the American Dream, but I benefitted from it nonetheless.

Our spiritual heritage was responsible for the abundance the Lord heaped upon our nation because we willingly shared with lesser countries and people. It was to America that virtually all the nations of the Earth turned for moral guidance and help in their times of need.

If you asked anyone in the fifties who knew about America, they usually described America as a "Christian" nation. We lived by a set of moral standards and laws that were so clearly drawn from the Bible that virtually every courtroom in America still has the Ten Commandments engraved on their walls—even behind the justices of the Supreme Court. Other Bible verses are engraved in concrete and stone throughout every government structure in Washington, D.C.

It is impossible to talk about the American Dream from an economic perspective without also viewing it from the social aspect.

I benefitted from America's spiritual underpinnings in an entirely different manner too. In those days I could hop on my bicycle and ride from my house in Winter Park, Florida to downtown Orlando, some five miles away, without any thought of being kidnapped or shot as I rode. As kids we played outside all day and never had a single kid snatched, raped, or robbed in our neighborhood.

The area I lived in was far from affluent. We were somewhere between poor and very poor, and yet I never heard about one neighbor burning down another neighbor's home because he was being "oppressed." Individual responsibility was the norm in those days.

My personal dream was that I didn't have to be poor forever. I knew that a good education and hard work would virtually assure me a good job. I knew also that you didn't get out of poverty by committing a crime. If I had burned down a neighbor's home I don't think the courts of the fifties would have cared much that I had grown up underprivileged; but that was when the courts still administered biblical justice instead of social values.

I attended public schools until college and I can clearly remember that our high school principal prayed before school assemblies, our coach prayed before football games, and some students even prayed before our proms. That may have violated my First Amendment rights, but we weren't much into "personal rights" back then. I guess I put my constitutional rights on hold while those who believed in God exercised theirs.

I do recall a growing awareness of God during those years. I really didn't know much about God, and I wasn't sure there actually was one but, just in case, I decided that I probably shouldn't offend Him by violating His basic rules. Fortunately that helped me to avoid a lot of foolish options that could have wrecked my life.

We weren't better kids back then, even though I never knew anyone who used drugs, carried a gun to school, or beat up a teacher. We simply were held in check by a society that had enough common sense to realize that we needed to be controlled for our own good; and that's exactly what God's Word suggests is the best plan to follow.

I grieve when I think what it must be like for teenagers today, with hardly any restraints on their actions. Even worse, our society is telling them they should have no restraints. I know I pushed the boundaries of our restraints back then; fortunately, they were a lot more confining.

A lot has been written and said about personal rights over the last 30 years. But the growth of personal rights, as currently defined, has resulted in a lowering of societal "rights." The net effect can be measured in the statistics on murders, rapes, burglaries, suicide, divorce, and even bankruptcy.

This is not a book on moral values, per se, but it is impossible to talk about the American Dream from an economic perspective without also viewing it from the social aspect. Clearly the financial situation merely reflects the moral and spiritual values of any society. Historians of the past accepted this as a given. Those of our "enlightened" generation don't like to equate the two because the evidence is too convicting.

A TRIP THROUGH TIME

I'd like to take a brief trip through time from the early fifties, when the epitome of the American Dream was alive and well, to the current decade where that dream is fading rapidly.

For those who weren't around before the so-called "cultural revolution" of the sixties and seventies, it may be almost impossible to believe there was really life before television, videos, and video games; but there was. Being born in 1939 makes me a part of the automobile generation (as opposed to horse and buggy) but still before the television generation.

Much has changed for the better over the last 40 or so years, but much has changed for the worse also. I find myself looking at the eighties and nineties through the eyes of one who grew up in the fifties. But if someone born after the fifties really wants to understand how far the American Dream has deteriorated, he or she would have to revisit that earlier era.

I remember World War II only from the perspective of a small boy. I don't remember gas rationing because I didn't drive. But I do remember that my dad worked in South Carolina for a time and couldn't come home because he didn't have enough gas ration stamps. I remember I had a cousin who could get bubble gum when none of the local stores had any—because of sugar rationing.

The war required the rationing of almost all essential goods, but I don't remember hearing anyone complain about it much. After all, it was a small sacrifice to make compared to what American soldiers were going through. Besides, my parents' generation had just gone through nearly ten years of depression; they were accustomed to sacrificing.

I can remember VE Day and VJ Day like they were yesterday because my mother said it meant my oldest brother would be coming home again. Now I realize it also meant an end to rationing and the beginning of the greatest economic boom of this century. Even with the GIs coming home, there would be plenty of jobs as Americans started buying en masse again for the first time in nearly twenty years.

Life for me was fun in the fifties. The country was on an economic roll, and opportunities abounded in housing, automobiles, aviation, and almost any other area. I could find an abundance of part-time work, which I needed if I were ever to own a car or go to college.

My oldest brother went to college on the GI Bill (one of the few productive government programs). He was the first college graduate in our family. Immediately upon graduating he had a variety of offers to teach and coach, which he did for a couple of years. But it was his training in computers while in the Air Force that ultimately landed him a good job with the rapidly growing IBM company. Right out of college he was making more money than my father ever had. The signal that sent to me was to work hard, get a good education, and the opportunities will abound. And they did.

It's easy to look back on your childhood and think things were either terrible or perfect; likely, neither is true. But the one thing I do recall clearly is that opportunities abounded in America. Jobs were relatively plentiful and new technologies were developing at a startling rate. It had been only thirty or so years since most American homes had gotten electricity, and indoor plumbing had been common in our area for only about twenty years.

Our society had its share of problems too, but many of them were externally inflicted, such as polio, spinal meningitis, and other incurable diseases. We actually had little self-inflicted morbidity, such as drugs, suicides, and teen murders.

As I think back on it now, the government actually did play a significant role in my generation and my own life—but not as the great provider. Coming from a poor background, almost none of my family was able to go directly to college. And there were no bankers (or government agencies) dumb enough to lend a college student money back then.

So, taking the lead from my oldest brother, we all went into military service first. This provided us with the necessary job skills to earn a living and receive a small stipend from the GI Bill to help with college tuition. But this wasn't welfare. We traded the government cheap labor for a chance to move up.

Since I served in the Air Force during peacetime, my benefits were greatly reduced (justifiably) from those of my brothers who served in World War II, Korea, and later, Vietnam. But by attending a community college for the first two years and then working while attending the second two years, I was able to finish. Besides, I had a great job at the Cape Canaveral Space Center that provided for my family and allowed me time to study during extended launch count-downs.

I attended college in the sixties, but the school I attended in central Florida, Rollins College, never got caught up in the protests that seemed to engulf other colleges and universities across the country. I disagreed with the Vietnam war—philosophically and morally. I long since had become an avid reader of biographies, and having read General Douglas MacArthur's biography I was familiar with his warnings to President Truman and others about the foolishness of getting trapped in a ground war in Southeast Asia. It was only by the grace of God that the U.S. had extricated itself from the ground war in Korea; and Vietnam was a far more hostile environment.

But I also knew that I owed my country a debt that I would have paid had I been unfortunate enough to have been born into the Vietnam conflict era. However, that war made it abundantly clear that our leaders in Washington were totally out of touch with the average American, and the media in our country was out of touch with any basic moral values.

Never before had the freedom of the press in America been so abused to the benefit of the extremists, especially those in Hollywood. The drumbeat of "American Imperialism" was just beginning in the media. It is this same group of celebrities who now lead the parade of extremists bent on shutting down American industry to save "Mother Earth."

It is difficult for me to comment on the effect of Christianity in America during the fifties and sixties, since I was not a Christian until 1970. But I can remember the simple faith of my grandmother. To her it was a matter of believing in Jesus Christ and obeying His commandments. Her faith translated into helping others who were in greater need, raising her family in a moral and God-fearing fashion, and teaching them the difference between right and wrong.

I grew up in a bigoted society in central Florida where nearly all the black people I knew came from migrant worker homes. We didn't have much, but we had a lot more than they did. And while only the lack of funds kept me from attending the college of my choice, discrimination played a much bigger role in their lives.

I can remember many times when I would shout something unkind at one of the black kids I played with, and my grandmother would call me into the house and chide me. "They're God's children too," she would say, "and in God's eyes we're all the same."

I wasn't sure I really believed that then, but it surely stuck in my mind when I was old enough to decide for myself. The many lectures on honesty and morality also stuck in my head as a young boy. I was benefitting from our Christian heritage and didn't even know it at the time. I wonder today how many of the families of murdered children and youth-related crimes even realize that they're reaping the results of Christianity being purged from our society?

If only we could take the technological advances of our present society and transplant the social and moral values of the fifties into it, I wonder what we could accomplish. But we can't go back. What we can do though is learn from the past and try not to repeat and amplify the problems as we're doing today.

LIFE IN THE NINETIES

If a man from the fifties were to become a time traveler and arrive in the late nineties, he would be awed by the array of material advancements. The cars are faster, smoother, and more reliable, and almost any family that wants them can have two or more cars. Virtually all middle-income American homes have air conditioning, color televisions, microwave ovens, and a plethora of other marvels of ingenuity and engineering; and the homes are nearly twice the size of those in the fifties.

If our time traveler visited any local hospital he would stand in amazement at the lifesaving devices technology has provided —from kidney dialysis machines to complete bypass coronary units. Almost gone from medical terminology is the dreaded word *polio* that struck down so many young and old in the fifties. As a result of better health care and diet, the average American's lifespan has increased nearly 10 years.

Any visitor from the fifties would be enthralled with the new computers now common to nearly every business and many homes. And the ability to pick up a telephone and dial anywhere in the world would seem to be a miracle. Just the idea of transmitting sound over glass wires would stretch anyone's ability to believe.

If our time traveler were to go into a busy airport, no doubt he would stand in awe as the big jets arrived and departed every few seconds, coming from and heading to every continent on earth. Flying from Atlanta to New York in the fifties was an all day adventure, full of bad smells and air sickness as the low-flying, piston-driven planes dodged in and out of thunderstorms that could not be scaled.

But our time traveler's real education would begin as soon as he discovered a television connected to a modern cable system. After all, in the fifties most cities had a single television station, and television for those living in rural areas was little more than snowy images of what was presumed to be real people.

For rural viewers, fall was the best time for television because the weather conditions were ideal. In the early fifties Howdy Doody, along with Princesses Winter, Spring, Summer, Fall were television's leading youth performers—certainly tame stuff compared to television programming today. "I Love Lucy" was about as risque as television got.

If our fifties visitor flipped his way through the endless variety of programs, he would have to wonder how anyone ever decides what to watch. Then if he happened upon one of the cable movie channels, likely he would stop and blink in disbelief as the television displayed, in living color, sex scenes that would have made a sailor blush in the fifties. He would soon realize that we're a sex-dominated society.

I can assure you that sex was as commonplace in the fifties as it is in the nineties, but it was condoned in marriage and condemned outside of marriage. Women who were known to be morally "loose" were shunned to a large degree by the general population. Certainly no thinking parents of the fifties would have allowed their children to watch adult sex films. Common sense in that day proclaimed "monkey see, monkey do." But now, on commercial television, our time traveler has a choice of several different sex acts to view—including some set to musical sounds on the MTV channel.

As our visitor continues to flip through the channels, he comes across a news program discussing the crime problems in New York, Miami, and most other large cities—whole neighborhoods rioting over the police crackdown and arrests of ethnic drug dealers. The violence displayed on the screen is so shocking it takes several minutes before he can decide if this is just another movie scene.

He stares at the scenes from the Los Angeles riots as waves of people form mobs bent on looting and destroying everything in their paths, without regard for the rights of anyone around them. Clearly our time traveler is beginning to lose some of his enthusiasm for the nineties.

Now our visitor ponders: *It has only been forty years or so since I left my own time. How could things have changed so drastically and so quickly? After all, many of the leaders now are children from my time who were raised by law-abiding, God-fearing parents. Could some of those rioters be my own grandchildren?*

What could we have done so wrong that would permit open sex on television, violence in the cities and, unbelievably, a society where drugs are sold openly on the streets to children? In our generation, a student caught smoking in the school bathroom was paddled the first time, suspended from school the next time, and usually expelled if it happened again.

It is apparent that our time traveler is beginning to have some grave doubts about his future. *The gadgets and gizmos of the nineties are marvelous, but society has lost something fundamental,* he thinks to himself.

Our traveler then decides to spend some time in the research department of a large library to see if he can discover what happened to America during the previous forty years. Wandering through the computerized files, he marvels at how much information can be retrieved in so short a time.

If these facilities had been available in the fifties, we could have avoided many of the mistakes of previous generations, he thinks silently. But then he remembers that it is *his* generation that has all this information available to them in the nineties and yet their problems are worse.

He skims through the headlines until he comes across an article about federal spending. In this article the reporter is attacking the president and the Congress for their lack of support for the needs of the poor and homeless; yet, as the article clearly points out, nearly two-thirds of all federal spending is directed to the poor and the elderly.

How in the world is such a massive welfare program funded? he wonders. *In the fifties even the most liberal economists agreed that national welfare would wreck the economy.*

The economy must be so productive that the working class already has all their needs met, he concludes. *Obviously the funds to support these programs come out of accumulated surpluses.*

The headlines from a financial publication read: "National Debt Now $4 Trillion and Counting." Our traveler blinks in astonishment. It's painfully clear that instead of these programs being funded from surpluses, they are being funded by huge accumulations of long-term debt. A quick review of the article shows that the largest line item in the federal budget is *debt* service.

Four trillion dollars in debt, he says to himself in amazement. *Even accounting for inflation, that would have been more than a trillion dollars in my day—four times what it cost to fight World War II. Any economist who even suggested such a debt was possible back then would have been ridiculed.*

How in the world did this happen in just forty years? he asks himself. *This generation must be a bunch of sheep,* he thinks grimly. *Think of the taxes they must pay!* And then he remembers: *I am this generation.*

*FHA, V.A., welfare—even Social Security. These are all govern-
ment programs sponsored by my generation,* he remembers with despair.
He shuts down the terminal and heads back out to the busy street, his
mind in a swirl of emotions.

It's astounding to see all the Japanese cars on our streets, he mutters
to himself. *The Japanese made some good toys back in the fifties, but cars?
Never!*

How could you let this happen? he shouts at no one in particular. A
few people stop and stare, but then they move on, shaking their heads.

*No wonder the American Dream is waning. What in the world has
happened in just four decades to transform us from prosperity to medio-
crity?*

He recalled that one of the headlines from the library read:
"Communism Defeated!" *I wonder if that's an advantage,* he notes dry-
ly. *We defeated Germany, and Japan too, if I remember correctly.*

At this point, our visitor has to fight a growing feeling of despair
and hopelessness as his mind retraces the countless stories of crime,
drugs, sex, and greed he scanned previously.

*How can anyone seriously think this is a better life. I'll gladly trade
these fancy cars for the well-being of my children.*

Suddenly the thought strikes him: *My children! They must be living here somewhere.* He rushes back to the library's computer system
and begins a systematic search for the location of his oldest son. He
finds his name listed in the computer directory for Birmingham,
Alabama.

Well at least Birmingham is still a fairly small city, he tells himself,
*and located in the heart of America's Bible Belt. Surely it has to be safer
than what I saw in Los Angeles and the other big cities.*

Armed with little more than his eldest son's name, he was as-
tounded by the amount of information available from the computerized files. He found that his son was actually living in Irontown, a
suburb of Birmingham, and was employed by a small printing company. *It's an eerie feeling to realize that my son is almost my own age,* he
thinks somberly. *Or at least the age I was in 1957.*

He sadly notes that his son was twice divorced and had filed for
both personal and corporate bankruptcy only four years earlier. The
recession that had devastated so many had wrecked not only his personal finances but also had resulted in the bankruptcy of the steel
company he worked for in Birmingham. As his son's financial situation deteriorated during a two year period of unemployment, his marriage had deteriorated also.

A quick review of his son's credit records revealed that, although he was again employed, his income had dropped by nearly 60 percent. He was living below the national poverty level. Despair again swept over him as he realized that his son was trapped in an economic era that his generation had made for him. The job he lost would not return to Birmingham—ever! That job had been driven out of the U.S. and was now going to China, by way of Japan.

How could we have been so blind and selfish? he asks himself over and over again. *How could we have let this country run down so quickly?*

Of course, as you know, the scenario I have presented is fictitious—in part. There is no time traveler from the fifties to bring into focus the decline of the American Dream. But in the next few chapters I will try to identify what has happened to erode the dreams of the American people.

Without a dedicated and determined effort on the part of the majority of Americans, it is quite possible that we are seeing the end of the American Dream. For those who seek to serve the Lord, I fear that we are in the early stages of class persecution. The liberal "left" sees us as the greatest impediment to "social progress."

Obviously, since most of us were raised in an affluent nation, we accept our affluence as being normal. But anyone who watches world events also realizes that affluence is not normal for a good part of the world and never has been. But could our nation sink to the level of bare existence? Could the failing economy spark open hostility against Christians in America?

As sin increases, the contrast between light and darkness becomes more and more apparent. Ultimately Christians will be forced to take stands against the sins of abortion and euthanasia that will bring us into direct conflict with the prevailing authorities.

In a time of great trial, scapegoats are usually in demand. Christians would seem to be the perfect goats for a failed or flagging economy. We are the only politically "incorrect" minority left in America.

The real American Dream should be to restore God to a place of preeminence in our country. The longer God's people delay in returning to biblical standards themselves, the less chance we have of being lights in a world of darkness. If we have to suffer, let's at least suffer for doing what's right.

"Therefore, let those also who suffer according to the will of God entrust their souls to a faithful Creator in doing what is right." (1 Peter 4:19).

CHAPTER THREE
Our Heritage

A s I look at the direction our society has taken, I am reminded of a statement made by a senator to his peers, "I fear for
our nation. Nearly half of our people receive some form of
government subsidy. We have grown weak from too much
affluence and too little adversity. I fear that soon we will
not be able to defend our country from our sure and certain enemies.
We have debased our currency to the point that even the most loyal
citizen no longer trusts it."

Sound familiar? Well those words were spoken by a Roman senator in A.D. 63, but they just as well could have been spoken by a
United States senator.

Wherever I go, discussing the problems facing our nation, I am
continually amazed when someone suggests that the "negatives" are
being emphasized too much.

Not long ago, while participating in a debate with some secular
economists, one speaker implied that those who report the negatives
do so because crisis-type books sell well. I beg to differ. The best-
selling books are consistently those that promise the readers uninter-
rupted prosperity and problem-free lives. Religious books on health

and wealth top the best-sellers lists, along with those dealing with prophecy—especially those relating to the rapture of the church prior to the Tribulation. It's very popular to minimize problems and maximize rewards.

In fact, the only best-selling books dealing with real problems are those where the authors have name recognition from previous writings. In general, people having problems don't want to be reminded of their troubles. As in the days of Rome, there is also a tendency to blame the messenger.

The best I can do is share the facts, try to draw some conclusions as I see them, and then suggest a realistic plan of action. What others do as a result is between them and the Lord.

As I was doing the research for this book, I found it hard to develop a positive perspective about our future. The election of President Clinton speaks volumes about where the average American is today.

One in four of all the evangelical Christians who voted cast their ballots for Bill Clinton, in spite of the fact that he clearly endorsed policies supporting abortion and homosexuality—lifestyles contrary to Christian principles. The economic promises he made were clearly more important than the social issues. This does not bode well for our society if and when a bigger crisis hits. It suggests that a large number of Americans will sacrifice their convictions for the sake of their comforts.

In reality, what we're concerned about in America today are comforts, not necessities. When you look at the statistical information available, it's clear that we have basically bankrupted the most prosperous economy in the world for the sake of bigger houses, expensive cars, multiple televisions, better vacations, and indulgent lifestyles.

Please understand that I am not condemning the success of our nation and its people—only how we have sacrificed more important values to achieve it. When a government and its people pile up debt as we have during the last 30 years, it's little more than a get-rich-quick plan. Any generation before ours could have done the same thing and left us with a legacy of debt and high taxes, but they didn't. It wasn't for lack of opportunity either.

A study of economic history shows that there have always been "spend now and pay later" advocates in every generation. What kept them from destroying our economy as others had in Greece, Rome,

Germany, and the British Empire was a strong commitment to future generations and an economic philosophy based on biblical principles.

I think it is vitally important to contrast the attitudes of the present generation with those of previous generations. There have always been shiftless people who migrated into government service because of the power a political office commands. To be sure, some were corrupt and worthless. But clearly they were always in the minority, especially when it came to doling out tax money to buy votes.

As bad as the nineteenth century was in the midst of a civil war (where brother fought brother), no rational politician would have suggested that the government could do a better job of managing business than the average American businessman. Most politicians had the good sense to stay out of the free enterprise system to the highest degree possible.

They knew what we are now discovering: Big government has, and always will, make a mess of anything it touches outside of national security (and that too, sometimes). Our founders understood this and specifically limited the federal government's jurisdiction.

Since shortly after the turn of this century, our politicians have been trying to prove the founders wrong and show that big government can manage an economy well. The results are what we see today: a nation nearly bankrupt and continuing to spend more than it can generate in taxes—presently at a rate of more than $600,000 a minute!

America is an experiment in "Christianomics," meaning economics as practiced in the Bible. When we turn our backs on that truth, we cut our economic system loose from its roots—just as surely as taking God out of the schools of America cut them loose from their moral roots.

Allow me to share a brief history of our nation's economic heritage.

THE PILGRIMS' DREAM

Clearly, America's economic foundation is biblically based, regardless of what any modern socialist may say to the contrary. The pattern for American enterprise goes as far back as the Plymouth colony.

The year is 1623. The place is Plymouth, Massachusetts.

The settlers, many of whom have been dumped at the pilgrims' door fresh from the debtors' prisons of England, are cultivating the meager crops of corn, potatoes, and beans, which will mean the difference between life and death for most of the settlement that winter.

The new governor, young William Bradford, recently established a policy that would have a profound effect on the colony and, ultimately, the nation. After surveying the miserable condition of the separatists (who had followed him from sanctuary in Holland) and the conscripted immigrants (sent as replacements by the trade company), Bradford realized that if any of them were to survive the harsh New England winter they had to practice both discipline and thrift. Instead, many of the men often sat around grumbling about the poor conditions and cursing the trade company that supported them in a fashion less than they deemed suitable. The dialogue of the time would likely have gone something like the following.

"Well I ain't workin' my fingers to the bone for no fancy lord," the poorly dressed ruffian mouthed to his companions. "Why, we ain't even got enough ale to keep body and soul together here. The guv'ner can sure spare us a little from his larder."

"The guv'ner says if we don't get busy and harvest them crops we'll all starve this winter," the smaller man added nervously.

"Now don't you go spreadin' lies," the big man growled. "There ain't no way they's gonna let us all starve this winter. I'm tellin' you they got plenny a stores hid out somers here."

Of Governor William Bradford it has been written, "He was of magnanimous temper, resolute but patient, devoutly religious but neither intolerant nor austere."[1]

Bradford had sensed the growing rebellion in the worst of the ruffians sent over on the last boat. He had seen the slothfulness of some and knew the results would be more than just lower morale in the colony. The harsh New England winters would extract the full measure for indolence: death. He looked at the other small band of hardworking families as they made their way out to the fields. The women's dresses were well worn and more than a little frayed at the edges, but they were clean and as well kept as possible, considering the pitiful conditions of the settlement.

"These are good people," he said quietly as they passed by, a cheerful smile on their faces. "They're of the stock to settle a country as harsh as this one. They work hard; they conserve what they have; and they're always willing to help anyone in need. God surely is pleased with these people who call themselves 'the way.'"

His smile turned sour as he glanced down the muddy path that passed for a street at the band of complainers who daily sought more privileges, less work, and more rations.

"Good for nothing sluggards," he muttered as he put his Bible away.

As was his custom every day of his life, William Bradford started each morning reading from the Bible. He not only was impressed by the thrift and compassion of those who believed in God, he was impressed that the answer to each and every problem facing mankind was to be found in God's Word. That morning he had found the answer he was seeking.

The Christian compassion of the pilgrims caused them to help and support those who were working against their very survival. He knew that there would be precious little surplus this winter at the very best, even with every man, woman, and child carrying their weight. But with that group of malcontents doing little but loafing and eating up the meager reserves of the diligent, the whole group could easily be condemned to starvation.

With fire in his eyes, Bradford snatched the hastily written note from his desk and walked into the street, shouting to the pilgrims and the loafers alike to meet him at the little church that served as the town meeting hall.

As the crowd assembled around the church, Bradford tacked his proclamation to the door. It read, "If any man would not work, neither should he eat (The Second Epistle of Paul the Apostle to the Thessalonians: chapter three, verse ten)."

"From now on, this will be the rule of our community," Bradford said firmly. "Those who believe in the Holy Scriptures are bound to observe its teachings. Those who do not are to be bound by its consequences."

Bradford directed all detached persons in the colony to live with families, and then he temporarily divided the Indian field, upon which the settlement had been established, among the several families in proportion to their numbers, leaving each household to shift for itself or suffer want. "Any general want or suffering hath not been among them since this day," he wrote in his daily diary later.[2]

That winter the little colony survived and even prospered some as their numbers grew. The sluggards did their share after testing the resolve of the pilgrims to see whether they would turn their backs on those who didn't work; they did, and eventually all in the community pulled their weight. The prospect of starvation proved to be a great motivator, especially when accompanied by some early hunger.

The next year Bradford did one further act to solidify the colony's survival: He divided the land permanently into small tracts, assigned each family a tract by size and told them they could keep all they produce, except the tenth for the trade company.

Confronted with this opportunity to own their own land, a prospect beyond their wildest dreams in England, the colonists worked even harder. From this stock came the settlers of America and the most productive economic system the world has ever seen.

The pilgrims' idea of the American Dream was not based on the ownership of *things*. The basis of their dream was freedom—freedom to worship as they chose; freedom to succeed or fail, based on their own efforts; freedom to lead their own lives independent from the dictates of a monarch; and freedom to live their lives according to God's plan. It was that heritage that influenced the framers of our nation in the eighteenth century.

THE COLONIAL DREAM

It clearly was not the desire for materialism and government handouts that motivated the colonials in 1775 to resist the oppression of a king who commanded their absolute obedience. The men who took a stand against the unfair taxes levied on the colonies by England were willing to jeopardize their material possessions as well as their own lives to provide freedom for their heirs. To the founding fathers of our country, the American Dream was more ideological than material.

The Declaration of Independence, drafted in 1776, has some simple, yet profound, proclamations in it: "We hold these truths to be self-evident, that all men are created equal, that they are endowed by their Creator with certain unalienable Rights, that among these are Life, Liberty and the pursuit of Happiness. That to secure these rights, Governments are instituted among Men, deriving their just powers from the consent of the governed."

King George was not about to concede a successful and prosperous element of his empire. England had the greatest military force on Earth, and its Navy truly ruled the seas. King George and his advisors knew they would have little difficulty in subduing the rebels. After all, nearly 60 percent of the "colonials" supported the British position.

When Washington and the others committed themselves openly to rebellion, they all knew the ultimate conclusion would be either freedom or the gallows.

In the winter of 1777 the Continental Army was all but defeated. General Washington warned that the prospect of defeat by the

British was all but certain, "except for the intervention of the Almighty," he added.

The ragtag colonial army of 8,000 men was trapped in York Town —its back to the river, and its front to 21,000 crack British troops.

Three thousand colonial solders were already in the hands of the British and, as the remainder of his army filed by, Washington wondered how long the rest would escape the same fate. Their uniforms, those who had any, were rags. A few wore flimsy riding boots to guard against the biting cold of the winter snow; but most had burlap wrapped around their feet in an unsuccessful attempt to keep the bitter cold from freezing their toes. Many had toes amputated because of frostbite. They barely felt the pain as their stumps were quickly refrozen. Almost unbelievably, some tattered veterans wore no shoes at all, their feet blue from the bitter cold. More American soldiers would die from the cold and disease in the winter of 1777 than from British guns.[3]

Two things drove the nearly defeated army as it retreated to the last stand along the river: a burning desire for freedom and the hope of a better life for their children beyond the reach of the English king. General Washington often rallied his men in desperate situations with the cry, "If God be for us, who can stand against us?"

But now the situation was beyond desperation. If General Cornwallis pressed his advantage, the doleful little army of rebels would collapse and the traitorous leaders would quickly be led to an English gallows. The elder statesman, Benjamin Franklin, was absolutely correct when he told the conspirators at Philadelphia, "We must all hang together or assuredly we shall all hang separately."

A short way down the river the English gunboats waited for a favorable wind so they could maneuver to a position where they could shell the rebel army into submission. Unbelievably, Cornwallis elected to withdraw his line rather than risk a final assault. His generals knew the Americans were beaten and urged him to press on. Instead, he decided to wait for the gunboats.

Desperate from starvation, the continentals ate bark from the trees, boiled and ate leather harnesses, and consumed all the dogs in the camp. They stopped short of eating their horses, knowing that without them the cause would be utterly lost in the Spring. The American Dream was still alive—barely flickering.

Washington, in a move born out of total desperation, decided to try to evacuate his army by rowboat in the darkness of night. His generals counseled against it.

"General," his chief adjutant said, "If the wind shifts the fog while our men are caught out in the open, they will be slaughtered like fish in a barrel. The British will show no mercy. That we can be certain of."

"I am persuaded that God would not bring us so far to let us fail," the General replied. "With God's providence we will succeed."

Early that evening a heavy fog had rolled across the river, blanketing the troops from all sides. Washington recruited men from every battalion who had any experience in boats and silently began the evacuation. They all knew that just one slip of an oar could alert Cornwallis to the plan and instantly bring the Redcoats down on them.

The wind held calm throughout the night as boat after boat crossed and recrossed the river carrying both the healthy and the wounded to the opposite shore. Horses were pulled along behind the boats, and precious powder and arms were packed in beside the freezing soldiers.

Only when the last boat left the bank and was well out into the river did the fog begin to lift. The British lookouts patrolling the shore throughout the night had not heard even a sound as 8,000 men, animals, and equipment slipped away. Now the sentries spotted the last of the retreating colonials and sounded the alarm. Troops rushed to the shoreline and fired in vain at the boats, now well beyond musket range. By the time cannons were moved into place, the American army was safely ashore. God had prevailed, and the real American Dream was born.[4]

The dream that the founders gave us was not one of perverted materialism—indulgence for the sake of indulgence. It was an idea: that God had created all men to be equal in opportunity, so that each could elect to work hard and prosper or lay around and suffer hunger. Obviously the founders also knew the biblical admonitions about helping the needy. They certainly realized that those who obeyed the word of God would not stand idly by while those who could not help themselves suffered from want. The Lord's admonition about helping the poor was not lost on them.

But, without exception, the leaders warned against allowing public monies to be spent to support the citizens. A republic was not a new concept to these men; it had just never been tried before. The very idea that a country could be governed by the general population was unthinkable to many who had grown up under the heavy hand of a monarch.

The arguments made by Madison and Hamilton in *The Federalist* papers gives good evidence that popular rule was on shaky ground. The electoral college was part of the eventual compromise, giving an alternative to total control by either the aristocracy or the commoners.

The greatest fear of men like Jefferson was the eventual rise of a central authority that could undermine the freedoms of the populous. The checks and balances he built into the Constitution were specifically designed to allow compromise without undermining the rights of the individual. Sadly, later in his life, Jefferson accepted the doctrine of unitarianism, rather than Christianity. He believed in the "brotherhood of mankind" rather than the omnipotence of the Lord Jesus.

Thomas Jefferson, John Adams, Abraham Lincoln, Grover Cleveland, and countless other great leaders warned each successive generation that the greatest threat to freedom was not in an external enemy conquering America. It was in greed and corruption taking over the government and giving the people what they want, because once the public treasury is open to barter, the people will vote for those who support them in the best style. Unfortunately, once the process begins it is terminal. How long it can continue is the only issue in question. The real question is not *if*, it is *when!*

Some years back there was a song about helping a butterfly that describes what our leaders are doing to their "wards." The song described a kindhearted soul who, upon seeing a butterfly struggling to escape from its cocoon, decided to help. So he took a sharp knife and slit the outer layer of threads holding the cocoon together, thus helping the struggling butterfly to free itself.

In a short time the butterfly had escaped the cocoon and, within another few minutes, had died. The effort required to free itself from the silk enclosure was an essential part of its life process. The circulatory system had not fully developed, and the intense effort to escape was absolutely necessary to its long-term survival. The last thing a butterfly needs is a kindhearted person to help it out. The same can be said of a society and its government.

We need a government that will protect us from our external enemies, domestic violence, and discrimination, and then stand out of our way—not treat its citizens like pets in a zoo.

THE FADING DREAM

Well here we are, slightly more than 200 years after the founders of our nation risked lives and fortunes to secure their dream of freedom. Today that dream is in danger, not from any external enemy—we defeated those handily—but from within.

It is my firm conviction that unless we act swiftly the dream that was passed down to us will be turned into a nightmare of unparalleled proportions. This is by no means a certainty. We can stop the erosion of our nation and, ultimately, our freedoms. If history teaches us anything, it is that people who are too attached to their possessions will surrender their freedoms to preserve them.

There are some specific solutions available if enough people just understand the problems and are willing to deal with them. But first we must be convinced that the problems really exist. Over the next few chapters I will try to present irrefutable evidence that *real problems* do exist. These problems, if allowed to continue unabated, will collapse our economy and perhaps our government.

The second lesson that history teaches is that early interdiction to resolve problems costs a lot less in the long run. Adolf Hitler could have been stopped in 1937 by a mere show of resolve by England. The spread of communism could have been halted after World War II by decree of the allied armies. Mao Tse-tung could have been driven out of China by American support of the nationalist government. The examples go on and on, including virtually every major economic crisis for the last 100 years.

Keep an open mind, review the facts for yourself, and then decide what you can and will do about the crisis we face. If the crisis, as I perceive it, begins to unfold in our economy, at least you'll be aware and able to react early.

As I said previously, it is my personal conviction that we will *not* resolve the problems and, therefore, are on a collision course with a major economic and social collapse.

I honestly don't have any objective way to know how long we can continue without a major economic crisis. Based on the 1992 elections and the promises made by President Clinton (assuming that he actually implements them), I would project five to seven years— depending on taxes, spending, and the size of the annual deficits.

The simple truth is, when the government's need for money exceeds its ability to tax or borrow, a crisis will occur. I believe we will first enter a period of declining productivity (recession or depression). Then we will enter a period of very rapid inflation caused by monetizing the debt (printing money). It is this inflationary cycle that can destroy the economic base of our country. We could survive a depression, if necessary. But no economy can survive hyperinflation for long.

It is hard for the average, law-abiding citizen to imagine the consequences of national bankruptcy on our country. Just consider the anger, frustration, and potential violence, if millions of Americans see their lifetime dreams evaporate and they lose their jobs, their homes, and even their retirement savings. The flame of resentment will probably be lighted by the inner-city poor who see their subsidies cut to the bone and inflation rob them of all hope. But it is the anger of middle-class America that represents the greatest threat. They may not riot. Even worse, they may vote in a "dictator."

CHAPTER FOUR

What's Killing Our Economy?

A s I said, our economy is facing some serious threats from several factors: debt, health care, aging, declining population, declining industry, lawsuits, and ever-expanding government regulations.

We might be able to absorb the impact of one, or even two, of these problem areas and still survive economically (with the exception of the soaring deficits), but when several of these converge at one time, no economy can remain functionally sound. I'm sure there are some surrealists out there who will tell you otherwise, but I believe I can prove them wrong. Failure to understand just how serious these problems are can ruin your day—and the rest of your life as well.

The key to economic stability in the coming economy is a realistic understanding of the problems and what can or will be done about them. To do anything personally, however, you must look beyond the evening news and the daily paper. They will not bring the truth to you until it's too late. The secular media are not simply reporting the news anymore; they're helping to make it.

In my judgment, the period between now and 1995–1996 is the last opportunity to bring this economy under control. Once the inflexible problems (too few workers, an aging middle class, an eroded industrial base, and uncontrollable health care costs) hit us, there will be no possible "fixes."

To be fair, it is not impossible that President Clinton and the Congress will deal with the real problems and bring our economy back to sanity. But, based on past experience, that's not very likely to happen.

The president has been met with a lot of enthusiasm by the members of his own party, but enthusiasm and *real* spending cuts are two different things. Real spending cuts require that this year's budget be less than last year's budget.

In addition, the president and Mrs. Clinton have their own agendas that require even more government spending. Look carefully at all the proposals coming out of Washington. I can practically guarantee that the net results will be more taxes up front and promises of spending cuts later—shades of the Gramm-Rudman Budget Reduction Act. All projected savings are cloaked in "governmentspeak."

Allow me to use an example. Because of a variety of factors, rarely does either the Congressional Budget Office (CBO) or the Office of Management and Budget (OMB) ever give accurate projections of future budget deficits. The longer the prediction, normally, the worse the error.

Simply put, the Congress and the administration look at projected income (based on their estimates); then they allocate the funds to be spent and, thereby, project the annual deficits. However, if the income estimates are too low, the funds already have been spent, so the deficit simply increases further. There is no effective mechanism to punish the budgeters by reducing the next year's spending to compensate.

The Gramm-Rudman Act of 1985 established guidelines that required automatic spending adjustments and congressional sequestering if the necessary spending cuts could not be made in the normal committees. The goal of this act was to bring the federal budget into balance by 1991. However, since this goal could not be met and still spend the money on social programs that the Congress and the president wanted, the target date was extended. Finally, the Gramm-Rudman Act essentially was scrapped altogether when the 1990 Omnibus Budget Reconciliation Act was adopted "requiring" automatic cuts to balance the budget. As you would imagine, the cuts never have been made and the deficits continue to rise.

No law can replace individual responsibility on the part of our elected officials, and they can always find somebody else to blame. As long as they fail to grasp the severity of the problems and can spend more money than they have to raise in taxes, they will. More taxes won't help either. For every new dollar of taxes raised since 1980, the government has spent one and one-half times the new revenue.

As of this writing, we have a new president who has pledged to reduce spending and cut the size of the government. He has also pledged to provide health insurance for 37 million uninsured Americans, invest more money in the infrastructure of our country, and lower the taxes now paid by 80 percent of the taxpayers. That really is voodoo economics.

The pork barrel junkies in Washington will carve up his new infrastructure programs between them in the first pass through the Congress. If all goes normally, our taxes will be raised and used to line the pockets of special interest groups and their constituents. We'll have roads to nowhere and more government employees to track how the money is being wasted. At the end of four years, we'll have higher taxes, bigger deficits, high health care costs, and more uninsured; and the new administration will tell us it's someone else's fault.

In *The Coming Economic Earthquake*, a lot of statistical evidence was presented which showed the economy was approaching a meltdown because of accumulated debt. But in reality, the national debt is a symptom, not a problem. Let me clarify. Nearly every plan that has been presented to bring the deficits back under control include some form of tax and spend. It is universally recognized by conservatives and liberals alike that raising taxes and cutting spending will not bring the deficits into balance. Why? Because you end up in a catch-22.

If taxes are raised, the government's income goes up temporarily. But since consumers have less money to spend, the overall economy slumps and, in a remarkably short time, the tax revenues that were gained through the increases are lost as businesses cut back.

Theoretically, if the government could raise enough taxes on the wealthiest taxpayers only, the average consumer would not be affected and overall tax revenues would increase. But the long-term effect of taxing the wealthy is that they usually shift their savings to nontaxable investments, such as municipal bonds, which removes this cash from the productive sector. Even if they pay the taxes, the money still shifts from private sector to the government. And since this group provides much of the investment capital for the business community, it results in less capital for creating and expanding business and, eventually, fewer jobs for the working class. Once again the net effect is lower tax revenue for the government; it just takes longer.

I can demonstrate this catch-22 with some actual statistics: From 1981 to 1990 the tax rate of the wealthiest taxpayers fell from 70 percent to 28 percent. During this time the actual taxes paid by this group rose from approximately 48 percent of all personal income taxes to nearly 54 percent. In other words, their tax rate fell but they contributed more to the overall taxes of our government.[1]

The reason for this phenomenon can be explained two ways. First, as the tax rate fell there was less incentive to invest in risky tax shelters. Second, more of their real income was reported as the shelters were eliminated. At tax rates approaching 70 percent, people are less motivated to work extra and more prone to cheat on their taxes.

Conversely, in the 1990 Budget Act, Congress placed a 10 percent luxury tax on expensive cars, yachts, airplanes, and the like. It was estimated the new tax would bring in an additional $31 million in 1991. Such projections from our politicians are static models, meaning they don't take into account the lost sales due to the higher tax. So instead of $31 million in new taxes, the 10 percent surtax generated just $16 million.

At first glance you might say, "Well we still got an extra $16 million from the wealthy but, in reality, we didn't. According to a paper prepared for the House Joint Economic Committee, the net result of this tax, because of lost jobs and additional costs to the government, was a loss of $24.2 million, even with the increased tax revenues![2]

The mistakes of the past should be studied and not repeated, but here we go again with a different president and the same old deal: tax and spend. The cuts are symbolic, the tax increases are real.

Even cutting spending is not the entire answer to the deficit problem, because this requires laying off some existing taxpayers. Taxes must be reduced (on all income groups) to allow for more consumer spending, as well as more savings. The spending stimulates more business. The savings provides the capital—but not if the government grabs it all to feed more deficits.

As with a family who is overspending, it does little or no good to increase income until spending is reduced. The old cliche is, "More money in, more money out." However, just as with a family's overspending, reducing it is not always easy. It takes time to sell a home, trade down cars, even to take the kids out of private schools. The same is true with government spending. Much of it is committed for years at a time. Spending cuts must be made, but they must be orderly. So the solution includes a combination of spending cuts, spending controls (future increases), and economic growth.

> *Unless . . . we force the government out of micro-managing the private business sector, the economy simply cannot grow sufficiently to pay off the debt.*

A major roadblock to economic recovery at the national level is the fact that too many politicians are hooked on the high that comes with spending other people's money (OPM). Over the last two decades our government has consistently raised spending on its own internal operations at a rate twice that of the annual consumer price index.

All the rhetoric you hear about responding to voters' demand is just so much nonsense. If government leaders *really* wanted to cut the deficit, they would start with the portion that is *totally* under their control. As James said (in another context), *"Prove yourself doers . . . not merely hearers"* (James 1:22).

Any debt or deficit reduction program that has any chance of succeeding must also encompass some form of economic growth stimulus. The advocates of bigger government say the stimulus must come as a result of more government spending on *infrastructure*. In Franklin Roosevelt's day, the term was *direct economic stimulus*. We have been trying that approach for more than 50 years now, and the economy is in the worst shape ever.

Look at any element of our society—from welfare to education —that has been fattened on government money, and see if you can find a true success story. All you see is waste and fraud: bigger programs loaded with staff and little-to-no tangible results (unless you count the negatives).

Welfare creates more poverty and a higher crime rate; education at the national level yields less learning, more dropouts, and gun-toting students. And those are the *success* stories of big government trying to solve social and economic problems.

Private enterprise may not be great, but it's light years ahead of public enterprise.

THE ECONOMY NEEDS REAL GROWTH

The primary difficulty in bringing the deficits under control is that the underlying economy is so burdened by excessive government controls that it is unable to function the way a capital-based economy (free market) must function to succeed. We no longer have a true free-market economy. Instead we have a "fascist economy." I have used this term before and received letters from people who took exception to it. But, in reality, the term *fascist* merely means government controlled and privately owned. I challenge anyone to look seriously at our economic system today and deny that it fits that definition.

Unless (and until) we force the government out of micro-managing the private business sector, the economy simply cannot grow sufficiently to pay off the debt we have accumulated. As you will see later, if we don't voluntarily solve this problem the basic rules of economics will solve it for us. And we *won't* like the fix.

Government regulations are crippling our economy just as certainly as too much debt is. It is almost considered unpatriotic to speak out against government regulations today. The environmental extremists make anyone who questions a new regulation seem like an earth-ravaging polluter. This small band of elitists believes that only through government control can the environment, or any other social ill, be cured.

More recently they have even begun to attack government agencies, such as the forestry service—for allowing loggers to cut trees (as they have been doing for nearly 100 years) and allowing cattle owners to use national forest range land for commercial purposes. Never mind where the timber and beef will come from—they already own *their* homes. It's the same mentality that French partisans attributed to Marie Antoinette: "Let them eat cake."

I believe in protecting the environment as much as anyone from the Sierra Club, and I believe in worker safety as much as anyone from Ralph Nader's group but, at some point, common sense must also be a part of protecting the environment and the workplace.

Many of the environmental extremists today were the socialists of the seventies and eighties. Communism and socialism have been branded total failures wherever they were tried, so the activists simply shifted their agenda to regulating everything from the environment to handicapped access. Their goal is the same: total government control from cradle to grave—only their methods have changed. Those who believe in total government are not beyond rewriting the history books, using mystical science to support their claims, and telling outright lies to accomplish their ends.

Let me make it very clear that I am not taking exception to the entire environmental movement. Those people who have challenged bad policies on PCB pollution, careless dumping, and a myriad of other legitimate issues, have helped to clean up some very bad problems caused by irresponsible developers and industrialists. I greatly enjoy the outdoors and have actively supported several well-balanced groups that helped to establish some of the early local regulations in our community.

But when the extremists (activists) hit upon the environmental issue as their "cause," all reason went out the window. Their agenda is to restore the environment to its "pristine" condition. To do so requires that we accept their notion of what pristine really is: a world without people in it.

For a long while now these activists have been using their primary tool—the media—to re-educate the American public on the evils of industrialization. These people, many of whom are well-known celebrities and media personalities, will allow no rational discussion on the issues they deem sacred.

It is interesting that this group is living proof that if you just shout loud and long enough (and you have access to ABC, NBC, CBS, and CNN), you can convince the public you're right, even if the facts say otherwise. I trust that as you read the next several chapters you will come to the same conclusion that I did: We cannot afford them.

Over the last decade this extremely active and committed group has been able to pressure Washington to pass legislation that is not just questionable, it's downright harmful to our children's economic futures.

I can only conclude that the worst is still to come, unless we speak up now and demand that reason be brought into the environmental equation. Our government is attempting to regulate everything from the ozone to global warming, based on little more than mystic science.

Government regulations aren't limited to just global warming and ozone depletion. They now transgress every area of American life. Invariably, they hit small businesses with rules too complex for the most skilled engineers to understand, laws too complex for the government's own attorneys to explain, and a gestapo-like police force that can violate nearly every constitutional restriction placed on the government with impunity.

I would like to look at some of these areas of regulation individually because they represent such a direct threat to our economic survival. But first let me share some observations I made while collecting information for this book.

In reviewing some of the statistical data from the government, I noticed that one of the often-quoted expert witnesses on the environment was a scientist I had met some years earlier. In fact I discovered that he was going to be speaking only a few miles from my home. So I called and asked if he would be willing to meet with me to discuss the Environmental Protection Agency (EPA)—his area of expertise. He was not only willing but enthusiastic. He was interested in talking with someone (off the record) who was not a radical proponent of the EPA.

We are trading jobs, lifestyles and, ultimately, lives (through lower standards of living) for the whims and wishes of a few radicals.

In talking with this scientist (who wished to remain anonymous), I discovered that he was a Christian and, in fact, we had many mutual friends. Once this barrier was crossed, he relaxed and began to unfold a tale of deception and intimidation that is almost unbelievable.

He is concerned that his current views, which run contrary to the extremists' views, could ruin his career as a university professor.

He said that once the environmental group targets someone they will keep on until that person either relents or gets fired. He also said he knew of more than one instance when the academic community blackballed a "rebellious" member.

He began working with the EPA as a private consultant during the Reagan administration, when former President Reagan was committed to reducing the number of government regulations and dismantling much of the government's ability to regulate. As the chart below shows, Reagan did succeed in reducing the number of regulations in force, as well as the number of government regulators assigned to this branch of the government.

Growth of Federal Regulations

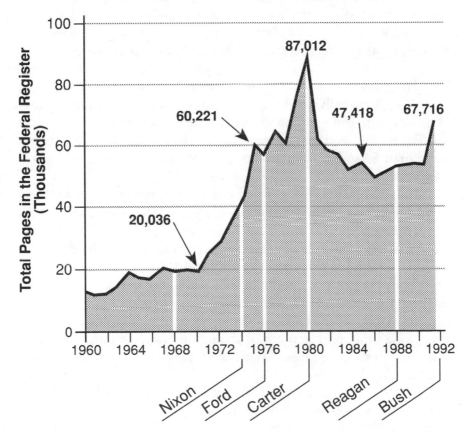

Source: Office of the Federal Register

This scientists' area of expertise is air pollution and, while working on several research projects for the EPA, he became a convert from the traditional position that our world environment is being destroyed and that global warming will be the death of us all (if the hole in the ozone doesn't get us first), to a belief that the environmental problems aren't nearly as bad as the public has been led to believe.

"In fact," he said, "the more data we are able to gather, the more it would appear that modern man has made little or no long-term impact on our global climate. Simply put," he said, "the environmental changes made by nature are so immense as to totally dwarf our negative or positive impact."

In fairness to the environmental movement, he noted that initially it had done a great deal of good in pointing out industrial water pollution, misuse of chemicals, and improper disposal of nuclear waste; but once the movement became politicized and popularized by the media, it took on spiritual dimensions. "Now it's out of control," he stated with a degree of alarm. "And if we don't get some balance back into these regulations, there will be no industry left in America."

He provided me with scientific studies I will use later, showing that there is virtually no evidence to support the global warming theory, the deteriorating ozone theory, or the sudden demise of multiple species. He also said that the federal government is planning to spend more than $3 *trillion* in taxpayers' money to solve these nonexistent problems.

In a comment I found to be common to many of the studies I reviewed, he said that we are trading jobs, lifestyles and, ultimately, lives (through lower standards of living) for the whims and wishes of a few radicals armed with little knowledge, faulty scientific data, and a zeal to establish a zero-defect environment.

The cost to our economy in jobs and living standards for implementing these regulations is staggering.

In a study on the cost of regulatory law, it was estimated that for every $7.25 million taken out of the productive economy, one life is lost through reduced income (lack of proper health care, stress, diet, and the like).[3]

According to the Office of Management and Budget (OMB), the direct cost of government regulations in 1990 alone amounted to about $500 billion. Translate that into lost lives!

But there are more hidden costs in these regulations, as you will see when we examine a few specifics. For instance, many of the EPA laws hold lenders (banks) and customers liable for violations, even though they exercised no degree of control over the offending companies. And the contingent liability is forever! Who would want to invest, lend, or do business with any company under these rules?

The professor said that when President Bush took office in 1989 there was a dramatic resurgence in government regulatory control. In fact President Bush restored many of the regulations and staff dismantled by President Reagan. The government's position shifted from one of no enforcement without absolute proof to that of "side with the extremists at all costs."

All I can conclude (without personally talking with President Bush) is that either he believed in more regulatory controls or he was trying to buy off the activists, which clearly didn't work in his case since they opposed his reelection.

In any event, President Clinton came into office with some of the strongest regulatory laws of any industrialized country on the books and a massive army of 125,000 bureaucrats ready to enforce them vigorously.

One example of regulatory excess is the Americans with Disabilities Act (ADA) of 1991. I hesitate to even discuss this law, lest I be branded insensitive to the disabled. But I can assure you, I am not. I have several good friends, including my own brother, who are disabled; and my record of speaking against any form of discrimination is clear. So I feel justified in speaking out against bad legislation, even for the handicapped.

The organization I head, Christian Financial Concepts, hires handicapped people. We always have and always will—not because the government says we have to, but because many handicapped people make great employees. However some don't—just as some black people don't, some white people don't, and some Christians don't. I hope you see the point. Any employer has to be free to hire those who will work best for his or her company. And any law that restricts that freedom punishes everyone in our society.

The ADA sets standards that virtually no employer without a staff of lawyers and regulatory experts can meet. The ambiguous language of the ADA makes it possible for any handicapped person (who even thinks he or she has been discriminated against) to bring suit against an employer, with huge penalties, using government lawyers to press the action. Just the cost of defending such a suit can ruin most small businesses.

I have a friend engaged in one such suit presently who says it will cost him at least $1 million before a decision is rendered. He would have been better off financially to settle, but he refused to do so—on principle. As he told me, "I'm not guilty of discrimination and I will not be bullied into paying someone who is using this law as a retirement plan."

The net effect of legislation like the ADA is twofold. First, it costs all consumers huge amounts of money as businesses pass on the costs of conforming their facilities to the legal requirements. Second, it discourages potential employers from hiring the disabled because they fear the repercussions a discrimination suit might bring. In practical truth, it is easier to discriminate by not hiring someone than it is to obey the mandates of the ADA law.

As I said, the language of the ADA is so vague that it virtually guarantees lawsuits, as lawyers tap into a new source of revenue, courtesy of the federal government. Although the ADA was estimated to cost approximately $2 billion a year for five years to implement, the estimates now range closer to $20 billion a year. [4]

This will translate into lost jobs as businesses scale back to absorb the costs that cannot be passed along to their customers. Just modifying existing buildings to conform to the new regulations will cost nearly $1 million per building, or about $45 billion; and that's just for office space.

In addition, every public building, bus, train, or van must be modified to accommodate a wide variety of equipment for the handicapped. Consider the costs of converting every public telephone to accommodate the deaf, changing every sign to include braille, or desensitizing every public facility to accommodate those who are chemically sensitive. The total cost to our economy may run into the trillions of dollars over the next decade—just when the economy is most vulnerable because of declining industry and rising debt.

I'm not implying that we shouldn't provide fair access and opportunity to the handicapped, or anyone else for that matter, but government regulations are notorious for smashing a gnat with a sledge hammer. The ADA is no exception.

I have a disabled friend whom I have probably alienated forever over this ADA legislation because he feels I am not supportive of the disabled. That simply is not so. For me the practice of federally mandated regulations controlling every aspect of our lives is the bigger issue. After all, where does our trust lie? Certainly not in the government, I hope.

It's interesting to note that the ADA had barely been in effect when someone in California decided to test it.

Becker CPA Review, a CPA exam preparation company in California, offered a free two-week introductory course for accountants who were interested in taking their full exam preparation course. One male attender, who was deaf, requested that a sign language interpreter be provided for the sessions.

The company declined the request, noting that all the materials were available in written format, and visuals would be used for the course. "Besides," a company official told the attender, "the course is free."

The deaf accountant filed a complaint with the labor department under the ADA, claiming the company must provide a signer for the deaf.

Facing pressure from the Department of Justice, Becker agreed to provide a signer for the student, but said they could not comply in the three days before the session was scheduled. The Justice Department demanded that Becker comply and provide a signer—without delay.

Becker officials scheduled a negotiation meeting with officials from the Justice Department, during which time they argued that many previous classes had accommodated deaf students. They were always provided a front row seat, clearly written materials covering all of the course content, and opportunities to ask any questions they had in writing.

All arguments were irrelevant to the Justice Department officials and they demanded an interpreter, regardless of the cost, inconvenience, or the fact that the course was offered free.

Facing an expensive legal battle, Becker decided to acquiesce to the Justice Department and agreed to provide a signer. What the people from Becker didn't know was that the Justice Department was searching for an example, and they were it. Two days later Becker was notified of a lawsuit filed against the company for non-compliance with the ADA. The notice came by way of the local newspaper; the Justice Department never officially notified the company.

So, less than three weeks after the issue arose initially, a full-blown lawsuit against the company was initiated, even though the company had agreed, although reluctantly, to fully comply with the Justice Department demands.

The Justice Department is asking for civil penalties up to $50,000 from the Becker company and damages to be paid to the alleged victim as compensation.

So a student at a free seminar is now in line to collect what could be thousands of dollars in damages because a company initially refused his request to provide, at their expense, a sign language interpreter. According to John Dunne, U.S. assistant attorney general for civil rights, "The filing of this action demonstrates the Department of Justice's strong commitment to effective enforcement of the ADA."[5]

I would further add that such action speaks of a government that no longer serves the interests of the majority. The rights of the minority are not protected by abridging the rights of all others. The cost to the economy for the enforcement of the ADA is yet to be felt by the average American. Just remember that this $50,000 and the cost of maintaining the federal bureaucracy to enforce these regulations are a tax on our children—just as surely as any other tax.

A large part of our problems originate from Washington. Too often laws are drafted based on "political correctness" and narrow social issues, to the detriment of the country as a whole. What sense does it make to pass laws that benefit a few people and destroy the opportunities of millions of others? If this economy fails because of our selfishness, we all go down together, handicapped or otherwise. The ADA regulations are not the problem. The attitude of government as our protector *is* the problem.

CHAPTER FIVE
Trends in Government

I t was enlightening to search through hundreds of articles dealing with the increasing control that our government is exercising over our lives. It was also enlightening to note that, in the history of our country, the fewer government controls that were in place, the greater the average economic growth of our economy.

Conversely, the more government controls in place, the slower the economic growth. That should not be surprising since dozens of communist countries have provided us with a casebook study on the end result of central government control.

In virtually every other country in the world, the leadership is desperately trying to shake the bonds of central control and central planning before the starving masses revolt. Here in America our leaders are expanding the role of government and centralizing economic planning. Eventually, this system will equalize the differences between the "haves and the have-nots." There won't be any "haves" outside of Washington.

In analyzing the effects of government on our economy I have tried to be objective about the data. Obviously any economy will show greater statistical growth in the early stages simply because the overall economy is smaller and more rapid growth is possible. There also may be many factors influencing an economic slowdown other than just government regulations. So I attempted to look at trends rather than get trapped into short-term cycles.

I want to share a few observations about our past economic and social trends and where we are today. If we are to correctly assess where this economy is going, we have to determine if we are in a long-term downward spiral or merely in a short-term down cycle.

For instance, the Great Depression of the thirties was difficult and long but, in reality, it was but one of many severe economic short-term down cycles. We have had many similar down cycles in our country's history, with one occurring approximately every sixty to seventy years. As I discussed in *The Coming Economic Earthquake*, these cycles are the normal result of successive generations making the same basic mistakes.

A depression occurs when several negative factors converge at one time. Basically, most depressions are the result of too much speculation, too much debt, and too many people thinking they are smarter than their predecessors.

The Great Depression was a classic example of this. There was widespread speculation in the stock market. The country had just come through the Roaring Twenties, and Americans thought they could get rich without working. The prevailing mentality in stock market trading was: Buy some stocks, hold them for a few weeks, then sell them to another speculator for a profit. Common sense should have told even the novice investors that this cycle eventually would run its course. But each generation seems to think their growth spurt will never end, no matter how many times it has in the past.

The difference between the Depression of 1929 and the previous depressions was not the severity of the economic collapse. In reality, the Great Depression was not all that severe in the early stages. In fact, there is good evidence that the collapse was prolonged by the New Deal government trying to force a quick recovery.

What was unique about the Great Depression was that Americans decided to trade their personal freedoms for economic gain. Franklin Roosevelt was elected almost exclusively on the premise that he would restore economic prosperity to America. Americans had grown accustomed to the prosperity of the twenties and they simply were not willing to suffer the loss of that prosperity.

Whether we like to admit it, our parents and grandparents traded our freedoms for the government's handouts during the thirties. From that point forward, the government has intruded further and further into our daily lives until the average American now considers our massive federal bureaucracy to be normal. But we have not seen the extent of these intrusions yet. Most of the controls we see now are economic in nature. The next wave likely will be aimed at the family structure.

When FDR initially attempted to redefine the role of government in the economy through public works programs, strengthening of a central banking system (the Federal Reserve, which had begun in 1913), Federal Deposit Insurance Corporation (FDIC), welfare, and the like, he was stopped cold by a Supreme Court that consistently declared his programs unconstitutional. The language of the Constitution is simple and clear: All powers not *specifically* granted to the federal government shall be reserved for the individual states.

This provision in the Constitution was not an afterthought by the framers of our law. It was deliberate and precise. They realized all too well that the greatest threat to freedom and liberty is a central government that is able to exercise too much power.

Those who drafted our Constitution attempted to build enough checks and balances into the central government's management system to keep one branch from overpowering the other. They also realized that the greatest threat to freedom would come if the central government were able to confiscate and then redistribute wealth. Thus they issued many warnings about never allowing a central bank, or personal taxation, or redistribution of wealth (entitlements).

Thomas Jefferson wrote: "I place economy among the first and most important virtues, and public debt as the greatest of dangers. . . . We must make our choice between economy and liberty, or profusion and servitude. If we can prevent the government from wasting the labors of the people under the pretense of caring for them, they will be happy."

Americans in the 1930s forgot that lesson or, more correctly, they probably had never heard it. Time has a remarkable way of dulling memories. Our educational system is supposed to keep the important lessons of the past fresh, but how many students do you know today who have even read the Constitution in school, much less studied its meaning?

Any student of American history knows that the Constitution was not a last hour impulse by a bunch of revolutionaries. Since the first pilgrims landed in New England, the experiment in individual liberties and self-government had been going on. It is critical to our

future to remember why these pilgrims, and later the puritans, came
to America: to escape the oppression of the English monarchy and
the persecution of the English church.

The pilgrims, who wanted total separation from the crown and
church, established the pattern for self-government—even to the
drastic step of allowing commoners to vote for their elected officials.
The Puritans, who wanted to reform the church away from the ever
watchful eyes of the English clergy, instituted the doctrine of self-
government, but under the balancing influence of the more educated
clergy.

You can clearly see both influences in the compromises made by
the drafters of the Constitution. On the one side are the self gover-
nors who wanted the one-man, one-vote rule (the House of Representatives). On the other side are those who were concerned that
commoner rule might degrade into mob rule so they established the
Senate.

The office of chief executive is clearly the compromise by those
who feared any democratic government and, therefore, kept the vestige of the old monarchy. So we find in our Constitution the original
three forms of government established by the pilgrims at Plymouth,
the puritans at Boston, and later the establishment of hierarchy rule
at Salem, under the tutelage of Roger Williams.

For teachers or lawyers to argue that the Constitution requires
separation of Christianity from our government, or any branch there-
of, is to demonstrate their ignorance of American history. For parents
to allow this to happen to their children is to swallow the doctrine of
secular humanism today.

If we American adults were truly looking after the best interests
of our progeny, Christian or otherwise, we would be initiating class-
action law suits against the National Education Association and their
ilk for rewriting American history to suit their own agenda. Remember, they are making up their history; ours literally is cast in stone
throughout America, especially in Washington.

It is my conviction that the demise of the American Dream
started during the first two terms of Franklin Roosevelt, but the coffin
was nailed shut during and after World War II.

If we see the whole world as a stage, upon which the last great
battle between the forces of Satan and Christ will take place, it helps
to put America in the right perspective. A nation committed to
obeying and serving Christ is a stumbling block to Satan's plans. Therefore, he will do whatever is necessary to undermine that nation. War

is Satan's great tool for value changing. In the case of America, wars have solidified the social and moral changes we are now witnessing.

With many of the constitutional rights being suspended during World War II, President Roosevelt was able to entrench the Federal Reserve, the FDIC, and the federal government as the economic planners of American society. Coming out of the war, the government handed out loans for college, homes, and businesses. Parents, who once were the concern of their children, in old age, became wards of the government.

States accepted a lesser role in education, transportation, and government, as the federal government flexed its muscles and doled out taxpayers' money liberally.

The average American also accepted the new role of the government as millions of GIs were educated by government grants and bought their first homes with government loans. The concept of conscription (the draft) redefined personal liberties in America. During World War I, the government assumed the right to involuntarily conscript men into the armed services. But during World War II, virtually any male under the age of 35 was subject to the draft. Never had a draft been done on this scale. Remember that both the Revolutionary War and the Civil War were fought almost exclusively with volunteer soldiers. Americans were hooked on handouts and pledged to a strong central government—just the tools needed to undermine a Christian nation.

Roosevelt's decision to politicize the Supreme Court in order to push through his economic policies greatly narrowed the separation between the executive and judicial branches. We can see the real significance of this during the sixties and seventies as the federal courts (up to and including the Supreme Court) began to manipulate and mold our society into their interpretation of what we should and shouldn't believe.

In the name of civil rights, the federal government established its authority over the states. Obviously the majority of Americans thought this action was the right thing to do—including me. But with each progressive step the government intruded into what had been states rights and individual freedoms. Private businesses that had no link to interstate commerce suddenly came under the jurisdiction of the federal government. Rather than the federal government helping and molding the state laws to prohibit discrimination, all violations came under federal jurisdiction.

Suddenly state educators, who had readily accepted federal school loans and grants, found out that they came with a high price tag: federal authority over what the schools could and could not do. At first the controls were limited to achieving equal rights for minorities; again, a goal supported by most Americans. But the controls soon evolved to curriculum, teaching standards and, eventually, the famous "separation of church and state" clause thought to be found in the Constitution (which it is not).

Actually what is now called the "separation of church and state" clause is found in a letter by Thomas Jefferson to a friend, in which he wrote, "There must be a sure and certain wall of separation between the church and state."

It should also be understood that in the latter part of his life Jefferson, who never professed to be a Christian, adopted the beliefs of the unitarian universalists, who believed only in the "brotherhood of all mankind." Toward the very end of his life Jefferson also wrote, "I would that every man should die a universalist."

> *The federal government has evolved, by way of individual apathy, into being the great provider, protector, and general all-round decision maker for the country.*

It's interesting that the avowed "separationists" fail to consider the great preponderance of evidence that no such intention existed in the minds of the constitutional Congress members (or the Supreme Court until most recently). Consider the following evidence that is a small part of the much greater interrelationship between America and God.

Benjamin Franklin: "He who shall introduce into public affairs the principles of primitive Christianity will change the face of the world."

George Washington: "It is impossible to govern . . . without God and the Bible."

John Adams: "We have no government armed with power capable of contending with human passions unbridled by morality and religion. Avarice, ambition, revenge, or gallantry, would break the strongest cords of our Constitution as a whale goes through a net. Our Constitution was made only for a moral and religious people. It is wholly inadequate to the government of any other."

James Madison: "We have staked the whole future of American civilization, not upon the power of government, far from it. We have staked the future of all of our political institutions upon the capacity of mankind for self-government; upon the capacity of each and all of us to govern ourselves, to control ourselves, to sustain ourselves according to the Ten Commandments of God."

John Jay (first chief justice of the United States): "Providence has given to our people the choice of their rulers, and it is the duty as well as the privilege and interest of our Christian nation to select and prefer Christians for their rulers."

The United States Supreme Court, 1892: "No purpose of action against religion can be imputed to any legislation (state or national) because this is a religious people. . . . This is a Christian nation.

Earl Warren (governor of California and later chief justice of the United States): "I believe no one can read the history of our country without realizing that the Good Book and the spirit of the Savior have from the beginning been our guiding geniuses . . . whether we look to the first Charter of Virginia . . . or to the Charter of New England . . . or to the Charter of Massachusetts Bay . . . or to the Fundamental Orders of Connecticut . . . the same objective is present; a Christian land governed by Christian principles . . . I believe the entire Bill of Rights came into being because of the knowledge our forefathers had of the Bible and their belief in it: freedom of belief, of expression, of assembly, of petition, the dignity of the individual, the sanctity of the home, equal justice under law, and the reservation of powers to the people . . . I like to believe we are living today in the spirit of the Christian religion. I like also to believe that as long as we do so, no great harm can come to our country."

Samuel Adams: "Impress the minds of men with the importance of educating their little boys and girls . . . in the study and practice of the exalted virtues of the Christian system."

Abraham Lincoln: "But for [the Bible] we could not know right from wrong. All things most desirable for man's welfare . . . are to be found portrayed in it."

"The philosophy of the school room in one generation will be the philosophy of government in the next."

Daniel Webster: "Whatever makes men good Christians, makes them good citizens."

John Quincy Adams: "It is essential, my son . . . that you should form and adopt certain rules or principles . . . It is in the Bible, you must learn them, and from the Bible how to practice them."

Jedediah More (founding educator): "To the kindly influence of Christianity we owe that degree of civil freedom and political and social happiness which mankind now enjoys. In proportion as the genuine effects of Christianity are diminished in any nation . . . in the same proportion will the people of that nation recede from the blessings of genuine freedom. . . . All efforts to destroy the foundations of our holy religion, ultimately tend to the subversion also of our political freedom and happiness. Whenever the pillars of Christianity shall be overthrown, our present republican forms of government, and all the blessings which flow from them, must fall with them."

Harry Truman: "The basis of our Bill of Rights comes from the teachings we get from Exodus and St. Matthew, from Isaiah and St. Paul. I don't think we emphasize that enough these days. If we don't have a proper fundamental moral background, we will finally end up with a . . . government which does not believe in rights for anybody except the State!"

Anyone taking a thoroughly objective look at what has happened to the rights granted to us as American citizens by our founders has to be dismayed and shocked.

As I said, the federal government is empowered by the Constitution to settle interstate territorial disputes, settle tariff disputes, negotiate treaties with foreign powers, and fight external wars.

From that humble beginning the federal government has evolved, by way of individual apathy, into being the great provider, protector, and general all-round decision maker for the country.

State laws that conflict with federal laws are automatically overruled. All issues effecting race, religion, work, home, business, and school are now under the domain of the federal government. These gains by the central government were at the sacrifice of personal freedoms, and they will not be recaptured easily, if ever.

Given the trend toward more and more central control, and considering the degree of dependence of the average American on the federal government, any major crisis in the future will spell disaster for the rest of our freedoms if we don't act quickly to reverse this trend.

The first level of control has been surrendered to the government. We now accept the government's right to control the economy, print fiat money, and regulate businesses.

The second level of control is virtually assured: control over our schools, preeminence over the states' laws, and federal standards on everything from hiring to retirement.

Now we're seeing the third level of control emerge: federal regulations for business and personal conduct (under the guise of worker safety and environmental control). This is the area that most threatens the American (economic) Dream.

It is critical to understand that there is a fourth level of control coming. If you believe, as I do, that what we are seeing is just a part of Satan's plan to destroy the Christian foundation of this nation, the next level of control will be to wipe the visible signs of Christianity from America. That plan is already in motion.

From the beginnings of our nation's history there has been one real separation of church and state: taxes.

Former Chief Justice John Marshall put it well when he wrote: "The power to tax involves the power to destroy."[1]

The founders of our constitution strictly limited the government's ability to tax the church, or vice versa. Early on in church history, European governments taxed the organized church not only as a fund-raising tool but also a means to intimidate and control the clergy. Later, as the church's influence grew, the opposite became true. Often the church would levy a tax upon the government, as in the case of Catholicism in Europe, or simply become a paid branch of the government, as in the case of the Church of England.

The effect of both of these situations was not lost on the framers of our constitution. They had seen and experienced the oppression that a government-run church could exert, and they had seen the oppression that a church-dominated government could exert. Neither was acceptable.

The solution was to prohibit the federal government from establishing an official state religion. Thus they insulated all religions from the oppression of the government and vice versa. Second, they prohibited the government from exercising control over any established religion that was not acting in a subversive manner or violating basic human rights, such as murder and theft.

These rules are clear and simple and worked well for the first 150 years or so. In case after case throughout American history, the Supreme Court upheld the right of any religion to speak up about any issue, free from government control. The pulpits of America were not silent during political campaigns. In fact, they were the most sought after platform from which any politician could speak.

Noah Webster, that grand statesman who was influential in both education and politics, once said, "The religion which has introduced civil liberty is the religion of Christ and his apostles, which enjoins humility, piety, and benevolence; which acknowledges in every person a brother, or a sister, and a citizen with equal rights. This is the genuine Christianity, and to this we owe our free constitution of government."

It's a historical fact that, prior to the modern mass media, few national politicians could win elections without the support of the clergy.

Today the government, through the empowering of the Internal Revenue Service, has virtually eliminated the church from its traditional role in politics. That should not be surprising since the last thing the liberal activists want is a national forum against their agenda and their chosen candidates.

The lack of fortitude on the part of the organized churches in America, in standing up to this clear invasion of their rights, is appalling. Either it is because too many preachers are caught up in the rhetoric of the liberals and believe it, or they simply don't know enough about church history in America to understand what these rights are.

Recently one of the major denominations in America published a list of dos and don'ts for their associations' pastors. It both saddened and distressed me to see this traditionally sound denomination giving away their constitutional right to speak out on moral issues during an election campaign. The liberals had won without even having to go to court.

The next phase of control will test the fiber of Christianity in America even more, I believe. In the interest of "political correctness," the government will allow or disallow tax exemption of all non-profit organizations, including the church. Many Americans already question why churches and other religious organizations don't have to pay taxes, and why gifts to the church are deductible from the donor's own taxable income.

The second part: deducting gifts from personal income taxes is hard to defend constitutionally. It is really a matter of preference in our society. But not taxing religious organizations, especially churches, is a fundamental part of guaranteeing religious autonomy. Lose that right and the church in America can be controlled, manipulated, and eliminated—at the whim of the politicians. Is such a move unlikely? Hardly so.

In recent years two cases before the Supreme Court have served to weaken this wall so diligently erected by our founders. In a case brought by Bob Jones University, a religious school in South Carolina, the IRS had revoked the school's tax exemption on the basis of racial discrimination. Until 1975 Bob Jones University did not admit unmarried blacks. Thereafter, blacks were admitted but interracial dating was prohibited. The school maintained that such a policy was rooted in their religious beliefs and therefore was protected under the Constitution.

In an unprecedented decision, the Court sided with the IRS, saying that the government's interest in discouraging racial discrimination in education was more important that "whatever burden denial of tax benefits places [on a school's] exercise of [its] religious beliefs."[2]

Irrespective of how anyone might feel about the Jones' position, because of this ruling it will be much simpler in the future for the courts and the politicians to decide that other religious practices are not in the general public's best interest. This will most certainly involve speaking out against homosexuality, abortion, euthanasia, and a host of yet uncovered social issues.

The second precedent-setting case, *Employment Division v. Smith* (1990), involved two state-employed drug counselors who were fired after it was discovered they used the drug peyote (mescal) as a part of a sacrament in their native American church. Most of us would agree that the use of mind-altering drugs is bad, especially in our drug-laced society, but the Indian tribe to which these men belong have used this drug for centuries. The Supreme Court struck down their right to do so on the grounds that an uncontrolled substance cannot be used in violation of federal law, even in a religious service. Bear in mind that Indian reservations are not federal properties. For all intents they are small countries to themselves within the United States.

Most of us would probably agree with this decision on the surface; drugs are a major problem in America. But what is an unacceptable practice in religion? Could refusing to allow non-believers to participate in communion be interpreted as discrimination? Could the expulsion of a member for unrepentant sin be grounds for a discrimination suit? Where will it end? Not here; you can be sure of that.

The trend is clear: If the church doesn't wake up and stop putting economic well-being before spiritual well-being, one day the liberals in our society who would like to see all religion abolished will be standing at the church door with warrants in hand. Perhaps it will be for discriminating against a homosexual who applied for a position as youth pastor. Or it might be for counseling a teenager to keep her unborn child. But unless we draw a line in the sand here and now, it will happen.

I promised I would try to stick primarily to the economic issues related to the American Dream but, as I said earlier, they overlap a lot. You can't look at any one area in a vacuum.

For the next few chapters I would like to acquaint you with what appears to be the most organized and concerted effort in history to use governmental regulations to promote a new social agenda. Just as the moral base of our country is rapidly eroding through the dedicated efforts of a few determined activists, so the economic base is being gnawed away at an alarming rate.

If you have a hard time accepting all you're going to read, I would encourage you to go to the Appendix, order copies of the resource materials, and check the information for yourself. It really is unbelievable—but true.

CHAPTER SIX

OSHA: The Inside Regulator

Most Americans, when asked which federal agency has the most authority, would probably respond, "the IRS." However, the IRS's powers are minuscule compared to that of the Environmental Protection Agency (EPA) and the Occupational Safety and Health Administration (OSHA).

If you have ever received a letter from the IRS announcing that you have been selected for audit, it probably caused a queasy feeling in the pit of your stomach. But any business person who has ever been audited by OSHA will tell you that an IRS audit is a "cake walk" by comparison.

The IRS has to operate within very defined parameters in most instances. And although the powers granted to the IRS are far beyond anything the founding fathers imagined for the federal government, they pale in comparison to OSHA and EPA.

One reason for this is that very few politicians are willing to take on the activists who lobby for ever-more-restrictive controls over our freedoms. In fact, any politician brave enough to oppose safety or environmental legislation will quickly find a vocal, extremely well-funded group lining up to aid his or her opponent in the next election.

"To oppose new OSHA regulations is the equivalent of being accused of wife beating," one congressman told me recently. "In the frenzy of governmental control, all sense of logic and balance has been lost."

In recent years, attention has begun to focus on both the immediate safety benefits of OSHA regulations *and* on the long-term economic costs. Those who make their livings and reputations through government regulations and control, resist this approach because it focuses attention on the negative impact of regulations. We can count on less research into the economic impact of government regulations now that the regulatory agencies themselves will be under the control of the extremists.

Many regulation advocates strive for what must be called "zero-defect environments" for workers and the environment. This means that workers should have the right to expect *no* hazards in the workplace and there should be *no* emissions into the environment. It's really pretty easy to accomplish these goals—just eliminate all workplaces and shut down all industry.

Let me hasten to point out once again that not all of those concerned about the environment and safety are extremists. In fact, only a few at the core of these movements are what many of the scientists, whose articles confront these issues, call *eco-freaks*. But the evidence shows this minority to be extremely radical, very well-funded, and virtually in control of the media, the universities and, more recently, the government. With the degree of control they exercise, they are able to sell their agenda to the public. They may even believe that what they're doing is the right thing to do. But under the guise of "right," many wrongs have been promoted. The one certainty is, they are destroying the economic base of our country.

OSHA

For nearly 200 years the government thought that free enterprise did a pretty good job of protecting workers on the job. Today, few employers with any sense would willingly expose their workers to health and safety hazards, especially since worker's compensation insurance premiums are based on the company's safety record.

But in 1970, under the relentless pressure of groups like Ralph Nader's "raiders," Congress passed the Occupational Safety and Health Act. Later many senators and members of Congress who voted for the Act admitted they had never even read it. And no one could honestly say he or she had, since the bill and the documents it referenced would have made a pile of material in excess of 30 feet high!

The Act granted compliance officers from the Occupational Safety and Health Administration (OSHA) the authority to enter and inspect virtually any place of business simply by presenting credentials to the person in charge. This authority was given in total deference to the constitutional requirement of established cause before a search of private property can be made.[1]

Based on evidence gained through these searches, OSHA can unilaterally levy heavy fines on an employer for violation of regulations so complex that even OSHA's own attorneys admit that no single person on their staff understands more than a fraction of the rules.

From an economic perspective, the big issue with all government regulations is: What do they really cost? In the case of OSHA and EPA, that is very difficult to determine, as I will show later. But an even more fundamental question has to be: What do we get for our money?

Worker's safety was steadily improving long before the federal government got involved through OSHA. Obviously there are isolated examples of abuse by employers, as there always will be—even with OSHA. But, in general, the environment on the job was improving without 35,000 federal regulators to enforce it.

In the real world there will always be hazards of some type, whether it is opening boxes with a sharp knife, jacking up a car with a hydraulic lift, or cutting grass along the highways.

There is also no realistic way to remove the natural tendency of workers to do dumb things from time to time, as an article in a California paper pointed out.

It seems that a lawn care company employee couldn't get his hedge trimmer started, so he decided to use an alternative trimmer: the lawn mower. He started the mower, held it up sideways, and attempted to use it as a hedge trimmer. All he succeeded in doing was nearly cutting off his fingers. He found a lawyer and filed a suit against his employer for not warning him about the potential hazard.[2]

Or how about the business in Florida, cited by OSHA for failing to place a "Do Not Drink" warning on a bottle of dish washing liquid; or the Oregon contractor who was required by OSHA to equip all his vehicles with buzzers and alarms and then later fined because his employees weren't required to wear earplugs to avoid hearing injury from the alarm noises.[3]

In Massachusetts OSHA required a supermarket to install non-slip grating in the butcher department. The Department of Agriculture then promptly forced them to rip out all the grating and replace it with sanitary tile.

The EPA required a steel mill owner to install hoods over the mill's cake ovens to reduce outside air pollution. OSHA then cited the company for violating indoor air standards.

In Wichita, Kansas, a foundry, which was acknowledged as "the most outstanding foundry in the U.S." by trade publications, was cited by OSHA for several violations of worker safety "rules." The company closed its doors rather than spend the $500,000 to comply with rules that even the union agreed were unnecessary.[4]

Does this sound ridiculous? Well, that's about how ridiculous our regulatory agencies have become. In 1992 James MacRae, of the Office of Management and Budget (OMB), challenged the legitimacy of proposed OSHA regulations for controlling the more than 1,000 substances used in agricultural, maritime, and construction businesses.

His argument was that strict enforcement of these new regulations would force many small businesses to close and, in fact, there was no verifiable scientific data to support the contention that many (or any) of the listed items were harmful. Even for those substances deemed potentially hazardous, his argument was that with no viable substitutes available for substances such as formaldehyde and asbestos, the net result from the loss of jobs would be more lives lost through poverty than would be saved through the regulations.

Mr. MacRae argued that the cost of eliminating these substances would be hundreds of millions of dollars. OSHA argued that the new regulations potentially would save 13 lives. Mr. MacRae demonstrated that the cost through lost jobs and resultant health care problems would be significantly more than that.[5]

Almost immediately Mr. MacRae learned the error of his way in even suggesting that OSHA regulations could be wrong. Everyone from members of Congress to consumer activists labeled Mr. MacRae's arguments as anti-employee and pro-business.

Even when he pointed to an independent study showing that elimination of just one substance—formaldehyde—would cost more than $90 *billion* for *each* life potentially saved, the regulations were overwhelmingly approved. It is estimated that the new regulations will save potentially three lives, at a cost of perhaps 13,000 premature deaths as a result of unemployment. Safety at any price is too costly.

It is interesting that most of these new regulations are not opposed by corporate America. American corporations represent a well-funded group that has a very active lobbying effort in Washington, so why do they often support new OSHA and EPA legislation? It's really not all that complicated. Big corporations can afford to hire teams of lawyers to fight their individual battles, if necessary, and with each new law passed by OSHA and EPA, the corporations solidify their market position and eliminate potential competitors.

As the president of a Midwest foundry commented after complying with a mandatory OSHA regulation that cost his company nearly $1 million, "That million dollars turned out to be a tremendous investment for us—not because our safety record has improved or because our products are any better. What happened is that a number of our competitors could not afford these same demands from OSHA and are out of business. We're booming."[6]

At the heart of the American Dream has always been the goal of starting a privately owned business and thus "striking it rich." As I said earlier, this is but a small part of the real American Dream but, to many of the poor who are struggling to climb the ladder of success, it is a way to bypass the corporate structure. To those on the top rung of the corporate ladder, restrictive regulations are an ally. In fact, if the rules are restrictive enough, the small businessperson has virtually no chance to break in.

I have a friend who started a small electronics company in 1985 to manufacture printed circuit boards, which enhance the capabilities of personal computers. The companies that manufactured the basic systems tried to shut him down (so they could provide the same options). They first tried to challenge his patents. After some costly battles in the lower courts, they decided that he would win the patent challenge and would eventually recover his legal fees as well. So his biggest challenger dropped his lawsuit. But the company lawyers hadn't given up. They merely shifted their attack to Washington instead.

A disgruntled employee was persuaded to file a lawsuit claiming a violation of OSHA regulations. She claimed that exposure to various chemicals used to etch circuit boards was irritating a previous lung condition (she was a two-pack-a-day smoker).

The most potent chemical used in the circuit board process was a solvent that had been used commercially for more than 30 years, with no previous record of complaint by other workers.

Using the complaint filed by this employee, OSHA levied several fines on this company. When my friend complained, the penalties were increased. The standards imposed were technologically impossible to meet, without investing millions of dollars he didn't have, so he caved in and asked for a compromise.

The compromise reached was more than a little ridiculous, but at least it was workable. He had to equip every worker with a gas mask capable of filtering out any potential toxic fumes. This was fairly simple since none of the chemicals the company used were considered toxic to humans. From time to time an OSHA inspector came by to verify that all the employees were wearing their masks, which they did—when he came.

In 1990 the budget act signed by President Bush increased OSHA's monetary penalties dramatically and also criminal penalties. Suddenly the OSHA inspectors decided that the gas mask compromise was not enough and the company was once again in violation of the law. The fines were assessed to the tune of nearly $3,000 a day— for an offense that had no cure.

With no friendly ear in the White House, this businessman appealed to his senators and congressman, but to no avail. Without the support of the administration, his pleas went unheard. Even worse, the lobbyists for some of the major corporations were supporting strict enforcement of the OSHA regulations. And why not? They could handle the fines if necessary. As a small businessman, he could not.

After several months of frustration and anxiety, he gave up and accepted an offer from the same company that had attempted to usurp his patent. He ultimately received less than one-half of the company's reasonable value (without the OSHA regulations). What could not be taken legally from him was taken by an act of Congress. His business was destroyed just as effectively as if the communists had taken over our government and established a central planning committee.

Much to the dismay of his employees, the original company was liquidated within a few months and the production shifted to Taiwan, where no OSHA regulations exist.

Was this a deliberate attempt to destroy a small entrepreneur by using government regulations? Nobody really knows, but that is the way it turned out, as it has for many other small businesses in America; so the effect is the same—jobs are lost and a piece of the American Dream vanishes.

AIDS AND OSHA

There never has been a more political campaign waged against an infectious disease than that of Acquired Immune Deficiency Syndrome (AIDS). To say that the control and spread of the HIV virus has been mishandled is a gross understatement. Because AIDS is associated with the homosexual lifestyle to such a large degree, as far as the media and Congress are concerned, it has been placed in a special category.

But just as the potential hazards of AIDS are being handled in a cavalier fashion by the media, OSHA has gone to the opposite extreme in the medical community.

In 1992 OSHA issued new infectious disease control regulations (80 of them) requiring extreme measures in controlling and handling potentially infectious diseases, especially AIDS.[7] These regulations are clearly aimed at protecting health care workers from the spread of AIDS.

The intent is good and, in fact, the rest of us could profit greatly by adopting more stringent rules for controlling the spread of HIV in the general population—specifically by requiring HIV testing of all food service workers, medical personnel, emergency team workers, and the like. But, in truth, that is not likely to be forthcoming. What is forthcoming are horrendous regulations aimed at doctors, dentists, paramedics, and others, that will add billions to our health care costs.

No one in his or her right mind would question the need to control AIDS in the medical profession, including dentists' offices. But as a Christian dentist recently told me, "We were already taking all the precautions required by the American Dental Association, including the use of two pairs of surgical gloves, sterilization of all tools between patients, use of throw-away plastic garments, and so on."

The new OSHA rules require the purchase of special sterilizing equipment, which is understandable at least, even though the new procedures far exceed those required for utensil sterilization in public restaurants. But the regulations pertaining to the disposal of contaminated dental materials alone will add between $10 and $15 per patient. For example, under the new regulations, saliva is considered a potentially infectious material and, therefore, must be treated as biohazardous.[8]

The result could be that paper cups used by dental patients would have to be disposed of by certified medical waste companies at very high rates. The secondary business of disposing of so-called hazardous waste will far outstrip the incomes of many dentists.

Many doctors and dentists now admit that the new OSHA compliance costs have caused them to send more patients to hospitals for procedures that easily could be done in their offices, such as stitching a wound, removing wisdom teeth, and the like. As a surgeon recently shared with me, "Sure, it costs the patient more, but with potential $70,000 fines for improper disposal of 'hazardous' waste, who wants the risk?"

---

*S*eldom . . . is the economic
impact of these regulations ever
fully revealed to the politicians
. . . and almost never do the
regulations accomplish the
stated results.

By the way, practitioners are potentially liable for using non-certified disposal agencies, even if they aren't aware of it.

Under the OSHA regulations, medical practitioners, including paramedics, ambulance company employees, nurses, and doctors, must maintain a written record of every washing of hands, disposal of any materials, and changing of rubber gloves (for every employee) for 30 years after the date of last employment, or face a $70,000 fine.[9]

My dentist friend said, "We'll end up working for the companies who helped write the new regulations."

So it seems that *overkill* rules in Washington today, at least where regulations are concerned. All of the hazards of government regulations are not limited to the workplace, however.

It is also hazardous to your career in Washington to challenge the logic of government regulating safety in the workplace, as many public employees like Mr. MacRae have found out. Just the image of being anti-worker-safety is enough to bring down the wrath of the union organizers, the ACLU, and several other well-funded groups who earn their salaries by promoting government regulation of essentially everything in our economy—especially business.

That is not to say there are no abuses of employee safety; there are. But existing laws are quite sufficient to prosecute the violators without countless billions being spent on endless volumes of mindless micro-management by the government.

It's interesting to note that the employment-related death rate in the U.S. was falling steadily before OSHA came into existence in

1970—falling from 18 deaths per 100,000 workers in 1945 to 9 by 1970. Under OSHA from 1970 to 1980, deaths stayed essentially unchanged until the deregulation efforts by President Reagan, when deaths fell to 5 per 100,000 by 1987.[10]

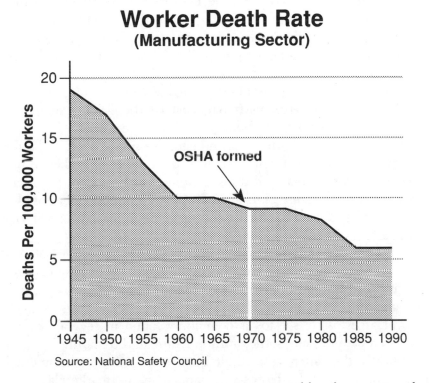

Worker Death Rate
(Manufacturing Sector)

Source: National Safety Council

Apparently business people are quite capable of protecting their employees without OSHA's help.

As I said, the free market has very effective means of regulating safety. If, for instance, an employer creates a hazardous environment for the employees, there are extremely high worker's compensation insurance rates to be paid. There are also lost work hours and enormous litigation costs. Remember there are more than 700,000 lawyers in America just looking for anyone who has a reasonably good case to take to court.

Regulation of private enterprise in America is a burden that will have long-term effects on future jobs. If the goal were simply to provide a *realistic* level of safety for workers, no thinking person would have any objection. But once the regulations start to flow, they take on a life of their own. They progress quickly from the regulation of child labor (a good law), to the regulation of asbestos (questionable at the very best), to regulation of farm tools (an impossibility), to regulation of the colors in an office building and the quality of the food served at lunch.

Seldom is the economic impact of regulations ever fully revealed to the politicians who vote for the laws that make them possible. Almost never do the regulations accomplish the stated results; and, yet, they remain on the books. It's been estimated that the OSHA Act and the subsequent regulations under it would require a full-sized semi (trailer) to haul them off.

Quickly the principle of diminishing returns takes over and regulating becomes a self-feeding frenzy. Perhaps the classic example of this principle can be seen in the regulation of asbestos.

Until very recently there was no effective substitute for asbestos as a flame retardant material, used in everything from brakes to fire blankets. Even now many of the substitutes, such as spun glass, are far less effective. Because of its abundance and low cost, asbestos also was used widely during the forties and fifties as an insulating material in homes and offices.

Then in the early seventies it was reported that miners of crocidolite asbestos developed an abnormally high rate of lung disease, including lung cancer. So, in their zeal to protect these workers, federal regulators issued new rules limiting the exposure of workers to all forms of asbestos. (Asbestos is commonly found in several natural forms—crocidolite, chrysotile, anthophyllite, and tremolite.)

Shortly thereafter, as a result of pressure from environmental groups, the use of all asbestos was banned in the marketplace. At best, the statistical study used to justify this ban was faulty. At worst, it was a concocted fairy tale.[11]

A group of activists looking for a cause jumped on the asbestos bandwagon. The study, which revealed only an obscure link between asbestos mining (crocidolite not included) and lung or other cancers, instead concentrated on the fact that mice injected with high levels of asbestos developed tumors. The study failed to note that mice injected with high levels of just about anything will develop tumors. As a result, asbestos became public concern number one.

This is not to say there are no hazards associated with the mining of asbestos and its subsequent use; there are. But generally the hazards, which include asbestosis (a pleurisy-like ailment) and mesothelioma (a type of lung cancer), have been linked to massive exposure to crocidolite asbestos in a non-protected environment. Crocidolite is found principally in Australia and South Africa and clearly has been linked to several types of cancer. Use of crocidolite was stopped in the United States well before the EPA and OSHA got involved.

The most useful form of asbestos, chrysotile, is also found in the U.S. and Canada. Numerous studies have shown that chrysotile is basically harmless in almost any normal commercial use. However, the EPA ban extends to this form of asbestos, just as it does to crocidolite.

According to Dr. John Kinney, a member of the USGS advisory committee and diplomat of the American Academy of Environmental Engineers, there has been only one cancer victim in Globe, Arizona since 1926, where chrysotile asbestos had been mined for more than eighty years, prior to the EPA sponsored lawsuits of asbestos mining companies.

Furthermore, the study upon which the EPA and OSHA relied in forming their regulations implied that a single asbestos fibre could trigger the start of irreversible lung cancer. All subsequent studies have proven this to be totally false. In fact, incidental exposure to asbestos in buildings and commercial products has been shown to be essentially harmless.

The EPA, with the assistance of the National Academy of Sciences asserted that all forms of asbestos were equally hazardous and equally responsible for causing cancer. That was all the Congress needed to pass legislation requiring the cessation of all uses of asbestos and its removal from all public buildings. The estimated cost of removal is $100 to $134 billion, with no measurable benefits, according to Dr. Kinney.[12]

One small result of the asbestos ban can be found in the brakes that you and I use every day when we drive our cars. Because there is really no equivalent substitute for asbestos in friction-use applications (stopping your car), the brakes on our cars don't stop us as rapidly as they would otherwise. It also means that your brakes will fade quicker in panic stops or in downhill use. Have you ever wondered what that awful smell is when you park your new car after using your brakes a lot? That's the materials being used to replace asbestos.

Another result of the asbestos law can be seen in the lawsuits against companies that mined and processed the mineral. Bear in mind that many of these lawsuits are filed for operations that occurred 50 to 60 years previously. Under the unlimited liability policy of OSHA and EPA, a company can be sued for violations decades ago, based on current standards. As a result, many companies were forced to file for bankruptcy, including the billion-dollar Manville Corporation, the leading producer of asbestos in the western world.

Recent studies done in Canada have shown that the exposure to chrysotile (white asbestos), even in mining operations, is not hazardous, as originally thought. In fact, the incidence of cancer has been demonstrated to be no higher than the public-at-large risk. In many cases, the cancer in miners who have been awarded large settlements has been traced to the use of tobacco and other substances rather than asbestos.[13]

This evidence in no way deterred the regulators who, along with the environmentalists, have persisted in keeping the product from the market entirely.

The town of Peru, New York is an example of regulatory overkill that reaches deep into the pockets of all Americans and, ultimately, into future jobs. It's important to remember that nothing takes place in a vacuum as far as the environment and the economy are concerned. The money used to remove asbestos from schools or office buildings and that used to build B-1 bombers come from the same source: the American workers.

A million dollars, used to comply with a federal regulation, is a million that cannot be reinvested in a business. One might argue that the dollars still go to an entrepreneur who removes the asbestos, but that is a make-work project—not significantly different from the WPA and the CCC of the Depression era. Planting seeds to grow food is productive. Digging them up and replanting them to keep your farmhands busy is not.

The Peru, New York central school district shut down their schools for a month and shuttled their students ten miles to afternoon classes that ended at 8:30 each evening, while a local contractor removed all the asbestos from the school building—asbestos that had been there for more than three decades. The cost was $3.5 million, or more than 15 percent of their annual budget. The school had barely completed the project when federal regulators announced that the hazard from the removal of the asbestos exceeded the risk of leaving it in place, and the entire complex of school buildings would have to be scrubbed, scoured, and all the old duct work replaced.

Based on more recent evidence presented on the asbestos issue, the U.S. Fifth Circuit Court of Appeals has overturned several EPA asbestos regulations. This is not a great comfort to those who have wasted countless millions of dollars attempting to meet impossible goals—nor to those who lost their jobs due to the federal regulations.

According to the EPA's own testimony, these mandatory asbestos regulations would have prevented perhaps *three* premature deaths over the 13-year period they were in force—at a cost of somewhere between $43 and $76 million per life. The loss of life as a result of lost jobs has been estimated in the thousands.[14]

If such examples were isolated cases, the excesses might be understandable. After all, people do get carried away in their zeal to protect the environment (or the workplace). But they aren't isolated at all. In fact there appears to be a concentrated effort aimed at strangling the life out of the American free enterprise system, and workplace regulations are an effective means of accomplishing this.

When I began this study of the American Dream, I was aware that there were extremists who would shut down a whole forest industry to protect an owl or stop a multimillion dollar dam project to save a one-inch fish called a snail-darter. I had assumed these were just a part of some eccentric fringe of the environmentalist movement. But I have come to realize: They are not the fringe; they are the leadership.

There is a major movement in America (and the world), which has become a religion (of sorts), that believes in total governmental control of the workplace, environment, and industry. To this group, the loss of jobs to accomplish their goals is totally acceptable—usually because they have already made their fortunes. They believe the world is too crowded, technology is too corrupting (except for their own microwaves and garage door openers), and they believe that only they can decide how to allocate the world's resources efficiently. They preach freedom of choice and free speech but continually work to remove that choice from others who disagree with them.

A few discussions with those who argue against their agenda verified how difficult the extremists can make it for any scientist, economist, politician, or educator who dares to challenge their decisions.

There is a legitimate place for both inside and outside environmental concerns, even regulations, but certainly not to the degree we see in America today. When whole milk straight from a cow cannot meet the FDA regulations to qualify as milk (as in the case of Mathis Dairies, Decatur, Georgia), then something is probably wrong with the regulations.

When a business cannot operate legally in the United States, but can move the plant one mile across the Mexican border and then sell its products in the U.S., something is out of kilter. And when the constitutional rights granted all citizens can be abridged by

OSHA or EPA without the benefit of a constitutional amendment, the system needs to be reformed— desperately.

It is a sad state of affairs when rapists and murderers have more civil rights in our justice system today than the average businessperson who is targeted by a government agency. Our system of government is not at fault here; the founders left us a truly remarkable heritage. Unfortunately we have allowed a few self-interest groups to dominate because of their zeal and their economic clout. The fault must lie with each of us who has been too busy to get involved.

I certainly don't relish taking on the extremists in order to bring some reasonable balance back to the workplace and the environment, but I would a whole lot rather take them on now than the totalitarian regime that will eventually be needed to regain control of our country if the economy fails.

In the next chapter we'll take a look at what can happen when the radicals target the environment. The issue is not protecting our natural resources from pollution and wanton destruction; any thinking person is for that. The real issue is whether the causes being promoted are real or imagined and whether our economy will be able to meet the needs of our children and grandchildren after the radicals get through with it.

CHAPTER SEVEN

EPA: The Outside Regulator

I really hadn't thought too much about the EPA and its regulatory control over everything outside of the office environment until I received a call from a close Christian friend one afternoon a few years ago.

My friend, whom I will call Henry, is a base metals broker—meaning that he buys and sells base metals such as lead, zinc, copper, and a variety of other metals used in manufacturing. I often had called to ask his opinion about trends in the economy. Since he made his living buying and selling the basic ingredients for most manufacturing businesses, he always had a very good feel for what was going on worldwide.

Without brokers like Henry, very little metals business would be transacted. He is a risk taker in an area where everything he owns is on the line every day. He calls hundreds of small-to-medium size companies regularly to see if they have any metals to buy or sell. Often he brokers sales and purchases for the same companies.

For example, let's assume he sells ten tons of aluminum ore, which he bought from a mining company in Canada, to a smelting company in Alabama. The Alabama company processes the ore to extract the aluminum they need to make pipe for electrical conduit. In the smelting process, many trace elements such as lead, zinc, copper, and iron also are extracted. Since the Alabama company can't use these minerals, they would like to resell them to other businesses that can. But they can't afford to pay an employee to dispose of the byproducts since they have only a small quantity. That's where my friend comes in; he brokers their waste to other companies for them.

Without brokers like Henry, consumers would be facing higher costs for virtually all the goods they buy. Companies like the one in Alabama would be forced either to dump the byproducts as waste or, even worse, pay a third party to haul the slag off and dispose of it. In the case of hazardous materials, such as lead and mercury, disposal can be very costly, if not impossible, in some areas of the country. In fact, before small metals brokers got involved, many of the small smelting companies dumped their waste illegally because they could not absorb the disposal cost.

But in order for Henry to make a profit he has to take some risks. The companies he buys from often have too little of any one metal to make it profitable to sell. So he buys from several companies, stores the material until he has a marketable load, and then sells it. The risk he runs is that either the market price will drop before he sells, or the demand will drop and he'll be stuck with a sizeable storage bill and no buyers. His actual profit on any one company's product is often as little as $100. His losses can run in the thousands of dollars.

All of this is to say that Henry, like the majority of other American entrepreneurs, is not a wealthy money-changer who lives off the labors of the oppressed poor. Although he employs only two people in his own company, his efforts provide jobs for at least 400 people (based on savings to the companies).

One of the companies Henry brokers metal for was involved in an investigation by the EPA. It seems that a large mining company from which they purchased raw materials had been found in violation of EPA standards and had been declared a so-called "Superfund" site. Superfund sites are dump sites or repositories identified by the EPA (under the Comprehensive Environmental Response, Compensation, and Liability Act—CERCLA) as potentially hazardous to the public's safety. At present approximately 1200 such sites have been identified. But remember that often what the government regulators consider hazardous is not necessarily what objective scientific observers would call hazardous.

The cost of cleaning up one of these sites can require hundreds of millions of dollars and may require the complete removal of all the top soil from the site. For instance, virtually any lead mining opera- tion in the state of Colorado could be declared a Superfund site, based on the amount of lead contamination found at the site. But for that matter, much of the state of Colorado fails to meet the strictest EPA standard for lead contamination. Under the strictest interpreta- tion of existing standards, EPA regulators could require the entire state to be dug up and buried in the caverns of Nevada.

No one who has seen or read about the harmful effects of lead poisoning in children who came in contact with leaded paints or toys would argue that some regulation of this potentially dangerous min- eral was necessary. Even today many people are exposed to excessive amounts of lead in their drinking water because of lead pipes and copper pipes with leaded joints.

In fact, recent exhumations of polar explorers have shown that many of them actually died from lead poisoning. Often the food con- tainers they carried to the poles were sealed with lead solder. There is no question that lead is a definite hazard when used improperly.

The improper disposal of old lead acid batteries can be a poten- tial hazard to drinking water supplies around land fills, as can drink- ing glasses containing lead. But none of this serves to justify the blatant disregard for contract law that holds a company liable for an- other company's actions, even if they had no knowledge of those ac- tions. In fact, often the laws and regulations being enforced were not even in existence when the offenses occurred.

The law is interpreted to allow them [EPA] to access any company even remotely associated with the sites to fund the cleanup.

Recent federal court decisions indicate that the courts are will- ing to go even deeper to procure funds—even to lenders. A friend who owns a bank wrote to tell me that his board of directors is panicked because a federal judge is allowing the Justice Department to sue his bank as a respondent in a Superfund site case. The bank's crime? Lending money to a company that did business with a "Superfund" site company that has since filed for bankruptcy protection.

His comment was, "How far does this liability extend? Suppose a bank holds the mortgage on a building where a company doing business with one of these Superfund companies is located. Will the bank be held liable, along with its board of directors, simply because they have the ability to pay?"

The precedent has already been set by the courts holding lenders liable for environmental cleanup on repossessed properties they financed. If this trend is not reversed, no lending institution will be willing or able to make any business loans. Again, the problem is not that all regulations are bad. It's just that what is logical and normal easily becomes extreme and bizarre in the hands of bureaucrats trying to appease the extremists.

Since the EPA Superfund Law holds anyone who has ever transported any material to or from one of these sites contingently liable for the cleanup, it gives metals brokers like Henry a queasy feeling inside. Actually the law says that *all* parties are individually and severally liable—meaning anyone who can pay will. That's bad enough, but the regulators have gone even further by declaring that *any* company that has ever done business, directly or indirectly, with a Superfund site is contingently liable.

The logic is pretty clear; it's called *deep pockets*. The EPA has a limited budget and an overwhelming potential cost. So the law is interpreted to allow them to access any company even remotely associated with the sites to fund the cleanup.

The Superfund Law has the potential of shutting down virtually all small manufacturing companies in the U.S. Let me describe the effect of this law on Henry's business.

The mining company filed for bankruptcy shortly after the assessment by the EPA, thereby eliminating that source of revenue. The EPA then promptly served notice on all the buyers from the mining company: They would be held liable under the Superfund (CERCLA) Law for the cleanup. Concurrently the EPA required the same companies to provide lists of those companies that had purchased any of the raw (or processed) materials originating from the mine site. That's where Henry's company came into the picture.

Obviously he had brokered some of the trace minerals that had been processed by the company in Alabama. The EPA sent him notice that his portion of the cleanup was approximately $60,000. The letter informed him that he was not "legally" liable for the cleanup, but if he refused their offer to release him from any further liability, he might be held liable for the entire bill.

Henry immediately contacted an attorney, recommended by another broker who had experienced the same problem. In no uncertain terms the attorney told him to pay up and then get out of the business.

"There may be 30,000 of these sites before its all done," the attorney informed him. "How many companies have you done business with that handle "hazardous" waste—like lead?"

"Probably three or four hundred," Henry replied.

"Pay your fine and then set up an offshore company to do your trading," the attorney advised him. "Then if you get another bill from EPA, dump that company and start another. Otherwise you'll be liable for these cleanups for the rest of your life."

Because he was a Christian, Henry had a problem with that counsel. But now, after having received a second fine, he is shutting down his company totally. Most probably, the business he was doing will revert to a foreign broker operating out of Hong Kong or Taiwan, both of which are far beyond the reach of the EPA.

Since it is not worth the time for a foreign broker to assemble small lot shipments, such as Henry was doing, the companies he brokered for will end up paying substantial fees to have the materials hauled and dumped. Then if one of those dump sites is declared a Superfund site, the companies will end up paying that tab too.

The Superfund Law isn't the biggest problem within the EPA, but it is growing to the point where it will be one day. It's as if government agencies are vying to see which one can shut down the most industries first.

I'd like to share a comment from a report by the Environmental Business Association (September 9, 1991):

> Superfund's system is virtually unique in American jurisprudence—strict liability based solely upon status rather than conduct. Under Superfund, a company is liable for response costs at a site merely because it bears the statutory label of Owner, Operator, Generator, or Transporter. In addition, parties falling within these categories are subject to retroactive liability.

In an EPA bulletin issued on November 15, 1991, EPA administrator William K. Reilly said that the agency's criminal and civil

enforcement actions (not just for the Superfund but for all its activities) set records in fiscal year 1991. Record fines were levied, jail time
more than doubled, and record numbers of people were convicted of
violations. A great report for a "public service" organization, huh?

According to a recent study, the Superfund has developed a list
of 1200 sites to be cleaned up. Thus far only 63 actually have been
"completed." Unfortunately, more than 70 percent of all the allocat-
ed funds expended, both public and private, have gone to litigation
expenses.[1]

It would seem that the Superfund laws are a great boon to the
legal profession and a real drag on the economy. Remember that every dollar spent on these projects in actual cleanup or legal fees is a
dollar that must be taken from the productive side of the economy.

If this mess were limited to the 63 sites already committed, or
even the 1200 or so presently identified, it would be a drain on the
economy at a time when more, not less, productivity is needed. But
according to a study done by the University of Tennessee's Waste
Management Research and Education Institute, more than 32,000
additional sites are being considered for Superfund status. The projected cost of cleanup, if it were done today, would be in excess of $1
trillion.[2]

It's important to remember that the Superfund project is just
one part of the overall EPA agenda. In addition there are thousands
upon thousands of regulations issued under the Clean Air Act and
the Clean Water Act. Annual public and private spending on pollution control alone has grown from $50 billion in 1972 to more than
$115 billion in 1989 (in constant 1989 dollars). It's estimated that
the regulations reduced our Gross National Product by at least $170
billion in 1990, translating into a loss of approximately four million
jobs.[3]

We have sat idly by while extremists have taken their agenda to
the media and then to Washington, often with little fact and a lot of
fiction to back up their "observations."

REGULATIONS AND THE AVERAGE AMERICAN

The tendency is to look at a topic as broad and complex as environmental regulations and think: *It must be true or the media
wouldn't support it.* Or think: *It must be true or Congress wouldn't approve it.* Or, even worse, to think: *I can't do anything about it and,
besides, it doesn't really affect me.* But, in fact, we can do something

about these regulations; they really do affect each and every one of us, and many of them are not only unnecessary, they're harmful.

I am constantly amazed that virtually everyone I meet says they know the media is biased and really can't be trusted on issues like education, the environment, or even political polls, and yet they believe what they hear about global warming, the ozone crisis, or nuclear energy. As you will see, the truth is: You can't believe most of what you read, and none of what you hear.

For most Americans, their exposure to federal land use control has been limited to the national and state parks they visit with their families. And, for the most part, these national and state parks serve a valuable service by keeping a portion of our land for public use in a nearly natural state.

But there's another type of federal land use control: federal control of private property. Once the control of private (non-public) land passes into the hands of federal regulators, Americans lose the right to use their own property. This is exactly what is happening under the guise of protecting "public interest."

A real estate developer in the South purchased a tract of land along the coast that he intended to develop into housing and condominiums. Before buying the land, he had a thorough search done to determine if there were any land-use restrictions placed on the property and to ensure that it had the proper zoning for his use. The zoning was correct and there were no restrictions on the property.

> *If just one animal on the endangered species list is found in your backyard, your property can be seized . . . for the "public's good."*

After paying nearly $2 million for the property, he applied for and received the necessary permits to begin construction. But a disgruntled neighbor, who wanted the property to remain undeveloped, filed a complaint with the EPA citing the Clean Water Act. Under the Clean Water Act, the EPA can stop any land use that threatens a wetlands area.

To be classified as a wetland, the land doesn't actually have to be wet. Any land with groundwater within 18 inches of the surface or which contains wetlands plant life potentially qualifies as protected wetland. Anyone who knows anything about beach front property knows that some groundwater usually can be found within 18 inches of the surface. In fact, in Florida you would be hard pressed to find land anywhere that doesn't have water within a foot of the surface.

Upon receiving the complaint, the EPA issued a restraining order against any construction. The contractor, who had already incurred considerable expense on the basis of the local building permits, had to pay the grading contractor to stand by while he hired an attorney and went to court.

After several weeks of delay he finally got a local court to hear his case. The EPA claimed the court had no jurisdiction and had the case referred to federal court. Nearly six months later the contractor finally got his day in court, only to hear that the court had no jurisdiction over the EPA ruling.

The contractor clearly proved that his development was no different than a hundred other similar developments that had been built along the same coastline, but all to no avail.

After several more unsuccessful attempts to either reach a settlement or have the EPA restriction overruled, the contractor realized that he would spend more in court costs than he would ever make from the development, so he sued the EPA to recover his initial investment.

After nearly two years he finally got his case heard in federal court. Unbelievably, the argument the EPA used in defense of non-payment was that he could have resold the property to another contractor who wouldn't have known of the EPA restriction and recovered his investment. That was too much even for the judge. He ruled in the contractor's favor—investment costs plus legal fees.

To date he has not seen one dime of settlement. The EPA filed an appeal that will wind its way through the legal system. If, in fact, his case is overturned by an appeals court, he will then be liable for all the legal expenses, which amount to well over $2 million for the EPA alone. In the meantime, the land sits idle as a mute testimony to a bureaucracy gone insane.

THE SPOTTED OWL

There is probably no more well-known bird in America today than the Northwest spotted owl. The spotted owl came into prominence when environmentalists, operating under the banner of the 1973 Endangered Species Act, shut down eight and one-half million acres of public (and private) timberland that was declared the habitat of the owl.

The Endangered Species Act (ESA) originally was meant only to protect any animal declared to be "endangered." The term is nebulous at best, allowing the radical group in the environmental movement to use the ESA to accomplish their goal: stop industry.

In December of 1992, a U.S. District Judge approved a revamped list that will add an additional 401 plant and animal species to the Endangered Species Act by 1996, and another 900 later.[4]

If the environmentalists have their way, they will add an additional 3,000 candidates to the list. If just one animal on the endangered species list is found in your backyard, your property can be seized by the EPA for the "public's good."

In reality, the issue of the spotted owl only recently came on the scene. The environmentalists had been battling the loggers in Oregon, Washington, and California to stop all logging on public lands for many years. Previously they had resorted to spiking trees (driving hidden nails in them to destroy the loggers' chain saws), chaining themselves to trees, even wrecking equipment in covert nighttime raids on logging camps. But without federal might behind them, they were little more than an irritation.

They also found that loggers are not of a mind to sit idly by while any group takes away their livelihood. In physical confrontations with the loggers, prior to federal intervention, it was loggers— 20: environmentalists—0.

The arguments generally evolved along the lines that the environmentalists wanted all logging stopped, especially in the virgin forest areas, while the logging companies argued that they had contracts allowing them to harvest trees according to federal land management rules.

Just from reading accounts of the confrontations, it seems reasonable to assume that some compromise might have been reached with the environmentalists before the "all-or-nothing" leadership took control. After that it was open warfare between the loggers and the activists.

I can sympathize with the tree lovers to some degree, because I love the forests too. We run a training center in Dahlonega, Georgia, in the heart of the north Georgia mountains. Our facility is surrounded by a national forest managed by the Department of the Interior. In the mid-eighties we had our own run-in with the National Forestry Service.

Someone in a position of authority within the Forestry Service decided that nature doesn't do a good enough job at regulating the growth of the forest surrounding our property, so they decided to clear-cut the land and burn the residue.

When I first heard about this idea, I went to our local forestry office and asked who had made this decision. It seemed to me that the forest was doing just fine and had been doing fine for about three thousand years without the government's help.

I understand the logic of periodically cutting fire breaks and cleaning out some of the undergrowth to lessen the possibility of a forest fire, but the few acres I had seen them clear so far looked like an atomic bomb had exploded in the middle of the forest. Literally nothing was left standing.

I guess we might have taken a radical approach and spiked trees in the forest, or poured sand in the equipment's gas tanks, but I doubt that the Lord would have appreciated such actions. So I contacted the head of the Forestry Service in our area. After discussing my concerns he came out to see for himself. After only a few minutes we had reached a mutually acceptable compromise. The Forestry Service would allow clear-cutting in non-visible areas, and leave us a border along our property lines. I would have preferred that the forest be left intact, but at least it was a workable solution.

Later I found out that the Forestry Service actually paid the loggers to clear the property, instead of selling the logs at a profit; which only helped to confirm my notion that the federal government should not be involved in "free" enterprise—especially when that free enterprize costs the taxpayers money.

We all need to realize that forests are beautiful, but they are also a part of our country's renewable resources. As long as we're going to build homes and print papers we will need to harvest that resource. Commercial companies have proved that industry and nature are not necessarily incompatible. One has to wonder where the environmental absolutists think the homes and other products will come from if no commercial development is allowed inside the borders of our country. I would imagine if we could look inside most of their homes we would find lots of items made from wood and plastic. But perhaps its that same old tired concept of "I've got mine already."

It is interesting that many of the leading environmental activists, including Hollywood celebrities, have net worths in excess of $1 million, live in homes of 5,000 square feet or more, and own at least two vehicles. Many also own large recreational vehicles that average less than ten miles per gallon of gas. But, that's also another story.

Somewhere along the way, the original intent behind the Endangered Species Act got modified. According to the Environmental Law Institute, regulators now rely on the public trust doctrine, meaning that the government can restrict the use or sale of private lands if, in the opinion of the EPA, the public's interest might be harmed.

Armed with such vague language and supported by a media barrage that made the loggers in Oregon seem like the SS in Germany, the environmentalists were successful in using the spotted owl to shut down almost all logging in these affected states and causing unemployment for several thousand loggers and their families.

It would appear that once an environmental issue has been decided in favor of the activists, it can never be changed, even in the face of new evidence that the conclusions were in error. As the search for more spotted owl habitats has expanded, it has been discovered that the little owl is a lot more resilient than previously thought. The mandates for protecting the owl prescribe that a 70 acre circle be set aside wherever one of the little feathered friends are found.

We now know that the spotted owl, once thought to be very territorial, tends to migrate a lot and "owl circles" dot private land throughout western Oregon, restricting the owners' rights to use their property in any fashion. One enterprising ornithologist added up all the "dots" and found they exceed the total estimated population of spotted owls thought to exist.

Perhaps Congress will pass a law requiring the spotted owl to stay within the designated "owl zones." In the meantime, a great many lives have been disrupted and a lot of taxpayers' funds have been wasted on little more than a notion that an endangered species can be rescued by federal law.[5]

The episode with the spotted owls would be little more than one more crazy idea promoted by a few radicals looking for a cause except for two things: thousands of unemployed loggers and an administration dedicated to the activist cause. I suspect there are a lot more spotted-owl-type causes yet to come.

There are more than 750 varieties of animals, fish, plants, and insects currently on the endangered or threatened species list. The little-known Oregon silverspot butterfly campaign stopped the construction of a golf course in 1992 at an estimated cost of $3 million and a loss of 80 jobs.

A handful of wild salmon enthusiasts are disrupting river traffic and hydroelectric power production along the Colombia River, and protecting the California delta smelt may dry up irrigation water for the productive California Central Valley.[6]

The cost in human misery and, inevitably, human lives, seems to have no bearing on these decisions. It's as if the environmental movement has a life of its own in America. And if history has any lessons for us, it will get a lot worse. It is my personal belief that the one-world government enthusiasts, who once used the threat of world communism to thrust the United Nations into a dominant peace-keeping role, now have settled on nature and the environment as their clarion.

The environmental movement has become decidedly anti-development and, yet, all the evidence shows that the industrialized countries are by far the most ecologically sound nations of the world. As affluence comes to a people, they are able to set aside more of their resources to protect both the environment and the animals. If a nation sinks back to the need level economically, as many have in history, every available natural resource is tapped to the fullest.

I'm reminded of the wisdom imparted by Solomon: *"He who tills his land will have plenty of food, but he who follows empty pursuits will have poverty in plenty"* (Proverbs 28:19).

I know to some who are involved in the environmental movement it may seem as if I am attacking them. I am not. As I have said repeatedly, the environmental movement has done a lot of good in educating Americans on the need to conserve our resources and manage what God has given us. But don't be duped by the extremists who would say that all development is evil and, therefore, all developers are evil. God told Adam to tame (subdue) this world and make it fruitful. Much of what man has done is productive and adds to the natural environment.

As I said earlier, I grew up in Florida in the fifties, and I'm convinced that pesticides, land filling, land clearing, and proper wildlife management has made the place a lot more habitable. With a little common sense and a cooperative effort between development and environmental protection, we have shown that animals can do quite well around people.

It is only through the efficient management of our natural resources that we even have the luxury of protecting our environment.

Talk to people from Somalia, Ethiopia, Bangladesh, or even Cuba, and they will tell you emphatically that ecology takes a back seat to survival.

The environmental movement, carried to the extreme, can and is costing our country jobs. What's even more critical is that this policy, if allowed to continue unabated, can virtually destroy the economic futures of our children and grandchildren.

CHAPTER EIGHT

The Global Warming Myth

T he information you will read on this topic is so incredible it's hard even for me to believe. I will readily admit that I'm skeptical about most things I hear through the secular media, so I assumed that much of the hype about our environmental problems was exaggerated. What I didn't realize is that virtually *all* of it is either exaggerated or non-existent!

What must be brought into focus is the staggering cost to our economy to support what is little more than the fabrication of a small group of extremists. Many people involved in the environmental movement are dedicated and honest and believe they are helping to protect the environment for their children, but they have been sold a bill of goods by the extremists who are well funded, organized, and fanatically committed to their agenda.

As I said earlier, obviously some good has come from public awareness about problems in the workplace and the environment. But the good effects, such as controlling groundwater pollution and eliminating child labor, have evolved into an all-out assault on the industrialized world—and America in particular.

In doing research for the American Dream, I had been collecting articles, pro and con, assessing the real value of the regulations passed by our government, when I came across some articles by Dr. Jay Lehr. What immediately attracted my attention was that he presented a balanced perspective. As the Director of the Association of Water Scientists and Engineers and Professor of Hydrology at Ohio State University, his scientific credentials were impeccable. Dr. Lehr's detailed scientific data presents a perspective contrary to the majority of articles I found in media publications, including many scientific journals.

Actually, articles which presented a view contrary to that of the extremists (labeled eco-freaks by many scientists) only began appearing in the late eighties, after the environmental activists began systematically attacking virtually everything in the industrialized world as hazardous.

Once I had read Dr. Lehr's comments and tapped into the cadre of scientists who supported his perspective, I found out why there was so little information available in scientific journals: Those who disagree with the extremists are methodically excluded from publication. That sounds a lot like censorship, doesn't it? The environmental movement has become so powerful that virtually no one dares contradict its agenda. To do so invites the severest consequences, particularly from the academic community that proclaims "freedom of speech" so loudly.

There is a rational reason why the academic community so readily has accepted what appears to be bad science. It's called *money*. There are huge sums of taxpayers' money being spent to "save" our planet and much more to be spent in the future. We're not talking about mere billions here; we're talking *trillions*.

For a long while, the traditional liberals in our society have been attempting to use taxpayers' money to cure all the ills (as they see them) in the world. Many of these people are convinced that the only way to bring lasting peace and prosperity to the world is to yield total economic, political, and military control to a single, unified governing body. Never mind that the concept has been tried on a smaller scale in socialized countries and found to be a disaster. They somehow believe that since socialism didn't work on a national level it will work on a global scale.

The clarion for global unity for a long while was the threat of communism, although many of the same people had cheerfully embraced the teachings of Marx and Lenin earlier. With the collapse of world communism, their platform quickly shifted to global ecology and the threat of worldwide environmental disaster. As I heard one commentator remark, "The Reds have turned into the Greens."

Not surprisingly, the major factor in uniting this group was the election of Ronald Reagan in 1980. Having a conservative Republican in the White House eliminated many of the plum positions in the Washington bureaucracy and forced the more liberal extremists into the academic world.

Through the interlocking groups within academia, the activists were able to promote their own "theories" of looming global disasters. They also found a ready ally in the media, who are always ready to take on the "profiteers" of American industry.

Lest you think this type of fact manipulation does not really occur in the academic world, consider this: It is the academic world that confidently declares the Earth to be at least 4.5 billion years old, with virtually no evidence except their word to support such a theory. It is also the same group that prepared the elaborate display depicting the evolution of monkeys to men in the Smithsonian—with absolutely no factual data to support their models.

This is also the same group that confidently announced that landing men on the moon would confirm the age of the universe once and for all. Simply put, the moon, being an airless planetoid would have been collecting cosmic dust since it formed, shortly after the universe cooled (according to their theory). So all the lunar explorers had to do was stick a long pole down into the dust and measure it. The minimum depth of the dust, based on the four billion year old theory should have been at least several feet. Instead, it turned out to be about one-eighth of an inch.

What was the explanation of the "scientists" once the empirical evidence disputed their theory? "Obviously, there is more dust falling in space now than there was in the past."

The truth is, those who are totally committed to their particular agenda will ignore all contrary facts and will ridicule anyone who dares to challenge them, including those within their own community. This is the same group that screams "censorship" when anyone challenges their x-rated sex education material in the public schools and then actively supports the removal of all religious content from history books. They will sue the cities to assure the rights of winos and drug addicts to sleep in, on, and around public facilities; then they will sue the same cities for allowing a nativity scene to be displayed on the courthouse lawn.

The majority of Americans are concerned with pollution and are committed to preserving as much of the natural beauty of our country as possible. But too often the "average" American is ignorant of the true facts and knows little, other than what is seen on television or read in the papers. We must be aware that just because a particular philosophy is espoused in the media, that does not make it true. In fact, the more research I do the more I am prone *not* to believe it if the media support it.

I readily admit that I also am biased in my evaluation of the radical leaders of the environmental movement. In reviewing the names that usually accompany environmental rallies, they're almost always the same ones that enlist with groups like Planned Parenthood, N.O.W., the ACLU, Queer Nation, ACT UP, and many others. These radicals also go to great lengths to keep any contrary views out of the media, and they are not against blacklisting anyone who disagrees with them.

I have a difficult time giving any great humanitarian accolades to those who will spend millions to save whales and dolphins, while heartily endorsing the killing of unborn humans to control population growth.

THE GREENHOUSE HOAX

Just in case you are not aware of the so-called "greenhouse theory," I would like to outline the essential argument.

Since about the early fifties a group of scientists and amateur ecologists have been concerned that the carbon dioxide emissions from many industrial factories, automobiles, and the like, are increasing the levels of carbon dioxide (CO_2) in our atmosphere, which is true. They also believe that higher CO_2 levels lead to higher atmospheric temperatures worldwide. Hence, the so-called "global warming" theory.

It is generally accepted that CO_2 in our atmosphere has increased by approximately 30 percent over the last 100 years although, interestingly enough, most of the measurable warming of our planet occurred before 1950, while most of the CO_2 buildup came after that date. In other words, the slight increase in global temperature came prior to the real energy consumption phase.

Fossil fuels such as oil, coal, and gas, are commonly thought to be the greatest single new source of CO_2. However, the basic issue is not whether CO_2 is being added to the atmosphere. It is.

The real issue is whether this additional CO_2, as a byproduct of the industrial revolution, is harmful to our world. If it is, then by all means we should take measures to reduce the output of CO_2. But if it is *not*, then we are spending hundreds of billions needlessly and strangling American businesses in the process—all because someone "says" we should.

Since the implementation of the federal Clean Air Act, the government has mandated the use of catalytic converters for all U.S. automobiles, strict enforcement of greater gas milage standards, scrubbers for coal-fired power plants, total elimination of wood-burning fireplaces in many areas of the country, and a general all out war on CO_2 emissions that is estimated to cost somewhere between $25 and $100 billion a year at present.[1]

Remember, these costs are borne by every working American (and many now-unemployed Americans). Regulatory costs are essentially hidden taxes.

At the Earth Summit in Rio in 1992, the basic premise was to force the industrialized nations of the world to drastically cut their CO_2 emissions by all possible means, even if it meant shutting down their industries. Fortunately the U.S. didn't support the conference agenda and no action was taken. But the pressure for the U.S. to join persists, and Vice President Gore is a leading supporter of the Rio agenda. It is a virtual certainty that the U.S. will support the Rio Accord, or something similar, in the future.

THE EVIDENCE OF GLOBAL WARMING AND RUNAWAY CO_2

Prior to the industrial revolution, the concentration of CO_2 levels in the atmosphere was approximately 280 parts per million (ppm). It is now approximately 360 ppm and estimates are that it could reach 600 ppm sometime in the twenty-first century, just as the global warming activists decry.[2]

According to the global "warmists" this will result in a temperature increase of four to five degrees centigrade, and the ice caps will melt away, inundating Miami Beach as well as a lot of other low-lying real estate—again, the so-called "greenhouse effect."

But here we are, well over half way to the catastrophic level, and we have had virtually no global warming. In fact, the average temperature of the Earth has not increased appreciably in the last 50 years.[3]

Although we did have approximately a .5 degree centigrade increase over the last 100 years, most scientists believe this is a cyclical warming from a little Ice Age that began in the fifteenth century and continued into the 1800s.

In Charles Dickens' day, the Thames River froze over and was used for ice skating—a phenomenon that has not been repeated in the last 120 years.

According to Dr. Hugh Ellsaesser, physicist at Lawrence Livermore National Laboratory and author of more than 100 articles in scientific journals on our global climate, "[the evidence suggests] that the bulk of greenhouse gases we have added to the atmosphere have produced no warming."[4]

In fact, some scientists believe that the increase in CO_2 will have a positive effect on the planet since it helps to boost the productive capacity of green plants (CO_2 is a natural fertilizer), leading to higher crop yields, more forests, and less water usage by plants.[5]

The contention in many of the articles I reviewed is that ice crystals in the atmosphere (H_2O) have a much greater effect on global warming than CO_2 does. In essence, there is a self-leveling system built into our atmosphere: More CO_2 yields more plant growth; more plant growth feeds more people; and more people put out more CO_2. One has to wonder if this is God's natural mechanism for the increasing population on our planet. As you will see later, population growth also is promoted as a crisis demanding regulation.

One interesting side note is that some scientists acknowledge that output of CO_2 from termites is more than twice that from all fossil fuel combustion.[6]

Mount Pinatubo in the Philippines last year hurled upwards of 30 million tons of material into the stratosphere. Also, the eruption of Mount St. Helens in Washington state in 1980 dumped more than 910,000 metric tons of CO_2 into the atmosphere, dwarfing the output of all industrial sources.[7]

The increase in CO_2 is real; global warming is a *myth*! How can something as obvious as the great global warming myth be perpetrated for so long and even attract major legislation to cure the "problem?" The truth is that global warming is a means to an end for the activists who want more government regulation and control. At stake here is the redistribution of hundreds of billions of dollars to their environmental causes.

Many Washington politicians feel the heat of the environmentalists' effective lobby, and the permanent bureaucrats see the possibility of another group of Americans dependent on the government. With this dependency comes a whole new bureaucracy and then thousands more federal employees who are pledged to the people who started the cycle in the first place. If you don't believe that's true, just stop and look around at what's happening today.

I won't take the time and space to detail all of the statistical data that, in my judgment, conclusively verifies there is no global warming threat. A review of the Appendix will provide a reference list of resource material. Needless to say, it is not a lack of objective, non-partisan evidence that keeps the activists and the politicians who cater to them ignorant. In fact, most of the available evidence demonstrates that an increase in CO_2 is potentially very beneficial; and even if it were not, we couldn't control it anyway.

An article by Dr. Sherwood B. Idso, a research physicist with the U.S. Department of Agriculture says: "Much of the world was a degree or two *warmer* about 6,000 and 1,000 years ago, when the CO_2 content of the atmosphere was fully 80 ppm less [22 percent] than it is today."

Dr. Idso goes on to suggest that, far from hurting our planet, increased levels of CO_2 will benefit the earth. As atmospheric CO_2 concentrations more than double, plant water use efficiencies more than double. Grasslands will flourish where deserts now lie barren. Shrubs will grow where only grasses grew before."[8]

In his article, "Global Warming Change: Facts and Fiction," Dr. Fred Singer, director of the Science and Environmental Policy Project, Washington Institute for Values in Public Policy, says that much of the temperature data collected over the last several hundred years suggests that global cooling has been more of a problem than global warming.

As Dr. Singer points out, "Actual climate cooling, experienced during the 'Little Ice Age,' or in the famous 1816 New England 'Year Without Summer' caused large-scale agricultural losses and even famines."[9] More recently, the early fall of 1991, losses of crops in the northern and western United States were due to early frosts.

This sudden and totally unexpected burst of cold weather certainly quieted the global warming alarmists, who had used the warm cycle of the mid-eighties as absolute evidence that their conclusions were correct. In truth, when dealing with long-term trends, such as global weather, neither side of an issue can use short-term cycles as "evidence." Unfortunately, once climate-related regulatory laws are on the books, it is very difficult or impossible to remove them. Global warming is becoming the rallying cry for one more obstacle in the path of our struggling economy.

It is almost impossible to calculate the real cost of the global warming "solution," but you can see its effect in the down-sizing of cars, the elimination of many coal-fired power plants, and the alarm over deforestation in Brazil. Of course, each of these have some positive aspects that benefit all of us—if kept in reason. But each and every benefit has to be weighed against the real need and long-term costs in jobs and lives. More often than not, a national solution is applied to a local problem.

For instance, Los Angeles and Denver both have local smog problems that require more intensive emission control. But does that justify the cost of millions of dollars and lost jobs for the rest of the country? Only by shouting "Global Warming" have the activists been able to attract national attention to what, in reality, is a local issue.

If the plants could vote, they would ask for legislation requiring more CO_2, not less, because after all, as Dr. Singer points out, atmospheric CO_2 is simply plant food.[10]

The next time you hear someone promote more legislation to control the threat of "global warming," you need to look at it from a different perspective: They're causing your children and grandchildren to give up their jobs to solve a problem that doesn't exist!

To be sure, this is not the last we will hear about "global warming" or a myriad of other environmental emergencies over the next several years. Once this kind of movement gets rolling it takes on a life of its own. Under President Reagan the trend was slowed down a bit but now, with an issue-sensitive administration in the White House and an environmentalist vice president, I suspect we haven't seen the beginning of the real regulatory phase.

What's so sad is that, 10 or 20 years from now, the next generation will be looking around at a stagnant economy, fewer jobs at lower wages, and have no idea how it happened. The blame will be shifted to the industrialists who failed to remain competitive and the greedy company owners who abandoned the American workers to give their jobs elsewhere; but in reality they were regulated and taxed and litigated out of America. The entrepreneurs certainly aren't pure, but it's like passing a law to shoot wolves and then wondering why there are too many caribou around. It's called "cause and effect."

Myths about the environment seem to abound today. Perhaps the greatest myth with the largest following is that the ozone layer is dying. In the next chapter we'll look at one of the really great hoaxes of the twentieth century. P.T. Barnum, who said, "There's a sucker born every minute," would be proud of this scam. It is perhaps the biggest in the history of mankind, with the greatest potential for economic disaster.

CHAPTER NINE

The Hole in the Ozone Myth

I n the world of the environmental extremists, virtually all technology is evil—even that which helps the poor and needy of
lesser countries. As a result, one of the greatest boons to humanity—refrigeration—has come under assault and is in danger of
being regulated out of existence for the poorest nations.

It's not really refrigeration itself that is considered the menace
by the environmentalists; it's freon, the gas used in refrigeration. Freon is comprised primarily of chlorofluorocarbons (CFCs) that are
widely condemned as the primary culprit in the destruction of the
thin stratospheric layer of O_3 molecules—commonly called the ozone
layer.

The ozone layer is beneficial in filtering ultraviolet (UV) radiation from reaching the Earth's surface. Anyone who does any reading
about threats to the Earth's environment is well aware of the battle to
save the ozone.

What you probably don't know (as I did not) is that our government agreed to one of the most expensive and restrictive regulations
ever imposed on any economy to rid our country of any commercial
CFCs by the year 1996. The agreement, known as the Montreal Pro-

tocol, sets stringent limits on the use of CFCs worldwide. Many Third World nations refused to sign on until the U.S. and other countries agreed to foot the bill.

In 1987 a group consisting of most of the industrialized nations met in Montreal to discuss the discontinuation of all CFCs worldwide. At this conference the environmental activists beseeched these nations to save the planet from what they termed "sure and certain destruction" and the ultimate annihilation of the human race, due to skin cancer caused by ultra violet radiation (as a result of the ozone depletion attributed to CFCs). Thus, the Montreal Accord was adopted.

Under the terms of the Montreal Protocol (as amended in 1990), all use of CFCs, including the world's primary refrigerant, freon, would be phased out totally by the year 2000. This was no small matter considering the number of refrigeration units already in existence that use freon, as you will see.

Then in November of 1992, shortly after the presidential elections in the U.S., a new conference was held in Copenhagen. At this conference the target date for eliminating CFCs in the industrialized world was accelerated to 1996, based on "new" data presented by then-EPA director William Reilly that ozone depletion would lead to 5 million cases of skin cancer and 70,000 deaths in the U.S. alone over the next 100 years, unless every nation accelerated the phase-out.

It is critical that you understand the scope of what has been proposed concerning CFCs, and especially freon—both economically and socially. If, as the EPA director proclaimed, the ozone is being depleted and massive increases in cancer will result, the phase-out still would be difficult to justify—considering the number of deaths that will result from a lack of adequate refrigeration, particularly in underdeveloped countries.

But, if the ozone problem is just a figment of some environmental group's imagination, then we are embarking on the greatest economic blunder in history.

The phase-out of freon for the underdeveloped countries is set ten years further back than that of the industrialized nations, but that is sure to change as new "evidence" is released by the environmentalists.

There is some element of truth behind every theory, including those espoused by the environmental activists. The difficulty is that when the extremists hear about a potential environmental problem,

they go into a frenzy, ignoring any and all data contrary to their conclusion that industry is destroying the Earth. Such appears to be the
case of the great ozone myth.

To understand the ozone debate, we have to back up a bit because the ozone scare really began with the supersonic transport
(SST) back in the sixties. As word of the airline industry's plans to
develop and build a fleet of some 500 supersonic planes (just to ferry
lazy rich people around the globe) reached the environmentalists,
they marshaled their forces to stop it. Based on little more than
hunches, these activists launched a campaign to have the SST program killed under the threat that a fleet of supersonic planes would
utterly destroy the stratosphere, including the lifesaving ozone layer.
The headlines of the time usually read something like, "If ozone dies,
humanity dies too."

Initially the ozone culprit from the SSTs was thought to be water vapor released into the stratosphere. This H_2O then would break
down into its elements, allowing the oxygen to combine with the
ozone, thus destroying it.

---

*One additional bit of data
"overlooked" by the activists
was that the ozone-destroying
chlorine . . . also occurs
naturally in huge quantities.*

Unfortunately for the alarmists, further studies showed that the
SST water vapor would have only a negligible effect on the ozone, if
any at all. Not deterred by this, the activists, now totally "anti-SST-
ites," scoured every test report looking for another reason to stop the
project.

They found it in a NASA document noting that sufficient quantities of nitrogen oxide, found in any combustion process, might destroy the ozone layer. Again the headlines carried the banner of
"Ozone Will Cause Skin Cancer! Melanoma!"

This time the activist lobby was successful in getting all government backing for the SST project canceled, thus effectively killing

the project. The activists went home confident that they had saved all mankind from a terrible death.

Later, further scientific study showed that vast amounts of nitrogen oxides occurred naturally, and the total effect of a fleet of SSTs would be negligible. Nary a word was carried by any major newspaper or network. Actually a subsequent study completed in 1978 showed that the net effect of the SSTs on the ozone would have been *positive!* Still nary a word from the environmental group.[1]

But nothing is ever lost on those who are seeking a cause—especially something as tasty as the ozone layer. Once their interest was sparked in "protecting" the ozone, the eco-activists simply went on looking for another potential threat, especially something produced by their major target—industry.

In 1974 two scientists working with the California Institute of Technology discovered a possible culprit: CFCs found in freon and used as propellants in aerosol cans. It was theorized that CFCs released into the atmosphere could potentially break down into their elements, thus producing chlorine that could attack the ozone layer.

Interestingly enough, what that study or any subsequent study did not demonstrate was how these CFCs, which are heavier than the surrounding atmosphere, would "float" up to the ozone layer some twenty to thirty miles above the Earth's surface.

Not to be deterred by something as trivial as the lack of scientific evidence, the activists concluded they had found their "smoking gun!" They confidently proclaimed that CFCs were destroying the ozone layer.

There was another theory that any ozone degradation might be the result of methane gas emitted into the atmosphere, but since the major sources of methane in the atmosphere are belching cows and volcanoes, no one could get particularly excited over those. Once the Congress was alerted to the potential disaster from CFCs, the politicians joined in the chorus. The activists finally had an issue: commercially produced CFCs. Now *that* was a target worth pursuing!

One additional bit of data "overlooked" by the activists was that the ozone-destroying chlorine, supposedly emitted by the CFCs as they break down, also occurs naturally in huge quantities. Volcanoes spew out some estimated 12 million tons of hydrochloric acid into the atmosphere each year. This natural chlorine, along with billions of tons of ocean salt (sodium chloride) dwarf all the puny efforts of mankind to produce chlorine from CFCs.[2]

Atmospheric Sources of Chlorine
(Millions of Tons)

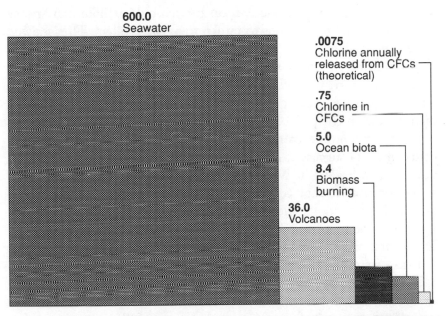

Reprinted with permission from *The Holes in the Ozone Scare: The Scientific Evidence That the Sky Isn't Falling,* by Rogelio A. Maduro and Ralf Schauerhammer (Washington, DC: 21st Century Science Associates, 1992), p. 13.

As you can see, the effect of man's contribution to the world's chlorine output is pretty minuscule when compared to that of a single volcano. I keep looking for congressional appropriations aimed at studying what it would cost to plug all the volcanoes in the world, but as of now no funding is available.

It is astounding how much scientific data is available that directly contradicts the theories promoted by the environmentalists. Surely this same information has been made available to the media and the Congress. One has to wonder why CBS, NBC, or ABC has not done one of their famous docudramas on this issue.

In spite of the best efforts of responsible scientists to require conclusive scientific evidence that CFCs were an environmental threat, by 1978 the pressure exerted by the eco-activists had resulted in a "voluntary" ban on the use of CFCs in aerosol cans.

It would seem that industry never really learns the lesson about compromising with the extremist groups. Once industry announced their voluntary ban on CFC propellants, it gave instant credibility to the idea that CFCs were destroying the ozone. The next target on the agenda was the total elimination of all CFCs from the world.

In reading over the newspaper articles and other data from the late seventies, I am truly impressed with the scope of the activists' vision. Getting a worldwide ban on freon would be like convincing all the industrialized nations to return to outside toilets. They may do the same job, but at a great inconvenience.

Or think of trying to force all Americans to give up running water and return to hauling it by the bucketful to conserve its use. There would be great opportunities for bucket manufacturers but open revolt on the part of average Americans.

The magnitude of this project is such that it truly dwarfs all other projects suggested by the environmentalists. They had to sell our political leaders in Washington on the idea of spending a *trillion* dollars or more to replace all the refrigeration systems in the world.

But trying to get the government to hear their pleas about saving the ozone by banning all CFCs, including freon, was not simple. In the first place, there were no practical substitutes, and those that did exist were highly corrosive, costly, and often poisonous.

Furthermore, neither the Japanese nor the Europeans were particularly interested in such a ban. The Japanese had their sights set on selling low-cost refrigeration to the hungry billions in the underdeveloped countries of the world. What the activists needed to push this agenda any further was a scare—a really big one.

The save-the-ozone campaign was rapidly dying out by 1980, based on more exhaustive scientific data disclosing that the projected depletion of ozone was not occurring. The extremists estimated in 1975 that 25 percent of the ozone layer would be gone by the year 2000 as a result of CFCs. But by 1980 their estimates were down to 18 percent. By 1982 they lowered their estimates to 7 percent, and by 1984 the estimate dropped to a minuscule 2 to 4 percent. In other words, no problem existed.

Then in 1985 a British scientific team studying the ozone layer above Antarctica discovered a short-lived decline in the layer above the South Pole of nearly 50 percent! When this announcement appeared in scientific journals, the activists shouted to the world, "There's a hole in the ozone!"

Finally the alarm could be sounded! Immediately the eco-activists pointed their fingers at the CFCs, demanding an immediate ban on this manmade chemical that would surely destroy all life on Earth.

Again the preponderance of objective scientific data was ignored. Writing in *The Washington Times* (April 12, 1992), Dr. Dixy
Lee Ray, former chairman of the Atomic Energy Commission, noted
that the dramatic new finding of the Antarctica ozone hole was neither dramatic nor new. In 1956 Dr. Gordon Dobson, a Cambridge
meteorologist who devised the instrumentation and techniques for
measuring the ozone layer and whose name is used to grade the ozone
layer (Dobson units), discovered a hole in the ozone above the Antarctic. When this same hole appeared again the next year, he reported it as a *naturally* occurring annual event.

In 1958 two French scientists measured the ozone "hole." It was
thinner than at any time since.[3] Drs. Rogelio A. Maduro and Ralf
Schauerhammer, authors of *The Holes in the Ozone Scare*, offer a totally plausible explanation for this hole in the ozone. They state that
it is the result of thermal drafts in the Antarctic (well known and
well documented) caused by the drastic temperature change between
the global ice cap (-80°C)and the ice pack that covers the ocean
(0°C).

Simply put: When the warmer air rising off the Arctic Ocean
meets the cold land mass, it falls. The result is a down draft that
creates a hole in the upper atmosphere, including the ozone. When
the sun heats the southern hemisphere again, the hole either closes
up, or nearly so, depending on the atmospheric conditions. There is
nothing mystical or chemical about the hole in the ozone over the
Antarctic area.

But, in spite of all evidence to the contrary (and fed by the
demands of the eco-activists), the media carried headline stories
about CFCs creating the "hole in the ozone." Then incredibly, with
almost no scientific evidence to support the idea, the activists, led by
EPA director, William Reilly, confidently proclaimed that skin cancer and, in particular, malignant melanoma in the United States had
increased nearly 100 percent due to the thinning ozone layer.

In fact, the incident of skin melanoma has increased but not as
any result of the ozone. Dr. Fred Singer, in his article "My Adventures in the Ozone Layer," points out that melanoma has increased
nearly 800 percent since records started being kept in 1935, with no
corresponding change in the ozone. It is thought that the increase in
skin cancer is related to the sun tan fad experienced in the U.S.—not
to ecological factors.

The eco-activists also failed to acknowledge clear scientific data
showing that ozone depletion of 5 percent results in an effective in-

crease in ultraviolet radiation that is the equivalent of moving 60 miles closer to the equator (UV increases as one moves toward the equator). In other words, people in Miami get more UV exposure than those in Palm Beach.

Facts notwithstanding, once the infamous hole in the ozone was announced, the politicians and business people who opposed the ban on CFCs simply "rolled over and played dead," according to Dr. Singer.

By endorsing the Montreal Protocol, the United States is now participating in a total phase-out of all CFCs by January 1, 1996.[4]

This effort is going to be unbelievably costly because there is really no acceptable substitute for the refrigerant freon. Most of the substitutes now available are caustic, corrosive, flammable, and generally don't work as well. For instance, a refrigerator using freon as the primary coolant costs about $500 (1993) and has an average life-span of something over 20 years. A refrigerator made with one of the next-best ecologically acceptable coolants—sulfur dioxide, methyl chloride, or anhydrous ammonia—will cost approximately $700 and will have a prospective lifetime of 10 to 12 years.

But far more significant than this is the possible side effect of many of these substitutes: death. In *The Holes in the Ozone Scare*, Maduro and Schauerhammer state that these refrigerants were used widely before synthesized CFCs were introduced to the market.

"The danger of the existing refrigerants was dramatically demonstrated in 1929, when more than 100 people died in a Cleveland hospital from a leak in the hospital's refrigeration system. *The New York Times* and other newspapers were waging a major campaign to ban household refrigerators as too dangerous, and fears about poisoning were the major reason at that time that 85 percent of U.S. families with electricity had no refrigerators in their homes. As a result of these disasters and the publicity, the future of refrigeration was at stake."

I doubt that most of us would rest well at night knowing that the ozone layer was safe but a leaky refrigerator could kill us in our sleep. Actually, one additional non-toxic refrigerant known as HCFC is available, and although it is nearly four times as expensive as freon, it does work well. But HCFCs are also under attack by the ozone activists and a permanent ban on HCFCs by the year 2030, with a 35 percent reduction by 2004 was part of the Montreal Protocol. Based on previous experience, we can expect those deadlines to be accelerated as the ecological movement gains momentum under the Clinton administration.[5]

The enormous cost of banning freon can not be accurately estimated. There is some $135 *billion* worth of industrial refrigeration equipment in use today and, in addition, in the United States alone we have 100 million refrigerators, 95 million automobile air conditioners, and nearly 100,000 commercial office buildings with central air conditioning systems. The total cost to convert or replace these systems is estimated to be somewhere between $2 and $3 *trillion* dollars—for a problem that many scientists don't believe exists![6]

I grew up in an era when air conditioning and, to some extent, home refrigeration were a luxury of the rich only. The memories of hot, humid nights in Florida are still quite vivid, as are the stories of heat strokes that killed many elderly people during the summers. I question whether the average American taxpayer would vote to return to that style of living plus pay the additional cost in jobs that a total ban on freon is likely to create. Particularly on such flimsy evidence as an oscillating ozone hole.

One very salient point made by many of the atmospheric scientists who disagree with the ozone activists is: If the ozone layer is really thinning (which is nearly impossible to measure because of the enormous number of variables), there should be a measurable increase in the amount of ultraviolet radiation being received on the Earth's surface.

To me this sounds like a logical argument since the effect of ozone depletion is supposed to be increased cancer, due to more UV penetration. In fact, based on the unequivocal statement by Mr. Reilly, director of the Environmental Protection Agency, 5 million Americans *will* develop skin cancer as a result of this increased radiation, and 70,000 *will* die due to ozone thinning.[7] Actually, according to an earlier statement made by the EPA in 1990, the cancer figure was estimated to be 12 million, with 100,000 deaths. In either case the position was taken that the ozone was deteriorating, and the deaths were absolutely attributable to the increased UV pouring through.

Even if that were true (which it has been shown not to be), perhaps a less expensive solution would be to issue sun block lotion to all the fair skinned people of the Earth. The darker skinned people have a natural resistance to UV and would be less effected.

Scientist John Delouisi of the National Oceanic and Atmospheric Administration (NOAA), whose job it is to monitor the increase in UV radiation, says meters at eight different monitoring stations throughout the United States show "an average surface ultraviolet radiation trend of *minus* 8 percent from 1974 to 1985."[8]

In other words, there has been a rather consistent decrease in the amount of UV striking the Earth. I rather doubt that this bit of information ever makes the evening news.

Perhaps the cruelest hoax of all is being played on the poorest nations. Think of what it would be like to live in America without the refrigeration we accept as a routine convenience. Then multiply that by about 1,000 percent for the poorer transportation, lack of food processing plants, and lower incomes of the third world countries, and you can see their plight.

One of the most basic needs recognized by almost all relief organizations is that of inexpensive food refrigeration. Instead, these poor countries will be facing an impossible barrier as more and more non-industrialized nations are forced to join the Montreal Accord and cease the use of freon. This single act is condemning millions, if not hundreds of millions, of people to early deaths through disease and hunger.

The majority of immunization vaccines and antibiotics require constant refrigeration. The health care needs of these nations will revert to that of the nineteenth century without ready access to inexpensive refrigeration.

One has to wonder if perhaps the real agenda of the extreme environmental movement isn't to reduce the population of the world. If not, the end result will be the same. Many of the programs the extremists promote, including elimination of CFCs, reduction of CO_2, elimination of DDT, and prohibiting the development of forest land, result in deeper poverty and, ultimately, in more deaths. Interestingly, this suggestion was made by many of the scientists involved in basic research on each of these areas.

Before leaving this discussion on the ozone and banning CFCs, I would like to summarize some of the basic facts about what a little research uncovered.

1. The hole in the ozone, supposedly caused by CFCs, was first discovered in the early fifties (long before the proliferation of freon and hair sprays).
2. The world's leading atmospheric scientist explained the phenomenon to the satisfaction of the other leading atmospheric scientists at that time, with no link to CFCs.

3. CFCs are significantly heavier than the Earth's air, and no one to date has explained how they would "float" into the upper atmosphere.

4. Virtually everyone agrees that the CFCs would have to break down to chlorine to attack the ozone layer, and while some probably do, the total output of the entire industrialized world is a blip when compared to even one active volcano and less than that when compared to the oceans of the world.

5. Even if the ozone layer were deteriorating, it would have little effect on human beings, regardless of the ultraviolet radiation. People at the equator survive multiple times the normal UV that anyone living in the higher and lower latitudes do.

6. Actual monitoring stations set up to check the increased UV show a steady decline in UV concentration striking the Earth. One should, therefore, logically conclude that the ozone layer is increasing rather than decreasing.

If all this is really so, then what in the world are we doing spending multiple trillions of dollars to solve a problem that only exists in the imaginations of some environmental fanatics?

DEFORESTATION

Most environmentalists deplore the deforestation taking place in the Amazon rain forests and other virgin forests of the world. The most common "alarm" that rings is the danger of oxygen depletion and global climate change.

There are many reasonable arguments for not clearing all the virgin forests in the world, but the oxygen content of our air is not one of them. According to many noted scientists, the clearing of the rain forests in Brazil and other Central American countries will not affect the supply of oxygen or the overall weather on our planet to any perceptible degree. Obviously that does not mean that we should encourage the underdeveloped nations to cut down every tree on Earth, but neither does it mean that clearing a reasonable amount of rain forest will disrupt the ecosystem.

According to Dr. Robert Buschbacher, a Fulbright scholar working in Brazil, only 1.55 percent of the Brazilian portion of the Amazon rain forest in Brazil has been deforested.[9] Certainly this land clearing will have little effect on the ecology of our world.

According to Dr. Sherwood Idso, a research scientist with the U.S. Water Conservation Laboratory, the world's plant and animal life would not suffer from a lack of oxygen even if all the rain forests were eliminated *totally*. Such vast reserves of oxygen have been built up over the centuries that it would take "hundreds of millions of years for the oxygen content of the earth to disappear," even if every tree, plant, shrub, and blade of grass were to vanish overnight." And, in fact, as the agricultural minister of Brazil points out, much of the deforested areas are quickly covered with new growth and revert to a nearly natural state. [10]

Dr. Petr Beckmann, author of *Access to Energy*, makes a further point: "Rain forests making way for agriculture in developing countries is a natural and human phenomenon that is unlikely to threaten anyone. None of these environmentalists in America would exist today if the Europeans hadn't burned the virgin forests that covered Europe to make room for agriculture."

Again, it's the "I've got mine, don't cut yours" mentality. Or as Proverbs says: "*Abundant food is in the fallow ground of the poor, but it is swept away by injustice.*"

Don't be duped by the activists who cry, "We're destroying the world ecological balance." There is no scientific evidence to support such a claim. However, there is a vast array of evidence to support the fact that millions of future jobs are being destroyed by their ever-increasing attack on any industrialized expansion.

I trust that Christians are not so easily duped by a lot of media hype and the shouting of the extremists that the world is being polluted beyond recovery.

As noted before, the early environmental movement did a lot of good in educating the average consumer on the need to clean up our rivers and streams, control our solid waste, and recycle wherever the costs justify it.

But we must speak out for reason and balance, which is in short supply among the extremist groups. They scream at the utility companies for burning coal to light our homes and then picket to stop all use of nuclear energy. They demand that the road leading to Aspen, Colorado be made ecologically aesthetic, at a cost of nearly $4 million a mile to the taxpayers, and say nary a word about the non-aesthetic chair lifts that take them up the mountains to their ski runs. They counsel the Congress to make the "little people" drive smaller cars, while driving motor homes to and from the film studios. And on it goes.

It is amazing to me that we allow so many people with so little proven character to set our national policy on issues that will ultimately be paid for by the rest of us. Edmund Burke was absolutely correct when he said, "The only thing necessary for the triumph of evil is for good [people] to do nothing."

Or as Proverbs 14:15 says, *"The naive believes everything, but the prudent man considers his steps."*

CHAPTER TEN

The War Against the World's Hungry

I rather suspect that very few Americans have ever thought much about a link between world hunger and regulations in our country. After all, many of the environmental activists are involved with relief organizations that help raise funds to fight world hunger. There's no logical reason to think that most of them are anything other than humanitarians, regardless of how misdirected their personal lives might be.

However, the more information I gather, the more convinced I have become that either these people are terribly naive or else they are so committed to their environmental agenda that even the needs of the poor take second place.

The evidence shows that the real burden of environmental regulation falls most heavily on the poorest people of the world. Our economy suffers because of stifled productivity, but our daily survival is not an issue—yet. However, in the poorest nations, anything that decreases their food production even a small percentile translates into hunger and famine. No amount of benevolence can supplant the need for any nation to be able to feed itself.

Benevolence sustains life at the lowest level, and once it diminishes, as benevolence always does, the hunger returns. Most people are willing to help short-term; few are willing to help forever.

It is not surprising that rules and regulations passed in the U.S. will affect virtually everyone else in the world. We are, after all, still the world's largest economy, and we represent nearly 80 percent of the world's benevolence. But even more impressive is the fact that we either directly or indirectly control most of the world's most vital commodity: food.

Our farmers are so productive that less than 5 percent of the American work force is able to feed the other 95 percent and still have enough left over to feed half of the industrialized world. The term *industrialized* is an important one. We could theoretically feed the impoverished, developing (or dying) third world countries as well. But it is not profitable to do so. They can't pay for the food they need, and their internal transportation system is almost non-existent, so just getting the food to them is extremely costly.

Even if we could get the food to them it would be only a temporary fix. Without a lifetime commitment to supplying and distributing food, the best we can do is delay the inevitable. History has shown that the only real answer to poverty and famine is to teach the people how to clear their land, plant the food they will need and, thus, maintain the supply indefinitely.

This certainly can be done. After all, when the pilgrims came to America there was no farmland (except a few Indian fields) in cultivation. And yet, in less than 100 years we were feeding ourselves and had become the biggest exporters of agricultural products in the world.

There are other factors that temporarily can keep a nation from being able to meet the basic needs of its people: poor quality land, lack of water, cyclical droughts, and so on; but, except in a few rare instances, these are not paramount factors.

In Central Africa, tribal wars fought with modern arms have taken their toll. Certainly that's true in places like Uganda, Somalia, Bangladesh, and others. But on a much larger scale, there are problems that can destroy any nation's ability to feed its people. Chief among these problems are the *insects*.

This prolific hoard of voracious eaters are constantly doing battle with human beings. We compete for the same land and the same food and, more often than not, we lose.

Some species of insects (including those that carry diseases) thrive off of man himself. Insect-borne diseases have wiped out countless millions of human beings over the centuries. In modern times, through the use of insecticides, especially DDT, science was on the verge of conquering insect-borne diseases. But because of the determined efforts of the ecological extremists to eliminate the use of pesticides, many diseases, such as malaria and diphtheria, are making dramatic comebacks.

This can be traced almost directly to the ban on the use of DDT. One has to wonder if those who spent hundreds of millions of dollars to stop the production and distribution of this cheap, effective pesticide care more about insects and birds than they do people. They seem to lean decidedly to the side of non-human species.

One agenda of the radical side of the environmental group is to reduce the world's population in order to maintain the environment in its "natural" state. A friend who attended an environmental conference sponsored by the state of Hawaii said he heard more than once that the "optimum" population of the Earth was about 400 to 600 million. That's bad news since our present population is nearly *ten times that.*

I would like to share an observation made by many of the scientists who write about the war on pesticides. To the best of my knowledge none of them are Christians, so their views are more that of humanitarians. However, their comments about the activists' efforts to ban the use of pesticides are worth noting.

It seems that many of the leadership in the world environmental movement believe the Earth is too crowded. They would like to put both voluntary and involuntary restrictions on new population growth in the developed countries of the world—much as China has done.

In 1992 the environmental group, the Sierra Club, suggested that California adopt laws to restrict the number of children state residents can have and create a state commission on population, resources, and economy.[1]

Anyone who follows the family planning techniques of communist China knows that fines, intimidation, and forced abortions are a part of their population control.

Other scientists go far beyond what this article suggested. According to Dr. George Reisman, professor of economics at Pepperdine University, the agenda of the extremist element is to depopulate the world considerably and, apparently, they feel the most effective way to accomplish this goal is through insect-borne diseases. If the use of pesticides is curtailed, the effect will be more disease.

As disease increases, the population decreases. Whether or not these allegations are true, the net result of banning the use of pesticides is a higher disease and death rate in the underdeveloped countries of the world.[2]

The case against the pesticide DDT was not based primarily upon its toxicity to humans but its alleged toxicity to animals, and particularly to birds.

Most people who follow these environmental issues are acutely aware of the horror stories about the American bald eagle population and several other species being decimated by DDT. Supposedly, the DDT, which leached through the soil and into the adjacent streams, was ingested by fish which were, in turn, ingested by the adult eagles. The effects of the DDT were reported to be thinning of the eagles' eggshells, resulting in lower birth rates.

In fact the primary culprit in the case of the bald eagles' was conclusively demonstrated to be PCBs, not DDT. PCBs are artificial molecules created as a part of plastics manufacturing, and were illegally dumped into streams and rivers prior to the early 1980s. Another major component in the thinning of birds' eggs was found to be mercury, commonly used in most mining operations. But mercury and PCBs are not the issue here.

Virtually no scientist I interviewed had any doubts about the ill effects of mercury, lead, PCBs, or other known poisons on both human beings and animals, and every article supporting DDT also specifically warned about the misuse of other known pollutants, especially lead commonly used in water pipes. These scientists do not support chemical abuse in nature; but they are simply saying we should be honest about what is and what is not harmful.

I will rely primarily on data provided by Dr. J. Gordon Edwards in his articles entitled "The Myth of Food-Chain Biomagnification" and "DDT Effects on Bird Abundance and Reproduction." Dr. Edwards is professor of biology at San Jose State University and, among many other awards, he is a lifetime Fellow in the California Academy of Science.[3]

In discussing the scientific data for and against DDT (and other general use pesticides) Dr. Edwards cites some very interesting statistics that are well known to both the scientific community and the activists who forced the ban on DDT.

It is important to understand the rationale behind the assault on DDT because, except for its value to developing countries, there does not appear to be any. As Dr. Edwards and many other scientists point out, there is no (repeat *no*) evidence to support *any* of the wild claims made about DDT—the most effective general pesticide ever made. The eradication of many insect-borne diseases can be credited directly to DDT, not the least of which are malaria and typhus.

Dr. Edwards cites numerous studies that show *increasing* numbers of birds (including quail, doves, turkeys, eagles, gulls, herons) during the years when DDT was most commonly used (1946–1960). The annual Audubon Society Christmas bird counts during this period show 26 varieties of birds increased dramatically. Other statistical studies also confirmed the Audubon counts.[4]

Dr. Edwards attributes this to a reduction in bird parasites (by the DDT) providing the birds with protection from avian malaria, rickettsialpox, Newcastle disease, and others. In fact, during this time bird populations became so dense that massive control kills were necessary, including the poisoning of some 30,000 sea gulls on Tern island by members of the Audubon Society.[5]

After 15 years of heavy DDT use in and around nesting areas of the bald eagle, the 1960 census of the Audubon Society showed 25 percent more eagles than did the pre-DDT 1942 census.

In 1966 Fish and Wildlife biologists fed large doses of DDT to captive bald eagles for 112 days, then concluded that "DDT residues encountered by eagles in the environment would not adversely effect eagles or their eggs."[6]

DDT has been blamed for the great peregrine falcon decline throughout the world by the environmentalists intent on banning the pesticide. What they failed to point out is that study after study shows that the peregrine decline occurred long *before* DDT was ever present.

Dr. Edwards also notes that, "No feeding experiments dosing captive pelicans with DDT or DDE were ever shown to cause any eggshell distortions. The EPA ban on DDT was based in large measure on the alleged environmental harm to birds caused by DDT!"[7]

Dr. Edwards points out that several factors do result in thinner eggshells in birds, including PCBs, oil, lead, cadmium, mercury and, most notably, a lack of calcium.

In one of the studies used as evidence of DDT poisoning, it was found that the researchers deliberately fed their birds calcium deficient food (.5 percent rather than the normal 2.5 percent). They then blamed the mis-formed shells on the presence of DDT. However, evidence from nearly every other study shows something totally different: DDT had practically no effect on bird reproductive systems.

I'll share this last bit of evidence and then move on. If you would like to read more in-depth material, it is referenced in the Appendix.

"It has been demonstrated repeatedly in caged experiments that DDT, DDD, and DDE do not cause significant shell-thinning, even at levels many hundreds of times greater than wild birds would ever accumulate. During many years of carefully controlled feeding experiments Scott et al. 'found no tremors, no mortality, no thinning of eggshells and no interference with reproduction caused by levels of DDT which were as high as those reported to be present in most of the wild birds where "catastrophic" decreases in shell quality and reproduction have been claimed.'

"Also, 'DDT did not have any deleterious effect upon the sex hormones involved in egg production and may indeed have had a beneficial effect upon eggshell quality.'"[8]

In fact, the misuse of pesticides has occurred in some instances but under the most extenuating of circumstances. To understand the problem, you must first understand the difference between what is called *point source pollution* and *general groundwater pollution*.

Point source pollution takes place when the same water source is used repeatedly to dilute the pesticide or to rinse the containers. This process can significantly increase pesticide levels in the immediate water supply.

Groundwater pollution is totally different. It requires the general application of the pesticide in such quantities as to leach through the soil and into the underlying water table. This would be extremely expensive for the farmer, and would be practically a full-time occupation.[9]

Totally removed from any influence by the EPA, farmers and others using pesticides have a great incentive not to pollute their own groundwater. After all, they and their families have to drink the water and eat the food, just like the rest of us. In most instances, a simple warning on the container is sufficient to convince most users not to abuse chemical pesticides.

For others, mandatory training on the correct use of chemicals is required. According to the vast majority of sources I reviewed, there is no evidence that the use of DDT or other effective pesticides contaminated either fields or groundwater to any measurable degree—with the possible exception being areas where heavy tilling of the soil was prevalent.

To control weeds, the majority of large scale agricultural producers shifted from tilling to local application of biodegradable herbicides. This technique is actually less expensive and prevents soil erosion, thus reducing pesticide runoff as well.

In the midst of early conflicting data about pesticides and their effects on wildlife, the environmentalists, who were pressing hard to secure a total ban on pesticides, such as DDT, were also seeking bans on the use of herbicides. To a large degree, they succeeded in getting the bans. Without herbicides to control unwanted weeds, most large-scale farmers returned to the process of soil tilling. Soil tilling involves cutting into the soil about six to seven inches and turning it top side down. As previously mentioned, the difficulty with this method of weed control is soil erosion (exactly what herbicides were designed to prevent).

Once the soil begins to erode, the long-lived DDT is carried into the streams and begins to concentrate in silt and fish. The environmentalists then claimed that the pesticides made their way up the food chain from the fish to birds and other animals. To date, there has been essentially no scientific data to prove that the DDT actually works its way up the food chain.

Here again I will draw from research done by Dr. Edwards. [10]

Dr. Edwards states that the process known as biomagnification, as touted by the anti-pesticide group, is untenable and contrary to experimental data, as well as virtually every field study.

In 1968 Dr. Virgil Freed performed an experiment in which fish living in identical water tanks with identical amounts of DDT present were fed different diets. One group was fed a diet high in DDT concentrations, while the other group was fed the same food, but with no trace of DDT. The amount of DDT in the fish tissues at the end of the test period were nearly identical, proving that any trace or accumulation of DDT came through the gill system, not the food chain.

In 1971 Dr. J.L. Hamelink reported that, "The hypothesis that biological magnification of pesticides through the food chain has been rejected, and an alternative hypothesis is accepted that accumulation depends on absorption.

In 1977 Dr. D.L. Gunn, in his address to the Royal Entomological Society of London, observed, "Here are some samples of scares that deceived laymen . . . the oft quoted food chain scare in general, often untrue, and at best dubious, and the Clear Lake food-chain story, which is totally false." (The Clear Lake food-chain report was used by the anti-pesticide activists as "evidence" that DDT had worked its way up the food chain.)

And quoting Dr. Edwards, "If there were no fecal elimination of ingested materials, no metabolism of chemicals in the body and no excretion of those chemicals and their metabolites, then animals would accumulate all of the chemicals they ever swallowed (including their food), plus all chemicals entering through their skin, gills, or lungs. Obviously those processes do occur; therefore, the long-term retention of those chemicals does not occur.

---

*T*he low cost of DDT and like products is what brought us the abundance of food we now take for granted.

"Unfortunately the popular press and some semi-scientific journals have been crammed with 'biomagnification' allegations for many years, and anti-pesticide activists have made profitable use of that myth. Environmental organizations welcomed the radical concept and used it to frighten the public into donating more money to 'help fight pesticides.'

"Scientists and other professional people who are aware of the truth should forcefully refute the 'biomagnification' propaganda at every opportunity. As long as news writers, teachers, legislators and laymen continue to be uninformed or misinformed about the facts, we cannot blame them much for being unreasonably concerned about traces of pesticides in the environment and for fearing that they might 'build up' in the food chain until ultimately they could even harm people.

"Whenever allegations of biological magnification are encountered the propagandists should be challenged to produce the actual data from analyses of each step of the actual food chain. They should also be required to specify which methods of analysis were used, which tissues were analyzed, how old the samples were and whether they were wet weight or dry weight. Of course, there must also be valid evidence that the animals really were involved primarily in the food chain under study.

"When all of these factors are considered, it becomes evident that there is really little or no increase in pesticide concentration attributable to 'biological magnification up the food chain.'"[11]

Without a doubt, pesticides do eliminate a broad range of insects, both good and bad (in the farmer's eyes). To affect higher level species, such as birds, the most convicting evidence shows that *extremely* concentrated amounts of pesticides would have to be present —a condition possible only through massive application *and* extensive erosion. So the problem, if there actually is one, is exacerbated by the environmentalists' ban on herbicides, which then results in a further ban on pesticides.

Dr. Leonard Flynn, advisor to the American Council on Science and Health and a member of the Nature Conservancy, says: "Most of the evidence for the existence or nonexistence of bio-magnification (pesticides moving up the food chain) within aquatic food webs has come from highly circumstantial and/or marginally relevant data."[12]

In other words, there is no real scientific basis for supporting the theory that DDT, or any other pesticide approved for agricultural use, works its way up the food chain. The environmental alarmists see a problem with thin-shelled bird eggs, hear that pesticides are leaching into the streams and unequivocally declare that the pesticides are the cause and therefore should be banned.

This problem is a real concern, both to the farmer and to his family. But almost any agricultural agent will admit that once the farmers are educated on the hazards of point saturation they quickly correct the problem. Education isn't enough for the extremists. Nothing short of a total ban on all pesticides will satisfy them. As a result, the most cost-effective and safest pest control known (DDT) is now being banned from the planet.

As Dr. Flynn states: "The use of substitute pesticides is ineffective, and the most efficient is nearly five times as costly as DDT and less than half as effective."[13]

The low cost of DDT and like products is what brought us the abundance of food we now take for granted.

Even more critical than the cost to agriculture are the long-term effects this ban will have on world health. Several outbreaks of malaria have recently been reported in California, brought in by Mexican immigrants who have been exposed to the illness in their own country due to increasing mosquito populations.

A classic example of extreme environmentalism trying to cure one problem and creating another can be seen in Alabama, a neighboring state to Georgia, where I live. In the western part of Alabama, farmers and ranchers are facing an ever-increasing threat from fire ants. These diminutive members of the insect world have been labeled land piranhas by farmers who have had the misfortune of disturbing their colonies.

Fire ants burrow into the ground, often creating rock-like hills above ground that can break plows and harrows. Domestic animals that wander into their path can be bitten and stung to the point of death. Cows grazing in a field infested by fire ants can easily be identified by their swollen legs where the ants have attacked them repeatedly.

The only really successful control for fire ants has been DDT, which cannot be used any longer. With virtually no effective control, the fire ants continue to march across the state, invading subdivisions as well as farmland.

Fire ants are a particularly hearty species that can adapt to short-lived pesticides quickly. Almost as soon as an effective control agent is discovered, the environmentalists find cause to ban it as well. In the confrontation over pesticides, few politicians are willing to risk the wrath of the activists.

The extremists, who often are involved in the media, are able to intimidate most politicians through adverse publicity. Certainly anyone who is pro-industry and pro-chemical-use is quickly labeled anti-environmental.

Understandably there are arguments on both sides of any issue, including the use of control chemicals. No one in his or her right mind wants the water or food supply poisoned by anything and, initially, the regulations were directed at curbing the *misuse* of manmade chemicals.

But, as I said before, in the world of environmentalism there seems to be no middle ground any longer. All chemicals are viewed as evil. It is either a total ban—or war. And no amount of solid scientific evidence confirming that most of the banned control agents are perfectly safe when used properly can sway the extremists, even in the slightest.

While working on this book I discovered that many "normal" people have accepted the extremists' views of ecology and the world environment. They, like many other intelligent people, cannot believe that so much of what they hear and read could be fabricated. And it's unfortunate most of our current regulations (and laws) are being dictated by those who seem to care less whether American industry succeeds or fails and whether our children have jobs in the future.

We won't change the perspective of the radical element. To the contrary, since they practically dominate the media, it is the conservative philosophy that is being redirected. The challenge now is to expose the lies, document the truth, and pray that rational people will be willing to listen.

A friend, who is an executive producer with one of the major networks (producing nature documentaries on the need to protect the environment), was convinced that the greedy, money-grubbing, American entrepreneurs were ruining our planet. He was sold on the idea that CFCs (chlorofluorocarbons) were destroying the ozone and that half of our planet's population would die from cancer because of it.

He also believed that the global warming menace would melt the polar ice and drown the world. And he swallowed the line that the environmentalists were saving the world from total chemical pollution. He vigorously supported the need for stronger, harsher environmental regulations and mandatory prison sentences for violators.

However, as a result of reading the evidence for the other side of these issues, he has reversed his position and is lobbying his network owner to present a more balanced view.

If he doesn't get fired, his future documentaries will focus on real environmental issues. Obviously there are problems that need to be addressed, such as the dumping of dangerous chemicals incorrectly and educating farmers and ranchers on how to safely apply the chemicals they need in the quantities that don't "overkill." But he assures me that he will also focus on the benefits of technology to mankind and the costs of totally abandoning the scientific advances that make life on our planet comfortable and safe for the majority of human beings.

As I was sorting through material from both sides of this issue, I noticed there were numerous references by the environmentalists to a book called *Silent Spring* by Rachel Carson. I had never read the book so I ordered a copy. Much to my surprise this book, which is referred to as "the environmentalists' bible" by many within the movement and is widely accepted by the public at large, is *not* a scientific analysis of any environmental issues. It is a poorly documented pseudo-scientific "factional" (part fact, part fiction) book.

In the words of Dr. Robert Devlin, professor of Plant Physiology and Weed Science at the University of Massachusetts, "There is no doubt that *Silent Spring* led eventually to the banning of DDT which, in my opinion, is the safest and most efficient chemical for its purpose ever produced by man. . . . It has been estimated that over one billion people are alive today because of DDT and that is something to think about!"[14]

I can only conclude that many activists have thought about it and don't like it.

I'm convinced that at the heart of the radical environmental movement, as well as other activist groups (such as Planned Parenthood), is the concern that the world is overpopulated and needs to be thinned out by any means necessary.

Such an idea may sound too farfetched to believe, until all the facts are considered. Look at their agenda and see if the net result is more or less people in the world.

As Thomas Jefferson once said: "Eternal vigilance is the price of liberty."

CHAPTER ELEVEN
Blueprint for Disaster

There is enough material available on the impact of government regulations and their effect on the economy to write an entire book. But, in reality, regulations are just one part of the overall problem. The sad thing is that, with all the misinformation being aimed at the public via our media, America's children are being brainwashed into believing that all those regulations arc in their best interests. After all, who can argue that recycling is good for the environment *and* the economy?

But the next step in the activists' agenda is to convince Americans that virtually all industrial activity threatens our environment and, then, press for stern regulations to control industrial "pollution." This sets the stage for the de-industrialization of America.

Think of where our economy would be without inexpensive electrical power for industry. If the government passes laws levying high taxes and restricting the use of fossil fuels to power electrical generators and, at the same time, nuclear power is being phased out because of environmental concerns, what alternatives does that leave? Fewer jobs and a lower standard of living.

Often the changes in an economy are subtle and hard to pin-point. A decision made by one administration doesn't always bear fruit for several years. For instance, if environmental regulations in the United States make steel processing uncompetitive, the jobs migrate outside the U.S. to Taiwan or Japan.

The U.S. steel mills die a slow death as new plants can't be built and remain competitive while meeting the new standards. Some older workers are terminated but, more often, attrition through retirement and death simply decreases the work force. The younger workers in the community are never hired and the plant is eventually abandoned.

A part of the American Dream disappears and they don't even know who is to blame. Is it really American business that is uncompetitive today, or do the regulations and micro-management by the government make them uncompetitive? Some of each, I believe.

In trying to find the causes of the disappearing American Dream, clearly, excessive government regulations are a major contributing factor. Perhaps I can put it in the right perspective by reviewing how regulations ultimately translate into fewer jobs, lower salaries, and diminished competition.

If we were still operating under the economic rules of the fifties, we could probably absorb the impact of these regulations without drastically altering our competitiveness and jobs. In the fifties the United States set the economic ground rules for virtually the entire world.

If you wanted a decent, reliable car, you bought American. The same was true for televisions, computers, refrigerators, washing machines, or even bicycles; but not so today.

Not only are we operating in an increasingly global economy, we no longer set the rules for that economy. Since the early eighties the rules have been set primarily by the Japanese.

The fundamental rules of manufacturing today are cost, quality, and durability. Until very recently, American industry has not been particularly cost or quality conscious and, as a result, they have seen an ever-decreasing market share.

Products and whole industries, where the U.S. once dominated, have been lost to the Japanese. Most of the consumer items, such as TVs and VCRs, have been lost to cost competitiveness because we haven't kept up with changing production technology. The Japanese produce quality products at lower prices through automation; and our industries have not been able to modernize, primarily due to the higher cost of capital in the U.S.

But in other industries, such as automobiles, we have seen our market share decline, not so much because of lower prices but because of better quality in the Japanese cars. Without a doubt, the Japanese have made better, more reliable cars than the big three U.S. auto makers since the early eighties. But also, the government regulations that dictated increased gas mileage and lower emissions after the Arab oil embargo helped the Japanese tremendously. Japanese companies were in the small car business long before most of the U.S. companies made the transition, and the mandated changeover gave them a competitive edge.

In addition, Japanese manufacturing plants are not burdened down with OSHA, EPA, workers' compensation, and union demands the way American companies are. Outside of any other factors, it has been estimated that the Japanese enjoy a $1,000- to $1,500-per-car cost advantage just because of government regulations. If the more recent estimates of regulatory costs are accurate, their real advantage is more like $3,000 per car. It's hard to compete with a 20 percent penalty tacked onto your product.

During and after the Arab oil embargo, the incentive to mandate higher gas mileage became a national security issue. Most Americans, including the Congress, actually believed there was a worldwide oil shortage. This fit well into the environmentalists' agenda, and they jumped on that bandwagon.

As with most issues the government has touched, the initial idea and the final product are worlds apart. Increasing gas mileage from 16 miles mpg to 25 mpg was feasible. It was achieved by simply downsizing the average family car and improving the standard gas-powered engines.

However, most recent regulations which mandate 40 to 50 mpg average will drive the cost of automobiles further out of the average family's price range, resulting in fewer cars being built. We will see smaller, less safe automobiles that have to be driven longer. The net results will be twofold: first, the death and injury rate in accidents will increase, unless costly safety equipment is added, because the smaller cars can go faster and sustain a lot more damage; second, more jobs will be lost in the automotive industry as fewer cars are sold at lower profit margins.

This is happening even now as the big-three manufacturers scale down their cars and their companies. The built-in cost differential for doing business in America can be absorbed and cushioned somewhat in the larger luxury cars but, as these are phased out, American companies, even with the same quality products, cannot compete. The question is: Is it worth sacrificing literally millions of American jobs to solve a problem that doesn't even exist?

I'm certainly not going to try to justify the automotive industry as a whole; both management and labor have hurt themselves over the years. But under the threat of global warming (carbon emissions), a great many Americans have and will become unemployed.

---

*T*he primary factors that cause companies to migrate are . . . regulations, cost of money, cost of labor, and availability of trained labor.

We operate in a global market, but we rarely play on a level field with the rest of the world. Actually we never did; but as I said, in the past we were able to dictate the rules of the game. We can no longer do that in any industry.

The classic example of this can be seen in the manufacturing of commercial aircraft. Forget for the moment all of the non-regulatory advantages that other countries' manufacturers receive, such as low-cost government financing, no anti-trust laws to keep companies from working together, non-competitive bidding on contracts, and much lower health care costs.

American aircraft manufactures must contend with high worker compensation insurance rates; OSHA regulations that add thousands of dollars a year to labor, both directly and indirectly; and EPA regulations that make it difficult to operate a manufacturing plant. But many of the indirect problems are hidden from sight.

When manufacturers order materials, such as stainless steel or aluminum, they have a whole cadre of suppliers to choose from, both domestic and foreign. The domestic suppliers also have the regulations to contend with, so their costs must increase accordingly. That leaves the foreign suppliers in a better competitive position, and too often the contract goes to a non-American firm, even in defense contracts. It is difficult to blame the primary contractor who is trying to stay competitive in the global market too, but U.S. jobs are lost, even on an American-built aircraft.

Once the cost differential reaches the point that building air-craft in the U.S. is no longer competitive, the whole industry ships out, which is exactly what is happening now. McDonnell Douglas Corporation is assembling their newest commercial planes in China. Boeing, America's largest private aircraft manufacturer, is now as-signing a large part of their 767 airliners to Japan.

The next series is scheduled to be built as a joint venture with Japan. In essence, because of a lack of development capital and a less-regulated environment in Japan, our biggest aircraft company is train-ing their future competition. If this trend continues into the next decade, there will be hardly any commercial aircraft manufacturers left in the U.S., and another industry with high-paying jobs will have migrated elsewhere.

Most knowledgeable corporate executives will admit that there is little, if any, real productivity difference between the average American and foreign worker. In the case of the Japanese there is essentially no cost-per-hour differential. So what is the basic differ-ence? Overregulation and litigation, in the majority of cases.

Many companies that have exited the U.S. have cited wage/cost differentials as the reason. This is probably true when the product requires unskilled, minimum wage labor. But where high-tech pro-duction is concerned, the cost differential quickly fades. The primary factors that cause companies to migrate are: (in order) regulations, cost of money, cost of labor, and availability of trained labor.

As these companies and jobs migrate elsewhere, eventually the trained labor pool in America will dry up. Not only is our educational system ineffective in preparing skilled workers for industry (to say the least), but the bright, motivated students won't train for jobs that don't exist. We'll end up with a nation of computer salespeople and securities brokers.

You don't have to search very far to see the end result of over-regulation. California is a classic example. It has been said that everything, good or bad, starts in California and works its way east-ward. I believe that's correct to an alarming degree, and not by de-fault. The fact that many of the extremists in our country make their homes in California gives them a media boost. Once they have an idea moving, the media pick up on it and soon it spreads across the country.

Certainly California has been the leader in environmental regulations. However, the unique problems of a heavily populated area, such as southern California, should not be translated into the needs for the entire nation; unfortunately, usually they are.

Even worse, the environmental problems of the Los Angeles basin (which existed even when only Indians inhabited the area) are often translated into national policy. Los Angeles does have its own unique pollution problem. The fact that some of Hollywood's most frenzied activists look outside their homes and see heavy smog creates a huge problem for the rest of us when they get on their "soap boxes" about it.

In 1990 the California Business Roundtable did a survey of the businesses in the state to see how the ever-increasing burden of regulations was affecting their companies. Of the 836 companies with 100 employees or more that responded, 12 percent were planning to move out of the state. Another poll of 250 smaller businesses showed 38 percent had already moved out of California or were planning to do so. Respondents to both polls cited the oppressive state regulations as one of their primary motivations for relocating.

As Peter Ueberroth, chairman of the Council on California Competitiveness said, "Laws that originally were passed to protect our quality of life now are being used to thwart environmentally sound growth without balancing job impact with economic needs."[1]

Sound familiar? David Westmorland, vice president at Ball Corporation (the Ball Glass Company), said in a July 1992 newspaper interview (after Ball made the decision to shut down its Santa Ana plant after more than six decades of business), "You could put millions into [refurbishing a plant] only to find out you've been regulated out of business."[2]

This same fundamental philosophy will apply to doing business anywhere in the United States if federal regulations are allowed to grow uncontrolled, as those in California have been.

One Los Angeles furniture manufacturer moved his entire operation from Southern California to Mexico primarily because of the stringent regulations issued by the South Coast Air Quality Management District (AQMD). His comment was, "The primary reason [for the move] was that the air quality rules were neither legitimate nor reasonable. We proved that what they were asking us to do was physically impossible and we demonstrated it, so they gave us a three-month variance. Why they thought we could comply in three months, I cannot say."

He went on to say that his company had to ship the materials to Mexico, have them assembled and finished (to comply with AQMD rules), then ship them back into L.A., where the company's primary customers are. His last comment was, "So the stuff [amount of pollution] we're putting into the air with trucks is probably more than we were putting into the air as manufacturers." But still, 500 jobs moved to Mexico.[3]

As Francis Paladino, senior vice president of Ball Corporation said about the air quality inspectors, "We've had people say, 'if you can't meet the [rules] . . . close down. We don't care.'"[4]

I wonder how the taxpayers who pay their salaries will feel about that statement after their jobs are gone.

One has to wonder if we ever learn from our experiences in government. One of the primary problems in California is identical to that of the federal government—the sheer numbers of regulators and agencies. In Southern California alone, there are 39 agencies with water quality control authority, 38 with hazardous waste authority, 17 with air quality authority, and 14 with solid waste authority.[5]

The problems of satisfying the overlapping authorities are enough to make any sane businessperson move to Nevada, Wyoming, or Utah.

In February of 1993 California Governor Pete Wilson convened an economic summit to discuss the problems of his state. Governor Wilson called upon every level of government in the state to lighten the burden on businesses by reducing the number of regulations and rules they must meet, citing the fact that excessive and abusive regulations, liberal welfare benefits, and disastrous worker's compensation rules had combined to create the worst economic slump in California since the Great Depression.[6]

Note: California's worker's compensation program is one of the most liberal and costly of any state in America. Businesspeople in California have dubbed the program, "The working person's retirement fund," since so many people use it to opt out of working for a living. This is a growing trend throughout the country and is just one more hidden tax being paid by consumers.

The image of California should be an example of what government abuse can do. California has a large economic impact on our national economy. In fact, if California were a country it would have approximately the eighth largest economy in the world.

Both Governor Wilson and Ueberroth blamed legislators for their failure to reform the state's regulatory nightmare and its anti-business attitude.

"California," said Ueberroth to the business leaders of the state, "has become an anti-jobs state."[7]

This sentiment was heartily confirmed by most of the subsequent speakers who testified that they were planning to escape the "regulatory clutches" of California as quickly as possible.

"I'd do anything not to hire an employee," said Judy Schuman of Hawthorne, California. She could no longer afford worker's compensation insurance.[8]

Such will be the sentiment of all small businesses in America if we don't wake up and demand some changes.

REGULATING YOUR PROPERTY

As difficult as it is to comply with all the regulations in a business, just think of trying to comply with them as a private individual.

Recently a friend in Congress decided to order a copy of all the EPA regulations that might potentially affect private citizens in his area. After having a staffer research the Clean Air and Clean Water Acts and all the associated documents, he ordered one copy of each from the Library of Congress.

The staffer received a call from a clerk at the library asking if he really wanted a copy of all the documents. To which the staffer replied, "Yes, why do you ask?"

"Because I wondered if you guys really have enough room to store a semi-trailer full of paper," the clerk replied.

Needless to say they didn't get a copy of everything the acts reference. But it does point out the absurdity of too many regulations over too many areas of our lives. I have not read the EPA Clean Water Act, but a friend who consults in this area tells me that no single human being can possibly assimilate all the information. He also mentioned that no sane human being can understand it anyway since it references documents, which reference other documents, which reference other documents, and all of these then become a part of the law.

We are a nation of private rights. In fact, if you talk to visitors from other countries, the one aspect of America they still marvel at is our personal liberties. Without the right to succeed or fail (on our own merit), our economic system can't function. American business, or at least 70 percent of it, consists of small, privately owned companies. These small companies provide 80 percent of all the new jobs in our economy, but most survive month in and month out only by the thinnest of margins.

Most of the previous business regulations have excluded companies of 200 employees or less because even the politicians realized how essential, but how fragile, they are; but no more. There is no mercy for companies and workers in the new environmental movement. The philosophy is, if it isn't totally clean, out it goes.

Once the battle to establish control over the small businesses was won (many new regulations apply to companies of 50 employees or less), the environmentalists didn't withdraw; they lowered their target.

The trend toward regulation of private property is the most disturbing element of the environmental movement. Once the environmental activists are able to regulate the use of private property, as well as public land, the economy is in real danger. It is the small entrepreneurs who create the companies that grow into bigger companies and create jobs. They cannot afford the legal battles with the government and environmental groups that it takes to free land and resources for development.

One of the worst examples of regulatory abuse is that of John Pozsgai, a 59 year old Pennsylvania resident who somehow thought that a piece of property he bought to build a repair shop on actually belonged to him.[8]

In 1990 Mr. Pozsgai bought a 14-acre tract of land across from his truck repair shop. The property had been used for several years as an illegal dump site for parts and hundreds of old tires. Mr. Pozsgai was given the go ahead by state agencies to clear the debris and begin filling in the low spots in order to build his new garage.

There was an old stream bed on the property (dry most of the year) that backed up during the rainy season due to the twenty-year accumulation of old tires. It was this dry stream bed that led to his undoing.

Based on a complaint to the EPA, filed by a neighbor who was irritated by the big dump trucks rumbling past his property, the U.S. Corps of Engineers was asked to review the site under the Clean Water Act. Mr. Pozsgai had total assurances from the state environmental agency that he could legally fill his land site and that the federal government had no authority to intervene. So Mr. Pozsgai told the local building contractors they could use his property to dump their (clean) landfill.

After surveying the property, the U.S. Corps of Engineers decided that, due to the presence of vegetation like "skunk cabbage" and "sweet gum trees," part of Mr. Pozsgai's property constituted a wetland, so they contacted the EPA in Washington.

Sure enough, the EPA decided that "swamp cabbage" was on the list of vegetation for wetlands designation, and they got a restraining order to prohibit Mr. Pozsgai from filling in the site.

In order for the federal government to get involved, the law requires the property to be connected to an interstate waterway. The little dry bed stream on the boundary of Mr. Pozsgai's property was declared a tributary of the nearby Pennsylvania Canal. The Canal was once designated as a part of the interstate waterway although, actually, it was never used for that purpose.

Under protest, but acting under orders from the EPA, Mr. Pozsgai erected barriers to stop the trucks that were dumping fill dirt on his land. However, over the next several days pictures were taken of the trucks continuing to dump the fill on the property.

Shortly thereafter, federal agents came to Mr. Pozsgai's home, handcuffed him, and locked him up. He was indicted on 41 counts of violating the Clean Water Act by allowing fill dirt to be placed on his property without a federal permit.

Unbelievably, Mr. Pozsgai was convicted in federal court on all counts and sentenced to *three years* in federal prison and five years probation. He also was fined a total of $202,000. His fine and sentence were greater than those given the majority of first-time drug dealers, armed robbers, and convicted rapists.

Since the federal government's whole case rested on the fact that the Pennsylvania Canal gave them jurisdiction as a part of the interstate waterway, Mr. Pozsgai's attorney appealed under the grounds that the canal had never been used as such. Both the Appeals Court and the Supreme Court refused to hear his case.

As of this date, Mr. Pozsgai is still in prison. As the federal prosecutor said at his trial, "A message must be sent to all landowners, corporations, [and] developers of this country" that light sentences for environmental crimes are a thing of the past.[9]

In case you might be thinking that Mr. Pozsgai's case is a fluke, or an isolated incident, I would like to share the story of William B. Ellen.

Perhaps you read about Mr. Ellen in the closing days of George Bush's presidency, when the Fairness to Land Owner's Committee organized a nationwide campaign asking President Bush to pardon Mr. Ellen. Unfortunately for Mr. Ellen, his crime of environmental pollution was not on the president's list of pardonable crimes.

Bill Ellen was convicted in federal court of destroying wetlands without a federal permit, according to Section 404 of the Clean Water Act. His crime wasn't dumping pollutants into the Everglades or the Okefenokee swamp, or even shoveling sand into the interstate waterway.

Bill Ellen's crime was creating a wetland sanctuary on a previously dry piece of property: a waterfowl habitat, complete with duck ponds, marshlands, and wetlands vegetation.

His troubles started when he accepted a job to create this waterfowl retreat on the property of a wealthy Maryland businessman who wanted a truly aesthetic scene on his 3200 acre estate. It was to be a 103 acre wildlife sanctuary where geese, ducks, and other wildlife could come and go as they pleased without fear of being hunted.

Mr. Ellen secured the proper permits from all the local government agencies. In addition, he regularly consulted with the Army Corps of Engineers, as well as the Soil Conservation Service. He also hired environmental consultants and had extensive studies done to ensure there were no wetland areas involved in the project. In fact the ground where the sanctuary was to be located was so dry that water had to be sprayed on it regularly to keep the dust down!

Mr. Ellen had been working on the project two years by 1989, when the Bush administration redefined "wetlands" and the entire Dorchester County area (where the estate is located) was declared a wetlands area.

The Army Corp of Engineers immediately served Mr. Ellen with a cease and desist order for all work on the estate.

Mr. Ellen immediately stopped work on the sanctuary except for the grounds management site where a house and kennels were already under construction. He felt secure in continuing that work because a Soil Conservation Service wetlands expert had just inspected the site one month earlier and assured Ellen that it did not qualify as a wetlands area.

However, a Corps of Engineers official insisted that all construction be halted immediately. Ellen offered to pay for an additional private survey to determine if any wetlands actually existed at the site and to shut down all construction (including the management area) if the site was reclassified as a wetlands. Otherwise, he explained to the Corps' inspector, he would be in violation of his contract with the building contractor.

After the inspector left he decided that, in light of further advice from his chief architect, it would be better to halt the project until the misunderstanding could be worked out. By that time two more truckloads of dirt had been dumped on the site. Those two loads of dirt eventually were to cost Mr. Ellen his freedom.

He was arrested and put on trial for violating Section 404 of the Clean Water Act. In order for the federal government to establish jurisdiction over private property, the law requires that the landfill must discharge into navigable waters of the United States or impose a threat to interstate commerce. Since the land in question was totally dry, without even a dry stream bed on it, the government was stuck for how to establish jurisdiction.

No problem. Since an interstate waterway was not available, the government declared jurisdiction by virtue of interstate fowl: ducks, geese, and other migratory birds being involved. In other words the government claimed that interstate commerce was involved![10]

Under the Carter administration wetlands were defined as areas flooded or saturated with groundwater often enough that, under normal circumstances, they would support "vegetation typically adapted for life in saturated soil conditions."

Under the new definition, says Senator Jake Garn of Utah, "You won't be able to spit on the ground without the Army Corps of Engineers coming up behind you and declaring the area a wetlands."[11]

The new guidelines are covered under the *Federal Manual for Identifying and Delineating Jurisdictional Wetlands*. This manual lists some 7,000 forms of vegetation that will qualify an area as wetlands. These include (but certainly are not limited to) dogwood trees, Kentucky bluegrass, poison ivy, ash trees, palm trees, cabbage palms (native to all of Florida), red maple trees, and just about every form of flower you ever heard of. You may actually have a wetlands right in your own back yard.

In a 1991 court case a defense attorney asked an EPA wetlands expert if a batter (in a baseball game being played on a field where the area had been identified as a wetlands) would be technically guilty of violating the Clean Water Act if he knocked the dirt off of his shoes at the plate. Incredibly the witness answered, "Yes."[12]

During the Ellen trial in U.S. District Court in Baltimore, Judge Frederic Smalkin asked why the government was prosecuting Mr. Ellen when, in fact, he was *creating* a wetlands, not trying to fill one in. Charles Rhodes, an expert witness for the EPA, said that the accumulation of fowl feces would flow into a wetlands tributary once the total project was completed and would have a negative impact on the water quality.

The judge questioned the witness further by asking, "Are you saying that there is pollution from ducks, from having waterfowl on a pond, that pollutes the water?"

Mr. Rhodes said yes.

Then the judge asked if the government had any regulations against ducks polluting other ponds that occur naturally, to which the witness replied, "No, your honor."

Still, Bill Ellen was convicted of wetlands violation and sentenced to six months in prison and a one-year probation. The prosecuting attorney had asked for the maximum sentence of 33 months in prison, "To send a clear message to other environmental criminals," he said. But Judge Smalkin refused and opted for the minimum sentence under the law.

To solve the duck feces "problem," the Corps of Engineers brought in a crew and blasted a 400 yard channel from the ponds to the Chesapeake Bay.[13] There will be no more territorial disputes over these ponds.

> *P*eople will put up with regulations when things are going well . . . but when their economy turns down they don't want unnecessary burdens that eliminate jobs.

As I said earlier, unless we begin to wake up and put some reasonable restrictions on government regulations, what will *really* be a thing of the past is private property . . . and jobs!

The step-by-step approach of encroachment used by the extremists has been likened to being "nibbled to death by a duck." They first get legislation passed that sounds both reasonable and necessary. After all, who wouldn't want to stop chemical dumping in our lakes and streams or stop the draining of all the natural wetlands used to collect water runoff? But once the laws are on the books, it is the unrelenting regulations that constitute the greatest threat to our economy and our freedoms.

The law merely establishes a skeleton to build on. It is the regulations and subsequent interpretations that "flesh out" the law. I'm sure the politicians who voted for the Clean Water Act had in mind big chemical companies dumping millions of gallons of PCB-laden chemicals into our rivers and streams, not Mr. Pozsgai dumping fill dirt on his land to build a garage or Mr. Ellen developing a wildlife sanctuary.

According to Rick Henderson, assistant managing editor of *Reason* magazine, "Preservationists [engage] in a form of bait-and-switch: They argue that wetlands provide unique, essential ecological benefits, but we don't know enough about the functions to quantify them and set priorities."

In other words, the protectionists insist that wetlands are essential but won't limit the definition to areas like the Everglades in Florida, the Okefenokee Swamp in Georgia, or the Louisiana Bayou. This would strictly limit their ability to apply the law. So the term "wetlands" becomes any property with groundwater within 18 inches of the surface that may contact a waterway or which contains any of 7,000 species of plant life.

"With [such] imprecise knowledge," says Henderson, "the 'safe' answer, ecologically speaking, is to define wetlands so broadly that everything is included."[14]

With this same approach being used to define the air we breath, the offices we work in, the chemicals we use to control pests, and the very land we use to grow food, how can the U.S. remain competitive in our world, and where will the jobs come from for our grandchildren?

Not everyone can work for the EPA or OSHA. Eventually we either must come to grips with the abusive regulations and test every new theory against known hard facts, or we will indeed revert to the Dark Ages economically.

It is interesting that apparently the majority of Americans agree that there are just too many regulations. People will put up with regulations when things are going well financially, but when their economy turns down they don't want unnecessary burdens that eliminate jobs. Unfortunately, once the law is on the books, it's too late. Only a highly productive economy can afford so many constraints to productivity, and we're rapidly approaching the point of no return.

It's the proverbial catch-22—only a highly productive economic system such as ours can afford the luxury of regulations to protect every species of fish and fowl. But when these regulations get established as national policy, the economy quickly begins to wind down, and then it can no longer afford them.

We are truly at a crossroads in terms of government regulations versus private rights. If the present trend is allowed to continue unabated, the bureaucrats will become so firmly entrenched that nothing will loosen their grip on the country short of a total economic collapse. And with these regulations in place, the prospect of such a collapse looms very large, especially when combined with the other problems facing our country. The only effective cure for the abuses of the federal and state regulators is a well-educated and vocal voter group who will remove those politicians who don't reform the system.

You need to study the facts for yourself, make up your own mind, and then do something! You also need to be aware that you aren't alone in this effort. Most other thinking Americans, Christians or otherwise, feel the same way; but they also feel powerless to do anything. Just one person who is committed to correcting these abuses can make a big difference.

The following are two graphs taken from a survey of Americans that questioned how they feel about government regulations. Note the overwhelming response on the non-regulatory side.

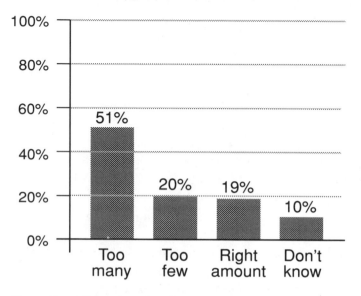

Is Washington issuing too many regulations, too few, or about the right amount?

- Too many: 51%
- Too few: 20%
- Right amount: 19%
- Don't know: 10%

Source: Penn & Schoen Associates, Inc.

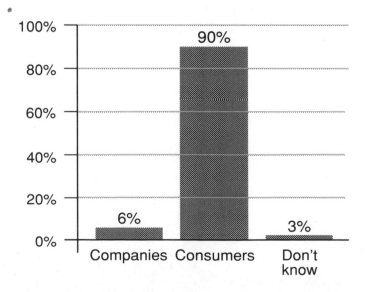

Who ultimately pays the costs of regulations?

- Companies: 6%
- Consumers: 90%
- Don't know: 3%

Source: Penn & Schoen Associates, Inc.

CHAPTER TWELVE

Regulation by Litigation

Consider the case of a 32 year old businessman who decided he would rather fly to his meetings than drive. So he invested $1,200 in flying lessons, during which time he spent some five hours in the cockpit with a professional instructor.

He then soloed the aircraft and was granted his restricted pilot's license. The restriction required him to fly visual flight rules (VFR), and he could not carry passengers. Visual flight rules stipulate that the pilot be able to avoid terrain and other obstacles (aircraft) by sight, rather than relying on instruments.

With roughly three hours of solo flying time, he took off one sunny day to fly approximately three hundred miles to a business meeting. Unfortunately, the aircraft he was flying was only carrying about two hours of fuel in the primary tank at the time.

The 40 year old plane had been purchased from another private aviator, who had owned it for nearly 5 years. The plane had been reconstructed after at least one known accident caused by engine failure on takeoff. That had been about 10 years earlier. Subsequently the airplane had been upgraded with new instruments and the engine overhauled. It was an old, but totally serviceable, aircraft. In fact, the manufacturer had made the little plane so rugged that even after a crash it had outlived its expected useful life by at least 20 years.

Flying at about five thousand feet over Mississippi, the engine coughed a couple of times and then died—out of fuel, or so it seemed. Actually there was still fuel in the reserve tank but, in his panic, the inexperienced pilot apparently neglected to switch over to the reserve tank.

Piloting a powered aircraft and piloting a nose-heavy glider are two totally different things. The plane he was flying had a very good glide ratio without power, and a more experienced pilot might have been able to guide it to a field or unused stretch of road and land safely, as many others have done in the past.

Experienced pilots know that the real key to keeping a powerless plane flying is two-fold: calmness and airspeed. This pilot had neither. He panicked and, instead of nosing the plane down to maintain his airspeed, he attempted to point the nose up, in a vain attempt to avoid the onrushing ground. This fatal flaw in judgment caused the agile little plane to lose airspeed; it simply stopped flying and tumbled from the sky. The pilot was killed in the crash.

The FAA investigation assessed the cause of the crash as pilot error. The pilot's first error: He didn't check his fuel properly before take off. And the second: He lost too much airspeed and caused the plane to stall. That should have been the last of a tragic accident caused by inexperience and bad judgment. But it wasn't.

Several weeks after the accident the widow was contacted by an attorney who specialized in private aircraft accidents. He told her that she had a potential case against both the seller of the plane and the manufacturer. That's correct—against the maker of a 40 year old plane that had been rebuilt and overhauled. He went on to explain that he had experienced great success in suing anyone even remotely involved with private aircraft accidents, and he was willing to take the case on contingency (he would collect only if he won). All she would have to cover would be the actual expenses, such as depositions and travel.

By this time the grief and shock of losing her husband had set in, as well as the realization that his life insurance was inadequate to provide for her and their two children for any length of time.

After negotiating a bit, the attorney settled for maximum out-of-pocket expenses of $5,000 and 40 percent of any awards. Now, serving as her attorney, he filed suit against the private seller and against the manufacturer for negligence.

One might legitimately question how either of the two respondents to the lawsuit could be considered liable, particularly the manufacturer. But it is the nature of litigation in America today that anyone can be sued for anything. Some states have laws requiring the loser to pay all legal fees and court costs but, at present, that is not the norm. With no "dis-incentives" to suing, many attorneys have made a career out of our greatly liberalized tort system.

The claim made against the previous owner was that he was negligent in selling a dangerous piece of equipment to an unknowledgeable and novice pilot. The suit claimed that to do so placed the deceased in a harmful environment which he could not fully evaluate, based on his lack of experience.

The suit against the manufacturer claimed that the aircraft lacked the proper alarms and monitors to signal the pilot that the fuel was being exhausted. Further it claimed that engaging the reserve fuel system required activity that an inexperienced pilot could not reasonably be expected to perform in a time of crisis—most notably, when the engine quit.

The lawsuit against the seller was dropped when the defendant's attorney contacted the widow's attorney and notified him that his client had no assets and no insurance to cover the suit if he lost. A brief deposition showed that all of the defendant's assets were held in his wife's name, and they had neither filed joint taxes nor shared joint tenancy. In effect, he owned nothing. With nothing to collect, that lawsuit was dropped.

The claim against the manufacturer was another matter, however. Although the company no longer made that same type of aircraft, it was still in business and had plenty of potential assets to attach. But the realistic prospect of winning such a suit against a company for a 40 year old airplane seemed pretty weak. Therefore, every offer to settle was summarily rejected by the company's legal counsel. Perhaps it would have been worth a few thousand dollars to avoid the greater expenses of a court case, but there was no way the company would allow such a precedent to be established.

After months of delays, costly depositions, and expert testimony, the case made its way into court. The most compelling evidence against the company was the widow's testimony that she would be financially destitute as a result of her husband's death.

Paid experts told the jury how potentially hazardous the fuel switch-over system was. A highly dramatized version of the last minutes in the cockpit was told by a veteran pilot who had lived through a similar experience.

The only witnesses the company could bring forth were those who sang the praises of the airplane and the company that built it. They also pointed out that technology in small aircraft had changed significantly since that particular plane had been built. The company's position was that it is not logical to hold a manufacturer liable for equipment that was built decades earlier and was subsequently modified and rebuilt without their knowledge.

In the world of tort law, logic plays little or no part in jury decisions. The jury decided against the company and awarded the widow several million dollars. Upon appeal, a higher court reversed the verdict, based on technical errors. So the company won. Or did it? The total cost to "win" this lawsuit was well in excess of $2 million.

An official with the aircraft company asked that their identity be kept confidential since a second civil suit on behalf of the decedent's children is anticipated.

This aircraft company and most others have ceased building any private aircraft for amateur pilots in the U.S. because of the potential litigation costs and ever-increasing damage awards.

Mr. Glenn Bailey, chairman of the Keene Corporation in New York, has an even more unbelievable story to tell about the American tort system.[1]

Mr. Bailey started the Keene Company in the sixties to get in on the building boom created by the baby boomers coming of age. It was not a Fortune 500 company, but it was successful and growing— the typical American Dream come true. By the late sixties the company was actively acquiring other companies to expand its product line.

In 1968 the Keene Company acquired another company called Baldwin Ehret Hill (BEH) for about $8 million. Unfortunately for Mr. Bailey, BEH made (as one of its many products) thermal insulation containing about 10 percent asbestos, a common insulating material of that period. From 1968 to 1972, out of total sales of nearly $500 million, BEH sold about $15 million in products containing asbestos.

When the first hint of any asbestos-related problems surfaced in 1972, Keene officials instructed BEH to totally eliminate asbestos-related products. In 1975 BEH was shut down totally, and the operations were merged or eliminated.

By the late seventies there were massive legal assaults on any firm even remotely related to asbestos, including the Keene Company. During that decade thousands of lawsuits were filed for asbestos-related claims. To facilitate the litigation, eventually most of these were lumped into a pooled, or class action, suit.

This was the largest class action suit in history and would set the stage for all major tort action in the future. Mr. Bailey and the Keene Company, along with industry giants such as the Manville Company, found themselves struggling for their very survival. Based on what was later proved to be faulty scientific data, thousands of litigants were awarded billions in damages.

It is important to note that not one single litigant was ever an employee of the Keene Company or its affiliate, BEH. In fact the vast majority worked in shipyards during World War II, years before the Keene company was formed. It is also interesting to note that the majority of litigants were not suing for injuries they had incurred or illnesses they actually had; they were suing for future problems they *might* have.

Under the "individually and severally liable" principle, adopted by the courts in the sixties and seventies, Keene was made a party to the suits (the "deep pockets" rule).

T hose who set the trends in law, just as those who set the trends in government regulations, are seeking zero risks.

Since the late seventies the Keene Company has paid out $400 million to settle claims brought against it by people who never worked for the company. Over $265 million of this money has gone to attorneys! Four plaintiff law firms have received more than the original $8 million Keene paid for BEH.

The trials of the Keene company are not over yet. There are more than 2,000 additional claims filed for asbestos-related "injuries" *every month*, and many of the original defendants have already filed for bankruptcy. Because of the "individually and severally liable" rule, as more companies seek bankruptcy court protection, those that are left face even greater liabilities. If the current rules of law remain in effect, it is only a matter of time until all the companies are forced into bankruptcy.

When the companies go into bankruptcy or leave the country, jobs go with them. So the few (in relative terms) winners cost the majority their jobs and homes.

The new tort laws can truly be called the working lawyer's friend. Tort has become the gold rush of the twentieth century for the working class and especially for their attorneys.

Of the nearly $9 billion already spent on asbestos litigation and settlements, nearly two-thirds or $6 billion has gone to attorneys![2]

HOW DID THIS HAPPEN?

Not being a lawyer, I did some research on exactly when and how the tort litigation we now accept as common began. After all, back in the fifties and earlier, there were very few lawsuits over defective materials, much less the misuse of materials. A little research in any library will verify that few Americans sued each other for personal liability prior to 30 years ago. The relatively few suits against companies were usually for breach of contract.

Today, liability insurance to protect against tort lawsuits is the norm, not the exception, and the cost of liability insurance alone runs into the billions of dollars a year. The hidden costs of additional testing to avoid lawsuits and the thousands of new products never introduced into our economy because of potential lawsuits cut deeply into our economic viability.

I have a good friend who, by any measure, is an excellent obstetrician, but he has stopped delivering babies because his practice could not absorb the $35-per-patient cost of liability insurance; nor could he handle the emotional trauma of potential litigation.

It is unfortunate for the poor of the world that many new drugs that could be extremely beneficial to the sick are scrapped prior to marketing, on the advice of the pharmaceutical companies' legal departments. Simply put, the potential profits are not large enough to justify the risks of potential lawsuits.

In reviewing this problem area in our economy, I found the same basic premise at work here that is feeding the regulations area: the zero-risk mentality.

Those who set the trends in law, just as those who set the trends in government regulations, are seeking zero risks to the public at large for any products they buy, no matter how those products might be used. The simple truth is: There are no zero-risk products! The only way to accomplish zero risk is to develop zero products. Sound familiar?

Former Vice President Dan Quayle often commented that the American legal system is out of control. Perhaps the best endorsements of Dan Quayle's comment were the constant attacks on his character by the American Bar Association. It is my opinion that anything or anyone the ABA opposes probably is working to the good of the American public at large. If the ACLU and other activists groups join in the attack, we can be certain that we should support that person or cause.

I would like to share a brief explanation of how we got in the mess we're in, from a litigation perspective. If we don't reform the present system, we'll soon have a business environment in which only the massive corporations with their staffs of attorneys will be able or willing to develop new products in America. And even these corporations will hide behind a myriad of legal entities, adding billions in cost to any new products.

As I said earlier, lawsuits in America have become the new "gold rush" of this century. Many Americans look at lawsuits the way they do lotteries: spend a little to win a lot. But in any gambling operation, the "house" always wins, whether the players do or not. In this case, the house is the cadre of attorneys whose wallets grow fatter in the court rooms of our nation.

Prior to the fifties, most of the law practiced in America was either criminal (crimes like robbery, rape, theft) or contract (disputes between two or more parties over contractual arrangements). The third element of law (tort) was usually limited to non-contract, non-criminal cases in which one party was injured by another non-related party. An example would be if a stranger runs a stop sign and hits your car and you sue to recover damages. Very seldom, if ever, did the rule of tort supersede the rule of contract.

For example, if you signed on with a circus act as a target for the knife thrower and were subsequently skewered, the law generally determined that you knew the risks and suffered the consequences. The contract, implied or written, was that the knife thrower was known to be good, but not infallible, and a reasonably sane person would know that. Therefore the knife thrower was contractually bound only to avoid purposely hurting you. If you could prove the knife thrower had *purposely* thrown the knife with the express intent of hitting you, you could sue for violation of contract.

Previously, if a customer bought a pair of roller skates, the manufacturer was not implicitly liable for any harm that might come to the wearer of the skates. The warranty covered the product (quality, durability) only as expressly stated by the manufacturer. Today, the exact opposite is true. The manufacturer, and anyone else in the chain of distribution, is assumed liable for any use of the product, no matter how foolish it may be.

The classic case in point has to be the Tylenol case in the eighties. The manufacturer of Tylenol medicine was held liable for the poisoning of several people after a lunatic opened some bottles and substituted cyanide-laced pills for the real ones. The jury, acting under the new interpretation of tort law, determined that the company should have anticipated such an event and prevented it.

As a result, the cost of buying any over-the-counter drugs went up, not just to cover the cost of "tamper free" containers (if there is such a thing), but also to cover the liability insurance for every other product manufacturer.

Such awards were not always as we now see them. A group of legal reformers in the fifties decided that contract law didn't adequately protect the rights of some victims, particularly those who might not understand implied warranties. Even more than that, these guardians of public welfare presumed that customers were not capable of assessing the risks of a product, so they needed a champion to intercede for them. Tort litigation was to become that champion.

One case in point is that of the Massengill Company of Bristol, Tennessee. In 1937 this company manufactured and sold a new sulfa drug suspended in a solution of diethylene glycol (similar to today's anti-freeze). Unfortunately, more than one hundred people who took the drug died. Under the rules of contract law, the company was not responsible for the fatal results. The company had only the responsibility to inform the purchaser of the contents, not the effects.

Clearly any caring person would agree that this company and all others should be held liable for not fully testing a potentially lethal product. But in their zeal to reform the obvious abuses, the reformers destroyed the legal system that had served well for nearly two thousand years.

The reformers, working through their positions at the major law schools, began to shape the minds of future judges, as well as the future attorneys who would actually handle the courtroom litigation.

The legal revolution came "with lightning speed." Once the first jury decided that the contract between a buyer and seller was not all-inclusive, the lid was off. In effect, the rule of law reversed from "let the buyer beware" to "the buyer has all the rights not specifically excluded by the seller's contract." In other words, the warranty had to spell out the specific exemptions the seller or his agents expressly declared.[3]

Let's go back to our knife throwing example again. Under the new rules of tort, the knife thrower would assume unlimited liability if he skewered his assistant—purposely or not. Even if the spinning wheel to which the subject is attached comes loose and injures her, the knife thrower may be contingently liable, as would be the circus owner. Thus, the tort game is being played under a new set of rules.

However, once the new rules were known, the manufacturers quickly adapted and compiled lengthy, elaborate exclusion contracts that covered everything from defects to acts of God. The reformers were furious that the nasty money grubbers were once more evading their responsibility (at least as they saw it).

In 1964 the California Supreme Court, once and for all, drove a stake through the heart of all contract law involving a potential tort situation.

In a case involving a brake failure in a Ford automobile, the court threw out all written and implied agreements between any buyers and sellers and their agents. The court declared that no citizen could sign away any future legal rights by way of contracts, disclaimers, or warranties. In essence the court said the defendant, Maywood Bell Ford dealership was liable, irrespective of any warranty contracts to the contrary. "Maywood Bell was liable because the court *said* Maywood Bell was liable for the accident, and that was that."[4]

From that point on, no contract signed by any potential litigant was a valid defense for any manufacturer or supplier of goods and services. Each case would be decided on the basis of what the jury concluded—period!

Few people actually realize that waivers, such as most patients sign before an operation, are essentially worthless in court. Under the rules of tort law a provider can be held liable, regardless of waivers signed.

One day I received a call from a man who was undergoing severe stress as a result of a lawsuit. It seems he had a farm with a small but deep lake on it. Before he purchased the farm, the lake had been one of the more well-known fishing spots in the county. After he bought the property he posted the lake to keep all the local kids out, for fear that one of them might drown and he would be liable.

Almost immediately some of the local people began asking if they could fish the lake. He agreed on the basis that they sign a statement stipulating that they were fishing at their own risk, and he was not responsible for their safety. On the advice of his attorney he included a clause that anyone using his lake would wear an approved life vest at all times.

One elderly gentleman, who had fished the lake for decades, signed the agreement and fished the lake frequently over the next two years; each time without a life vest (as was his lifelong habit). The landowner threatened to prohibit him from fishing if he didn't at least keep a life vest in the boat, so he agreed to do that.

One afternoon the older man's boat was found floating in the lake; he had suffered a heart attack, fallen out of the boat, and drowned.

About three months later the landowner was served notice that the man's wife had filed suit against him for $10 million dollars, claiming negligence in her husband's death since he had not been *required* to wear a life vest.

As lawsuits do, this one dragged out for nearly two years before a compromise was reached, during which time numerous depositions were taken and sizable attorney fees were paid by the landowner.

---

*A*s the problems converge,
they tend to amplify and
compound. This is especially
true in the area of tort litigation
and regulations.

Ultimately, the case was settled out of court with the landowner's insurance company paying only a few thousand dollars. The landowner told me, "I still believe we could have won in court, but there was no way the insurance company would take that chance."

So another case was "settled," and a frivolous lawsuit was turned into a profit—for the plaintiff.

The only real winners in a lawsuit are the attorneys. This land-owner paid out thousands of dollars in legal fees. Shortly thereafter he sold the farm and moved onto a property with no streams or lakes.

Since the Maywood Bell decision, the court room has become a great showplace where each side parades expert witnesses through the court trying to convince average laypeople on the merits of their cases. More often than not, the decisions are made on the basis of "feelings" rather than facts because one set of experts usually contra-dicts the other set of experts.

But the rewards for these experts and the attorneys on both sides have very nearly ground technology and innovation in many indus-tries to a halt. This is especially true in areas such as drugs and vac-cines. Quite often the possible side effects of new drugs and vaccines are similar to naturally occurring illnesses. This confusion leads many patients to believe their symptoms are the result of taking the drug rather than an unrelated disease. In these cases, a manufacturer or distributor is practically guaranteed to be sued.

REGULATIONS AND LITIGATION WORKING TOGETHER

In the first part of this book I mentioned that our economy can survive one, two, or even three major problems at one time. But as the problems converge, they tend to amplify and compound. This is especially true in the area of tort litigation and regulations, both of which overlap virtually every area of our economy.

Most private citizens, as well as business owners live in a cloaked fear of lawsuits. All too often these suits are originated with-out prior warning and potentially carry enormous penalties. The suit can be the result of an auto accident, a visitor slipping on your front steps, a customer tripping in your store, or a burglar falling through a skylight. The awards granted by jurors can destroy a lifetime of work and savings. In fact, just the very presence of accumulated surpluses attracts lawsuits like flypaper. In our society, in which we tend to punish success, litigation is an effective means of transferring wealth.

The media play a major role in the current attitudes about litiga-tion by selectively dramatizing what appears to be blatant abuses by companies. A classic example is found in the case of the Ford Pinto car.

Several TV news magazines did documentaries on what they termed the flagrant negligence by Ford concerning the dangers of fuel tank ruptures in a rear-end collision of the Pinto. Although the total number of deaths in the Pinto are not statistically higher than those of other vehicles of similar weight and size, some of the deaths in rear-end collisions were as a result of fire when the gas tank was punctured by an extruding bolt in the undercarriage.

It was pointed out (correctly) that some Ford engineers felt there was some potential of fire in a rear end collision, and at least one had suggested some design changes to correct the problem. What was not reported was that there were literally dozens of other potentially dangerous problems identified by Ford engineers resulting from the size, weight, and cost constraints of the car being downsized.

The same can be said of basically every other low cost, small car on the road today. Although technological advances are making small cars safer than ever, these didn't exist in the seventies. To have made all the changes suggested for the Pinto would have driven up the cost at least $1,000 and made the car non-competitive.

Remember that the design of the Pinto was in direct response to government regulations dictating higher milage which, by the technology of the time, necessitated much smaller, lighter cars.

There is no doubt that the Pinto could have been made much safer by the addition of a heavier frame, air bags, a roll cage in the doors and roof, and anti-lock brakes. In fact, if you really wanted these improvements, all you had to do back then was buy a Mercedes.

I'm not trying to defend the defects in the Pinto. But at some point, there is a trade off between cost and safety. Drivers of small cars must accept some risks or there will be no small cars built, or anything else for that matter. The trend in tort liability is driving businesses out of the U.S. and into the waiting arms of our competitors.

In November of 1992 NBC aired a docudrama depicting GM trucks equipped with side-mounted fuel tanks as being potential fire bombs. The television scenes were dramatic: a mid-sized auto crashes into the side of the truck and instantly a huge fire ball engulfs both vehicles. Who wouldn't be alarmed?

Later a lengthy investigation by General Motors revealed something quite different. In several previous side collisions no fire or explosions took place. So the NBC crew staged the dramatic explosion by wiring toy rocket motors to ignite the gasoline upon impact.

Later NBC publicly admitted the deception and apologized, but one has to wonder how many potential jurors were influenced by the previous program.

Less than two months earlier, a jury awarded $100 million to a couple whose son had been killed in a fiery collision of a similar vehicle. If that judgment stands, you can believe all future GM customers will pay a portion of the award.

I benefitted from one facet of America's litigation mentality. When I was in college during the early sixties, I worked at the Cape Canaveral Space Center and attended college about 60 miles away. So I was always in need of reliable, cheap transportation. I found it in the Chevrolet Corvair. After Ralph Nader classified these little cars in his book as being "unsafe at any speed," their value plummeted.

I had been driving Corvairs since early 1960 and had found them quite acceptable, provided I used common sense and drove the little car like a normal rear-engine car should be driven.

The Corvair had never been profitable for General Motors and was scheduled to be phased out in 1965. But because of their irritation over Nader's attacks, the leaders at GM continued the line until 1969, providing me with excellent, inexpensive transportation for many years. I wrote Nader a thank you letter. (By the way, I still own a 1965 convertible that I love.)

While working on this book I have come to realize that there is a small, dedicated element in our society who see the demise of industry and technology as their mission in life. In the case of the environmental extremists, they see jobs and people as secondary to their environmental goals.

In the case of the legal reformers, they view the masses as downtrodden, abused serfs who are preyed upon by ruthless merchants. Obviously neither extreme is good for our country. No one in his or her right mind wants a drug company to dispense a poisonous substance with impunity. But neither should any thinking person want to destroy a company financially because of an unintentional error. Once the atmosphere of litigation terror takes over, everyone becomes a potential target.

In a much larger sense, it is easy to see the struggle between good and evil in our world behind the scenes. America really is the grand experiment—not only in democracy but in Christianity as well.

We are the funders of the world's evangelism, or at least we have been in the past. If the enemy can destroy the economic capacity of the United States, much of the funding for world evangelism will go with it.

I believe God has a much greater plan that includes world evangelism. The only question is: Will we be a part of it?

CHAPTER THIRTEEN

The
Litigation Lottery

Americans seem to have a natural affinity for games of chance, which is why state lotteries have spread so widely. Perhaps it's a part of our national heritage. Many of the early settlers of our nation were truly risk takers. Why else would Europeans leave their homelands and settle in America where the average survival rate was one in ten. To escape religious and political persecution? That's true, but then more than 200 years later their descendants left established communities, such as Boston or New York, headed west to Texas, Oregon, Washington, and California, where the average survival rate was about one-in-five.

Clearly, a large part of the motivation to head west was the prospect of instant riches. When gold was first discovered in Georgia in the early 1800s, thousands of prospectors flooded the foothills of the Appalachians in search of the hidden treasures.

By the mid–1800s, as the gold in Georgia played out, the risk takers headed west. The risks were much higher, but so were the rewards. The few who actually struck it rich did so at the greater expense of those who didn't because, as they squandered their riches, the price for everything went up. So the get-rich-quick syndrome in

America is not new. Ever since the first explorers stepped off their boats, the dream has been to strike it rich and live in luxury.

The get-rich-quick mentality so ingrained in our society perfectly coincides with the activists' desire to stop, or at least control, industrial growth. Litigation is the new get-rich-quick plan and litigation is an effective tool in the environment battle. A few do get rich, but at a high cost to the rest of us.

In the previous chapter we took a brief look at the growth of tort litigation. Now I would like to look at the result of this new form of hidden tax, because that is exactly what the legal costs levied upon our economy are: hidden taxes that must be paid by every consumer.

HEALTH CARE

It has been estimated that the threat of litigation adds somewhere between 10 and 30 percent to the cost of health care practiced in our country. The exact figure is difficult to determine because some of the cost is direct (insurance, settlements, and actual judgments), but many of the costs are indirect (defensive testing, extra record keeping, lost wages, and so on).

After talking with a great many practicing physicians, I am convinced the real costs are probably somewhere between 20 and 25 percent. The threat of lawsuits is so real to most medical practitioners that it is foremost in their minds. Every physician knows at least one associate who has been sued for millions of dollars and most doctors live in dread of his or her own turn in court. In reality, most of the cases are settled out of court, without trial, but the costs are still enormous—both financially and emotionally.

According to a study released in 1993 by the National Medical Liability Reform Coalition, the real cost of defensive testing alone—not including malpractice insurance—was about $10 billion in 1991, and will rise to $15 billion a year by 1998. About $9 billion a year is also spent on malpractice insurance premiums.[1]

A good friend, whom I mentioned earlier, was a practicing obstetrician (OB) until recently. He was very helpful in my understanding just how bad the litigation problem has become for those in the medical fields.

He delivered babies in a small Midwestern city that is representative of most such communities in America. As an OB he was well respected and, until about fifteen years ago, had never had a lawsuit filed against him. In fact, he said he never thought about anyone suing him. His patients were special people to him; they were friends.

He made a good living in his practice but certainly wasn't getting wealthy at it. His average day was 14 to 16 hours, and he was on call every third night and weekend. He has a big heart and would never have thought about turning away a needy pregnant woman. He practiced medicine because he felt it was his calling from God, and he often took on so many nonpaying patients that his partners complained.

One day in 1981 a pregnant immigrant woman showed up at the obstetric office, about to deliver her first child. Because she had no money and no insurance, she had never sought any prenatal care. Consequently, none of the other doctors would take her as a walk-in patient; the risks were just too high. Rather than turn her out, my friend sent her to the emergency room of their local hospital and notified the attending physician that he would deliver the baby, if necessary.

True to form in many such cases, she developed problems in the labor room and my friend was called in to perform a caesarean section. After delivery the baby was kept in the hospital for several weeks because of a congenital problem and, eventually, the infant died. My friend said he was almost certain the problem was related to the mother's smoking, drugs, and poor nutrition while pregnant.

He was shocked a few weeks later when he received notice of a lawsuit filed against him and the hospital for the negligent death of the child he delivered—free. The amount of the suit was a staggering $10 million.

He said his first instinct was to dismiss the suit as a nuisance. After all, any thinking person would easily see that he had done the best he could under the circumstances. Besides, virtually no other OB would have even accepted her as a patient, much less have delivered the baby. The insurance company's lawyers assured him they were taking the suit very seriously. Litigation, particularly in the health field and especially in the case of obstetrics, is a growth industry for attorneys. As the insurance company's attorney said, "It's like mining the mother lode."

Attorneys know that juries often sympathize with mothers whose children are injured during birth. And since it is almost impossible to determine the actual cause of the difficulty, often juries will award judgments on the basis of compassion, rather than logic. As the attorney for the insurance company told him, "One crying mother is worth a hundred expert witnesses."

Over the next two years this doctor went through a life-changing experience with the legal system. He gave no fewer than ten depositions about the case, and saw the prospect of an enormously expensive legal battle raging over this act of benevolence. If he lost in court, his million dollar liability policy would be woefully inadequate to cover the judgment. Literally, he and his family could become destitute overnight.

As the case drew nearer, more and more of his time was occupied in being coached on what he could and could not say on the witness stand and in interviewing the hordes of expert witnesses his side would need to combat the expert witnesses from the other side.

His insurance company tried to settle out of court, but the plaintiff's attorney would not settle for the few thousand they offered; he smelled big money.

---

*T*he litigation system . . . had
just cost every one of this
doctor's patients about $8.00
each, per visit, and they didn't
even know it.

The doctor consistently tried to explain to his insurance company's lawyers that he had done nothing wrong and his practice of health care was impeccable. What they tried to explain to him was that it didn't matter that he was right; all that mattered was whether the jury felt sorry for the plaintiff and decided to soothe her with some of the insurance company's money (as well as his).

The insurance company's lawyers suggested that he secure counsel of his own since they could not represent him if the judgment exceeded the amount of his liability insurance. He did so and began to incur the costs of preparing his own defense—just in case.

My doctor friend, who was guilty of nothing more than compassion, saw his income decline and his expenses increase as he looked forward to the terrifying prospect of a court trial where a jury would decide if he and his family should lose everything they owned—all because he tried to help one of the less fortunate in our society. He wasn't even allowed to talk with the woman, at the instruction of her attorney, his attorney, and the insurance attorneys. After all, where would the legal process be if rational people were able to sit down and work out their own problems?

Just before the trial was scheduled to begin, the insurance company's attorneys began to get indicators that the plaintiff's attorney was willing to discuss a settlement. By this time the doctor had already incurred legal costs of several thousand dollars and had mentally committed himself to the trial, still believing that right would prevail; after all, that is part of the American Dream too.

His education in tort law came when the insurance company's attorneys notified him that they had reached a settlement. Even the amount the woman received was to be undisclosed as a part of the settlement. The doctor objected, but to no avail. It was simply cheaper to settle than to fight. Besides, the insurance company had an alternative recovery plan in mind.

Once the insurance company settled, the doctor's own liability was also settled as a part of the agreement, so at least he was off the hook financially and could get back to his practice—or so he thought.

Shortly after the last papers were signed, the insurance company sent him notice of a premium increase, effective when the current policy expired. The increase of nearly 100 percent shocked him into reality: Someone had to pay for the settlement, and it surely wasn't going to be the insurance company. Insurance companies don't pay claims. They merely lend the client the money temporarily and then recover it through increased premiums.

The litigation system in the U.S. had just cost every one of this doctor's patients about $8.00 each, per visit, and they didn't even know it. Two subsequent law suits, one over a delivery that he did nearly 17 years earlier, raised the average patient's cost to nearly $35 each and forced this doctor to retire from obstetrics altogether.

Space will not allow me to relate the dozens of other similar stories told by many of the physicians I contacted; but multiply their experience by about ten thousand cases a year, and you get a good feel of what litigation now adds to our health care costs.

DEFENSIVE TESTING

The advance of technology in medicine is something to behold. As in the earlier story of the time traveler, anyone from just 40 years ago would marvel at the changes, most of which are potentially less costly than previous technologies; that is, if it were not for the tort system we now have in place.

As medical technology has improved, so has the potential to use it as a weapon in lawsuits. Allow me to use a personal illustration. Ever since high school football I have suffered from a torn cartilage (meniscus) in my left knee. Usually it doesn't bother me but every so often it flares up. Since I don't earn my living in professional athletics, virtually every orthopedist I have seen has advised against surgery (even orthoscopic), opting to treat the problem with localized steroids—until recently.

A few months back the knee began to get sore and progressively got worse. Being totally familiar with the symptoms, I immediately went to a local orthopedist and asked if he would administer an anti-inflammatory steroid, which he refused to do.

When asked why, his answer astonished me. "You'll have to have the knee checked by an MRI (Magnetic Resonance Imaging)."

This marvelous bit of technology is now used routinely to get an image of the internal parts of the human body. But it is also quite expensive.

I argued for several minutes, insisting that I knew exactly what the problem was and did not require an MRI. I had experienced similar symptoms in the past and was more than willing to sign a liability release. He shook his head, and although he agreed with me, he still refused to give me a cortisone shot. It wasn't until I began the research on this book that I realized the courts don't recognize a waiver of personal rights anymore. In other words, patients can still sue, and win, even though they have signed a waiver acknowledging that they accept the risks involved.

Needless to say, I left the office more than a little irritated at the doctor, the medical profession in general, and the fact that I had to get an MRI to confirm what this doctor already knew.

Later I discussed this whole issue with a radiologist who operates a nuclear medical laboratory. What he said makes sense, in a distorted sort of way.

In the past a condition like mine was fairly easy to diagnose externally, and the treatment was also relatively simple. But as technology has progressed, it is now possible to look inside the body through a Computerized Tomography (CT or "CAT") scan and the MRI. If the doctor had treated me for a simple inflamed cartilage and

I had developed further complications, the failure to utilize all the current technology could be used against him in a court of law. So rather than take the risk, doctors now routinely run all their patients through essentially every possible diagnostic routine.

"Put yourself in his position," my radiologist friend said. "If he treats you for the problem you described (with which he concurred) and you develop cancer of the knee, you might say that it was the result of the steroid. Then the burden of proof would fall on the doctor to prove it wasn't so. Or you might already have cancer of the knee and you could sue him, saying that if he had required you to have an MRI it would have been detectable earlier. Either way he loses. So, from the physician's perspective, it is simply more prudent to require the tests." As I said, in a distorted sort of way it does make sense.

Technological advances have made complicated medical diagnoses simpler, but they have made simple medical conditions more complicated. In the near future a family doctor may require a complete body MRI (or whatever develops in the future) for every annual exam. Otherwise those who develop serious ailments could sue, claiming that the physician had not done everything possible to diagnose any existing problems.

In my case, I paid $935 for a cortisone shot in my knee—$900 for an MRI, and $35 for the shot. In reality, everyone on our health care plan paid a portion because we are self-insured. The same basic principle is reflected throughout our economy whether it is in health care, automobiles, or athletics. Excessive litigation raises the cost of products and services, and everyone pays the costs.

In our health care system there are thousands of examples of million dollar (plus) awards. Every time someone wins a large judgment against a health care provider, we all pay a share of the cost. The current tort system, like the regulatory system, lives in a zero-defect-mentality world. There is no such thing.

BUILT-IN LIABILITY

Whooping cough is practically unknown to our generation, but two generations ago it was one of the leading killers of infants in many parts of our country. Statistically, about three hundred thousand children would contract whooping cough each year if not for a very effective vaccine, and at least four hundred children would die annually. Even today, medical technology could save only a fraction of them. The old adage that "an ounce of prevention is worth a pound of cure" is absolutely true in the case of vaccines.

But no vaccine is totally risk free, and the whooping cough vaccine is created from a live virus, so it has its liabilities too. Statistics show that approximately 30 children out of the 3.5 million vaccinated each year will suffer some form of brain damage as a result of the treatment. Those whose children will be inoculated successfully against whooping cough would consider this an acceptable risk. But those whose children are damaged don't agree, and most will file suit against the manufacturers and suppliers, in spite of the ample warnings associated with the vaccine and its use. Hundreds of such lawsuits were filed in the seventies and eighties, costing millions in court costs and judgments.[2]

The whooping cough vaccine is universal enough for the manufacturers to risk the lawsuits and absorb the costs (pass them along in the cost of the product). But many other vaccines and related drugs are simply never marketed in the U.S. because the potential for litigation is too great and the profits too slim to absorb the costs. Those who wonder why our medical costs just keep going up need to look no further than our regulatory agencies and the courts for much of the blame.

There are thousands of "miracle" drugs available today, and *none* are without risk. Anyone from 100 years ago willingly would have risked any potentially negative side effects to have something as simple as penicillin available to them.

In the tort litigation system today, the accuser does not have to prove the guilt of the accused.

Tens of thousands of Civil War soldiers died from secondary infections, rather than their initial injuries, because of the lack of any infection-fighting drugs. Even a minor skin puncture from a rusty nail would often result in an excruciatingly painful death from tetanus (commonly called lockjaw). Even as recently as the twenties, tetanus was still a potent killer of young children.

As I said, any company should be held liable for selling faulty products, including pharmaceutical, but no progress or industry can be made in a zero-defect environment. At some point, reason and balance must be restored.

My own father probably would have lived many years longer if any one of the blood clot thinners used routinely in cardiac care units had been available in 1959, when he suffered a fatal coronary and died. Would he have minded that one of the potential side effects is internal bleeding? I doubt it.

A friend who recently suffered a heart attack is still alive today because the hospital where he was taken used this type of drug, as thousands of others do every day. One of the side effects my friend experienced was extensive bleeding after an angioplasty to restore a clogged artery to normal function. In spite of the bleeding, he didn't think about suing his doctor, the hospital, or the drug company; he was simply grateful to be alive.

Later his doctor told him that, even though it is still the most effective blood clot thinner ever developed, the hospital had stopped using the drug because a patient died of internal hemorrhaging after receiving it. This patient was admitted after an automobile accident, which was probably caused by his heart attack. After his death, the coroner could not say conclusively whether his internal bleeding was the result of the drug or the accident or some combination of the two.

But in the tort litigation system today, the accuser does not have to prove the guilt of the accused. The burden falls on the defendant to prove that the drug did *not* cause the death (so much for the innocent-until-proven-guilty concept). As a result, the hospital settled with the widow for something over $100,000, and the clot thinner was banned. In our seemingly mindless court system today, this attitude means that thousands may die needlessly because one person suffers a bad side effect.

The logical question now is whether the relatives of some future heart attack victim who dies because the drug is no longer available at that hospital will file suit claiming the deceased was damaged by the absence of a proven blood clot thinner.

In a larger sense, the cost of tort litigation for pharmaceuticals is much greater than just the damage awards, because no commercial company is going to develop drugs that cost it more than it makes.

It is not my intention to defend all the practices of pharmaceutical companies. I'm sure there are plenty of things they do wrong and, without a doubt, many companies charge excessive prices for patented drugs. But even a little research into the number of lawsuits flowing through our courts today will show how bad the tort system has become for drug manufacturers.

Between the Federal Drug Administration (FDA) reacting to every knee-jerk of the activists, and the legal system ready to file billion dollar law suits, developing and distributing drugs today is a very expensive process.

Fortunately the days of the sidewalk snake oil peddlers are gone. But now we have the opposite extreme: a system that requires multi-million dollar investments to produce any new drugs.

Since many of the diseases still common to Third World countries basically have been eradicated in the industrialized countries, the drug business migrates naturally to where the money is: in the industrialized countries. But often new drugs and vaccines are discovered as a result or byproduct of working on commercially viable products.

More often than not, the drugs with less commercial value, but of great benefit to underdeveloped nations, will be dumped—their commercial value deemed not to be worth the litigation cost. So, instead of doctors and research scientists making the decisions about what drugs will benefit us, the courts are doing it by proxy.

TORT REFORM

When the legal system is so distorted that strangers (physicians and laypeople alike) will pass by an injured or sick person for fear of being sued, something is fundamentally wrong with the system; and that happens regularly in our cities. The relationship between the ever-increasing awards and the ever-increasing number of suits is hard to miss. As the rewards for suing have climbed, so have the numbers of litigants jumping on the gravy train at the expense of the rest of us.

Just a casual glance at any of several cable television channels today will provide an insight into the various specialties that lawyers have acquired. One firm in our area has the owner/lawyer hawking just about every kind of tort suit imaginable—from malpractice to workers' compensation. The firm advertises that they will initiate a suit for as little as $100 down and, if their attorneys don't win, they don't get paid. Ambulance chasing has been outlawed, but modern media have taken the ambulance chasers right into the potential litigant's home.

According to the American Tort Reform Association (ATRA), the hidden costs behind our litigation mania costs the average family about $1,200 a year.[3] It's little wonder that in head-to-head competition with other nations' companies, U.S. businesses have some difficulty.

In addition to the costs of regulations and health care, the cost of operating our tort litigation system in the late eighties was some 2.6 percent of our Gross National Product (GNP), or about $120 billion. In contrast, the Japanese spend about .4 percent of their GNP on litigation.[4] Americans spend nearly 650 percent more than the Japanese do—just settling lawsuits.

The next time you look at a football helmet, a motorcycle, or your family car, just think about how much extra you paid so that someone else could sue the manufacturer of those products.

In the case of the football helmet, it amounts to nearly 35 percent of the actual sales price. Litigation adds about 4 percent more to the price of your car.[5]

For motorcycles, litigation adds about 17 percent. But, litigation adds some 135 percent to the cost of oral vaccines.

The next time you go skiing, ask what the cost of the resort's liability insurance is. And remember, no one is *forced* to go skiing. They're all volunteers.

As it says in Proverbs 16:8,11: *"Better is a little with righteousness than great income with injustice. . . . A just balance and scales belong to the Lord; all the weights of the bag are His concern."*

CHAPTER FOURTEEN

The Aging of America

There is no doubt that Americans, as a group, are getting older. The reason is twofold: aging baby boomers and a generation of abortions. Unfortunately, most Americans, Christian and non-Christian alike, have bought into the philosophy promoted for the last 30 years: that our country and our planet are being overrun with too many people. It just isn't true.

Our planet is underdeveloped, not overpopulated. The example shown by the free-market-based industrialized nations is that a large number of people can be fed, clothed, and sheltered by a relatively small percentage of the population. In fact, virtually everyone can live at a reasonably good standard of living—even in the inner city if the system works properly.

Welfare, not free enterprise, has been the destroyer of the inner cities. Where people are working and improving their lifestyles from generation to generation, business just naturally migrates to the area creating new jobs and better living standards.

Where welfare abounds, families break down, crime rises, lifestyles stagnate, and the only businesses that really thrive are drugs and alcohol.

America desperately needs young, bright people who want to succeed. With the population gap created by abortions and birth control, we can't afford to waste the people resources of the cities. In the next two decades older Americans will pay dearly for the lack of younger people in our work force.

This problem is the result of a determined effort to decrease our country's population, or at least control its growth severely. In great part, population control revolves around the philosophy that was discussed earlier: nature should be left intact, unspoiled by human beings.

Without question, as more people live on our planet some natural life forms do get crowded out; that's inevitable. That process was taking place long before human beings had any affect on these changes. Natural disasters, such as climate changes, meteor impacts, and volcanic eruptions always have played a much greater role in ecology than people do today.

But the idea that human beings might be the mechanism of ecological changes seems totally unacceptable to environmentalists who believe that saving the land requires eliminating the people.

Being pro-human does not imply necessarily that one is anti-ecology. Much the contrary. People who care about people are far better ecologists than any group of radicals who believe that the Earth is a "mother spirit" and human beings are a virus attacking her.[1]

Many of the same people who hold to this perspective also believe the elderly have a limited usefulness to society. The process of solving this problem is a subtle one—but quite effective. The model can be seen in some of the more socialized countries, such as Holland, Denmark, and Sweden, where euthanasia programs are in the early stages of development.

After the Supreme Court's *Roe v. Wade* decision in the seventies, the abortion movement in America began in earnest. Planned Parenthood and those within the abortion movement had long advocated population control, especially among the lower classes. In fact, the stated purpose of the Planned Parenthood was to reduce the birth rate among the poor.[2]

In 1973 the Supreme Court provided just the vehicle to initiate a large-scale birth control project: abortion on demand. Abortion has eliminated more than 30 million unborn children since 1973. By the year 2000 abortion will have eliminated more than 40 million people from our society.

This alone would be significant enough to stifle any productive economy. After all, what society can absorb the loss of 40 million consumers (not to mention taxpayers) and hope to remain economically viable? These losses must ultimately translate into lost product sales. Think of the millions of diapers, clothes, toys, and other consumable items that will never be produced and sold. And since this lost generation will never live to grow up, their loss will be felt in education, transportation, and housing.

> *We're going to have a whole generation of younger workers paying an enormous portion of their incomes to support an older generation.*

Assuming this lost generation would have had an average annual consumption of perhaps $10,000 (a low-side figure) by 2010, the retirement decade for the baby boomers, the net annual loss to our economy will be at least $400 *billion*. I would like to see the politicians of *that* era fit that into their budgets.

Additionally, it is this missing generation that normally would pay the taxes to run the country. But the simple truth is, they don't exist. I will be 71 in the year 2010, and I assure you I don't want to be dependent on the government or the working taxpayers at that age. The generation wars likely will be in full swing by then.

Think of what our society may be like in the year 2010 (assuming that our whole economy has not collapsed by then). It is projected that entitlement programs, such as Social Security and Medicare, will consume almost a third of the country's total Gross Domestic Product (GDP).[3]

We will have about 30 to 40 million baby boomers facing retirement in 2010, with another 30 million or so following them within 10 to 15 years.

Without question, the minimum retirement age will have migrated to around 70 years of age because there will not be enough money in the system to support retirement at a younger age. (That discussion is already underway in Washington.)

It is my personal conviction that private retirement accounts will be diverted to feed the deficits within the Social Security system as wage earners are tapped out for taxes. I have stated this publicly for several years and have drawn a lot of criticism from people who assert that it will never happen.

Recently, articles have been appearing in various newspapers about proposals within the government to utilize private retirement account funds to provide capital for inner city programs. There is no logical reason to think that the same rationale will not apply to protecting the Social Security system.

I doubt the government would be so bold as to confiscate retirement funds. It is far more likely that the rules governing retirement accounts will be modified to require the funds to be secured by government notes, much as the Social Security Trust funds are now—to "protect them."

Regardless of other funding sources, we're going to have a whole generation of younger workers paying an enormous portion of their incomes to support an older generation, who will live better than they do. The question we all need to ask is: Do I want to be dependent on a younger generation that has been raised on "situational ethics?" Their value system is significantly different than that of earlier generations.

Those who are feeding the current younger generation a steady diet of violence, pornography, and disregard for human life will live to regret it. We need to pray that the children of today will turn from the wicked ways of their parents and seek the Lord. Otherwise, there's going to be some tough times by the second decade of the twenty-first century.

THE BABY BOOMERS

As mentioned earlier, predominantly these are the people born to the GIs returning home from World War II. Presently there are more than 60 million baby boomers aging their way toward retirement. It was this huge population boom that created the sudden burst of productivity, and thus wealth, after World War II, as their parents bought diapers, cars, and homes for their families. The "boomers" also created an increased demand for new schools, second cars, trendy clothes, books, magazines, and movies, as they moved into their teen years in the sixties.

It was this great surge of humanity entering the job force in the sixties and seventies that made retirement economically feasible for the millions who now enjoy its benefits. The boomers, and a few of the rest of us, are paying the Social Security taxes that maintain most of the current retirees. But, as noted, when this huge group of boomers become age 60 plus, it will create some real problems for the few who are left to pay the bills and bear the taxes.[4]

HEALTH CARE COSTS

It is a statistical fact that the older a person gets the more health care he or she normally requires. In our era of life-support technology, it is possible to extend life beyond the point of viability (when the body can function on its own). This technology is a tremendous blessing to older people who can resume their normal lives after a major illness. But, when it is used to sustain artificially the lives of those who will never regain any degree of normalcy, the cost is overwhelming.

I will not attempt to address the issue of when to stop applying medical technology to the terminally ill, but you can be certain this issue will continue to surface as funds for all health care get more scarce. It has been estimated that almost 30 percent of what a person spends on health care during his or lifetime will be spent during the last two months of life.[5]

Older people continue to consume a greater ratio of our health care resources, even as overall health care consumes a greater ratio of our nation's economic productivity. Translated into English, this simply means that health care costs keep rising, and older people consume the biggest share.[6]

The insurance mentality (both private and public) of the average American helped to create the cost problem and until all Americans realize that someone *else* doesn't really pay the bills (we all do), this problem won't be resolved. I can tell you this: I don't want the current crop of doctors to make the decision of whether or not I am a "viable" asset to society or too much of a drain on the national health care system, as those in the Netherlands presently do for their patients.

In February of 1993 the Dutch Parliament passed a euthanasia law allowing Dutch doctors to do what they had, in reality, already been doing for nearly ten years: killing their patients.

Although in the strictest sense euthanasia is still illegal, the new law protects the practicing physicians from prosecution if they follow the prescribed government "Carefulness Requirements." They include: consulting with the patient first (that sounds like a good idea), consulting with a colleague, and filling out the proper forms.[7]

In an earlier article it was reported that the Dutch government had taken a survey of physicians in 1991 to see how many actually practiced euthanasia, and it was found that a high percentage had done so at one time or the other. The official euthanasia rate had been thought to be about 2 percent prior to this survey. In fact it is probably considerably higher since many cases go unreported.[8]

This says loads about government sponsored health care. You want to be sure that you don't become too much of an economic drain on the system or accumulate so much wealth that the state might be tempted to hurry along their inheritance tax share.

THE SOCIAL SECURITY DILEMMA

If I could offer some counsel to those who will be 60 or older in the next decade, it would be: don't totally stop working and don't totally depend on Social Security.

Changes are coming in the Social Security system whether we like them or not and irrespective of the political power of . . . (AARP).

Supposedly, the Social Security "trust" funds are going to make up the deficits in current contributions beyond this decade. But the question is: Where will the government get the money to replace the trust funds they now spend? Remember, to repay the trust funds means that the government must stop spending the trust fund surpluses and start paying the retirees.

Assuming that the surplus payments end in 2010 as the baby boomers retire, and the payments from the trust are $100 billion a year, that will be the equivalent of a $200-billion-a-year spending cut for our government.

I am convinced, based on the data I have reviewed, that Social Security and Medicare will *not* be available to most retirees (at least in its present form) beyond the year 2015, more or less. (The "more or less" depends on whether or not our whole economy collapses before that time).

This is not just my isolated opinion. It is shared by people such as Dorcas R. Hardy, former commissioner of the Social Security Administration, in her book, *Social Insecurity*. Apparently it is also shared by notable groups such as the Social Security Board of Trustees, whose 1991 report offered some possible solutions to this dilemma. I'll leave it up to you to decide if any of them seem reasonably feasible, given the current (or future) state of our economy.

In evaluating the future of Social Security and Medicare, I relied on an analysis provided by the National Center for Policy Analysis (NCPA), a non-partisan think tank in Dallas, Texas.[9] This analysis shows two assumptions for the future of Social Security: an intermediate and a pessimistic. I have chosen to use the intermediate rather than adopt the worst-case scenario. However, in the words of the NCPA, "People are encouraged to believe that the intermediate forecast is the most likely. But many students of Social Security think the pessimistic projection more closely reflects" what we now are experiencing in the Social Security system.[10]

Without wasting a lot of time in analyzing the future of Social Security, which I have already done in the book, *Preparing for Retirement*, let me summarize it: When Social Security began in the thirties there were approximately fourteen contributors for every retiree drawing benefits.

That ratio stayed fairly constant until the late fifties and continued to decline steadily until 1992, when the ratio was approximately three and one-half to one. Early in the twenty-first century it will decline to approximately two to one. As noted earlier, this kind of ratio creates a real funding problem.

I might add that all of the analyses provided are without the impact of AIDS on the health care (Medicare) side of Social Security. There is no scenario that will resolve that problem if no effective cure or prevention is found (other than one man and one woman for a lifetime, as God commands).

Number of Workers for Each Social Security Beneficiary

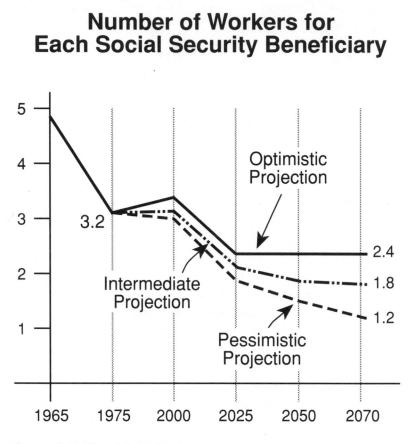

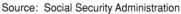

Source: Social Security Administration

By the year 2015 Social Security plus Medicare will consume approximately 22 percent of *all* employees' wages based on the "intermediate" assumptions. This amount will grow to approximately 33.5 percent by 2050 and 37 percent by 2070. Under the "pessimistic" assumption, Social Security and Medicare taxes will consume 66 percent of taxable payroll by 2070.[11]

This scenario obviously is impossible—socially and politically. When other taxes are taken into consideration, American families would have nothing left to live on. One thing about it though: The IRS Form 1040 EZ would consist of two lines and would be very simple: line one—total income; line two—all of line one remitted to the IRS.

Changes are coming in the Social Security system whether we like them or not and irrespective of the political power of the Ameri-

can Association of Retired Persons (AARP). The financial burden of
our health care system alone is quite sufficient (by itself) to sink us
into financial oblivion.

Unlike the retirement and disability side of Social Security,
health care is beyond anyone's ability to control at present. If the
system is allowed to progress down its present course, the cost of
Medicare and Medicaid will overwhelm us.

My concern is that those with vested interests to protect, including politicians, retirees, and health care lobbyists, will not see
the urgency of action in this area. One thing is certain: Placing
health care under government control won't solve the problem. In
fact, government involvement has helped to create the problem of
rampant inflation in health care costs. On the average, government
spends about two dollars to obtain one dollar of real health care
services.[12]

As of this writing, the official national health care package has
not yet materialized. I wish I could see the end product now because
it would allow me to do a better analysis. But by the time all the
proposals wend their way through the congressional process, I rather
suspect even the originators won't recognize the end product.

The following are some aspects of the plan that are fairly clear at
this time.

Higher taxes—The cost of providing health insurance to all (or
even most of the 37 million or so uninsured will cost about $100
billion a year. That's a lot of money in an economy strapped by massive debt and annual deficits in the $400 billion range. The only way
to fund such a huge cost is through higher taxes on everyone! The
keystone for these taxes probably will be some form of national sales
tax. I also suspect that employer-provided health insurance benefits
will fall into the tax plan as well.

Another aspect of the plan will likely be price controls on the
medical community. The last time price controls were attempted was
under President Nixon. They lasted about ten minutes . . . until the
special interest groups started getting "exemptions." Pretty soon the
only group not exempt was the taxpayers.

Standardizing government paperwork will help to reduce costs,
but until some means of curbing the litigation, standardizing costs
from hospital to hospital, and eliminating all the duplication of expensive medical facilities, health care will not be brought under any
degree of control.

With all the ingenious entrepreneurs in the medical field, I rather doubt that such reforms can be made without a total government takeover of the medical industry. If this happens the Department of Health and Human Services will become the largest and most costly department in the government.

THE NEXT GENERATION

It is important to reiterate that when the baby boomers are approaching retirement (and thus creating the greatest demand on the system), those who are now in their twenties and thirties will be in absolute control of our government. They will make the rules and control the health care system.

I don't believe they will sacrifice to sustain their elders in a lifestyle better than their own. But since I have already made this point before, I'll drop it. However, we do need to look at the proposed "fixes" we have created.

THE IMMIGRATION SOLUTION

The influx of immigrants into our country is both an asset and a liability. The asset is that many businesses have need of the low cost, relatively unskilled labor that many immigrants provide. Examples are the hotel industry, agriculture, construction—even fast food restaurants (usually teenagers would fill this role, except that there are fewer teenagers today).

During the early days of the Clinton administration, another factor was brought to light: illegal immigrants being hired for cheap labor. At least two of President Clinton's nominees for attorney general admitted to having hired illegal immigrants as baby-sitters for their children and one candidate even failed to pay the legally required withholding taxes. But that's another story: the underground economy in America. As taxes and regulations increase, the underground economy (non-taxed) expands.

If cheap labor is an asset to business, it is a corresponding liability to government. Because of our liberal welfare rules, many immigrants become welfare cases, absorbing vital resources while waiting for better paying jobs, which often never materialize. It is not unusual for first generation immigrants to contribute less to the system than they receive. This particular problem is significant in light of a proposed "Immigration Solution" to our generation gap of the twenty-first century.

When I first read the proposal, I thought perhaps it was a spoof. But, in fact, it is an actual proposal (or idea) from the Social Security Board. I can only presume that once the committee evaluated how bad the future problems are going to be they were grasping for any straws. After all, what do you do when faced with an unsolvable problem and told to come up with solutions?

The so-called Immigration Solution involves opening our borders to massive immigration. To adequately offset the declining population base beyond this decade, the U.S. will need approximately 100 million *new* workers. The only possible source of such a massive immigration would be Central and South America. An immigration of this magnitude would essentially strip those developing countries of their labor pool. And, still, it wouldn't solve our problem.

Common sense maintains that so-called Third World immigrants normally are not educated and trained in the skills necessary for a modern industrial society. It would take a whole generation before they would begin to fit into our economic mainstream.

The immigration proposal also requires that these 100 million immigrant workers agree to pay into the Social Security system, while pledging never to draw benefits from it. That sounds more than just a little naive (in my opinion)—especially when you consider that the workers and their families would represent approximately 240 million potential voters. I rather suspect they would vote us out and themselves in.

I discounted the Immigration Solution as anything but a political fantasy. A far more feasible solution is the "pooled fund" solution.

THE POOLED FUND

The pooled fund approach (commonly called the Social Security Trust) was established in 1983 after the Social Security Review panel evaluated the system's long-term funding needs and concluded that the pay-as-you-go method would not work when the worker-to-retiree ratio fell below three-to-one.

The pooled approach is fairly straightforward: Store some funds during the higher income years to be used in the lower income years. Joseph did this quite successfully some 3,000 years ago in Egypt, but he had the advantage of absolute authority over the trust. Not so in our political system.

The Social Security Trust will need approximately $2 trillion by 2010, when the worker-to-retiree ratio will become critical. Assuming

Annual Surplus/Deficit in
Social Security Trust Funds
(Percentage of Gross National Product)

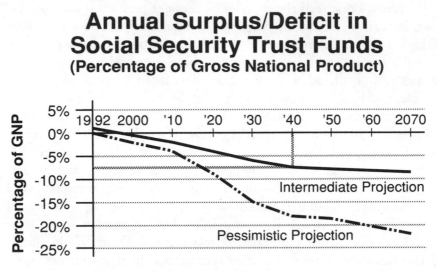

Source: Social Security Administration, National Center for Policy Analysis

the intermediate position shown on the graph above, these funds would carry the system until approximately 2040.

This plan makes two critically flawed assumptions (in my opinion): First, that the cost of operating Medicare will not increase beyond the average inflation rate of the economy (whatever that will be). By point of reference, the present rate of inflation in health care is nearly four times that of the economy in general and nearly five times greater than our annual gross domestic product (GDP) rate of growth.

The second assumption is that the trust funds will be left intact, along with the accumulated interest. As stated earlier, in spite of all the rhetoric to the contrary, the trust funds do not exist anymore.

Each year the trust funds are shifted to the general revenue side of the government's ledger and spent! The government then substitutes an IOU in the form of a zero coupon Treasury bond for the funds consumed.

Interest is not actually paid out on an annual basis on a zero coupon bond. Instead the bond is sold at a discount and later redeemed at face value. A U.S. savings bond works very much like this.

This type of security is ideal for the government, especially in the case of the Social Security trust funds because they don't even have to pay the interest annually. But the logical question is: How will the money be repaid when it is needed?

My experience as a financial counselor causes me to stop and consider that question logically. If the government already spends more than it makes (by about $350 billion in 1993, including the trust funds), and it owes more than $4 trillion already that cannot be repaid, how will the funds be repaid?

Federal pension laws now require that private companies set aside adequate reserves to cover future pension liabilities, and yet the same is not required of the government for their own pension trusts. Why would any intelligent person not perceive this as a problem?

I realize this sounds pessimistic but, in all honesty, I believe it is realistic. The tendency too often is to shoot the messenger bringing bad news, but I didn't create our economic problems. I don't think I even contributed to them appreciably. But I'll be right in the middle of the problems, along with the rest of the country, so it is in my best interest and yours to understand the problems and try to deal when them as best we can.

Later I will try to outline some things that we can (and must) do, the first of which is to get rid of those politicians who aren't willing to step forward and deal with the *real* problems. Those who increase taxes and then spend the money on *anything* other than debt reduction should be voted out!

By this point I have gone through disappointment, despair, and anger about what we are doing to our nation and especially to our future generations. Most of us didn't do it purposely; we did it ignorantly. We simply allowed ourselves to believe the lies that were being told because it was more convenient.

Any thinking person with the conservative background of most Americans has to realize that no one, our government included, can spend more than they make indefinitely. We certainly had adequate warnings from the leaders of past generations. President Abraham Lincoln warned, "You cannot keep out of trouble by spending more than you earn." He also said:

> You cannot bring about prosperity by discouraging thrift.
> You cannot strengthen the weak by weakening the strong.
> You cannot lift the wage earner by pulling down the wage payer.
> You cannot help the poor by destroying the rich.
> You cannot build character and courage by taking away a man's initiative and independence.
> You cannot help men permanently by doing for them what they could and should do for themselves.

Before him, Thomas Jefferson also warned us: "To preserve our independence, we must not let our rulers load us with perpetual debt.

I place economy among the first and most important of Republican virtues, and public debt as the greatest of the dangers to be feared."

But Americans have allowed their government to wallow in debt because it is easier than paying the taxes or reducing our benefits. After all, as Pogo said, "We have met the enemy, and he is us."

I spoke to a group of senior citizens in the early part of 1993, just after the budget proposals were made by President Clinton in which he recommended taxing the Social Security benefits of seniors making more than $30,000 a year. The response of that group is indicative of our underlying problems and why the future of our economy looks so glum.

Almost to a person they were opposed to the idea of paying higher taxes, in spite of the fact that the tax on their total income would still be considerably less than that presently paid by a younger worker with an equivalent income.

The central comment was: We have already paid our fair share and we don't want to pay more. Another common comment was: We paid into Social Security so it really is our money coming back to us.

In the first place, their attitudes reflected a lack of understanding about just how serious the problems are. It also says that the basic concept of Social Security as a safety net has been reversed totally. Older Americans are looking to Washington as their primary source of help—not their families and certainly not God.

It also speaks of an underlying attitude of selfishness that has taken over in America—one that will eventually pit young against old, as other groups are already pitted against each other.

The average Social Security recipient draws out all his or her contributions in the first four years of retirement. After six years they have recovered an average return of about 6 percent for the years of contribution. Beyond that, they truly are living on taxpayers' welfare. Some need the help; many don't.

One man I talked with admitted that he earned nearly $200,000 a year in retirement, yet he still drew Social Security benefits. In fact he had set up a dummy corporation to shelter some of his earnings so his benefits wouldn't be reduced further. Obviously this is not the norm, but it is common enough to set the attitude of greed in the minds of the younger workers who see their dreams being eroded. Each and every individual has to be responsible—including the retirees. Those who don't need the help should turn it down.

There are also too many military retirees and former government workers drawing multiple retirement benefits. Unless the trend away from a self-first mentality starts with God's people, there's little or no hope that others will follow.

The key principle from God's Word is found in Philippians 2:3: *"Do nothing from selfishness or empty conceit, but with humility of mind let each of you regard one another as more important than himself."*

The borrowed money that the current generation of older Americans benefitted from has been spent and now they want to relax and let the younger group pay the bills; well, watch out! The younger group may just decide they won't pay the bills; then what?

While we were enjoying the fruits of our labor (or so we thought), in truth we were consuming the seed corn of our children and grandchildren.

Proverbs 13:22 says: *"A good man leaves an inheritance to his children's children, and the wealth of the sinner is stored up for the righteous."* So what does that make us if we don't correct this situation?

"The wicked borrows and does not pay back, but the righteous is gracious and gives" (Psalm 37:21).

CHAPTER FIFTEEN
Defining the Problem

U p to this point we have been looking into our past decisions. I don't believe you can cure a problem that you don't know exists; nor can you cure a problem without understanding how it came about. Thus the old cliche': "Those who fail to learn from the past are doomed to repeat it." Now we need to look forward.

Time is rapidly running out on our economy and on any chance we might have of recovering the American Dream—both spiritually and economically. For too long, conservatives (especially Christians) have sat on the sidelines thinking the battle was someone else's. Well, the battle is coming to our front door now, and I'm not just talking about the moral battle being waged by the pro-abortion groups, the homosexuals, or the "new age" crowd in Hollywood. If they were the only problems we face, at least we could easily identify them. In reality, most Americans don't accept their agenda.

The majority of Americans still believe in God, pay their bills, help their neighbors, and want their kids to succeed in life. The difficulty is that, although they still believe in the correct values, they are willing to tolerate "sin in the camp."

The activists who support everything from gay rights to child pornography could not have gained the audience they have without a fundamental shift in the moral fiber of our nation. When I was a teenager we didn't bash homosexuals to keep them in line morally. The society in which I lived simply would not tolerate their immoral conduct anymore than it would have tolerated someone shouting four-letter words in public or going to school nude, as a college student in California recently did.

I grew up in an area of Florida that attracted a lot of transients because of the orange groves and truck farming, so we always had migratory workers in the community. And yet we didn't have to lock and bolt our doors at night.

The law was swift in punishing crime, and everyone knew it. I'm sure there were some police officers who were corrupt, but they were the exception.

I remember my sole confrontation with the law at about age fourteen. I was out with some other kids late one summer evening in 1955, and we happened upon a used car lot that had the misfortune to be located directly in our path.

Some of the guys suggested that we pop a couple of hubcaps off of one of the cars closest to us. I don't remember why; none of us had a car, and hubcaps were not big on our "need list." Looking back, I think it was just a bunch of teenagers trying to act like big shots in front of each other.

I volunteered to pull a hubcap and, as chance would have it, just about the time I had one loose, a patrol car came around the corner.

As the economy erodes (as ours has), the frenzy to sue grows.

The other kids saw the police car and took off, but by the time I saw it the policeman had his lights dead on me. It turned out that he knew me so, when I turned to run, he called me by name. Needless to say, I knew I was caught, so I just stopped in my tracks. I remember promising God that if He would get me out of this mess I wouldn't steal anything ever again—period!

I was handcuffed, put in the back of the patrol car, and hustled away to our city jail, where I sat on a bench for the better part of two hours contemplating my fate. I knew I would probably go to jail, if I was not murdered by my father first.

The police chief, who was also the magistrate, asked if I had tried to steal the hubcaps off of a car in the lot. By that time I was ready to take my punishment and go on off to jail so I said, "Yes sir."

"Why?" he asked in tone that gave me a little hope that perhaps he wasn't going to shoot me immediately.

"I don't know sir," I said honestly. "I guess it was just a stupid thing to do."

Fortunately that was the right answer, or at least the one he wanted to hear. Instead of locking me up or even calling my parents he said, "I want you to come to my office every Saturday for the next six weeks and wash all the patrol cars. Once you're done with our cars then you can go down to the used car lot and wash all of his. Got it?"

I gratefully agreed, and for the next six Saturdays I washed cars. It was one of those events that set me straight from a life of crime (no more hubcap stealing) and also gave me a good friend for the next four years. The owner of the car lot hired me after the six weeks was up and I worked for him off and on for as long as I was in high school. I had the chance to see how hard he worked to make a living and how selfish stealing someone else's property really is.

In my generation the law wasn't tied up with drug dealers and drive-by shootings. It was there to protect the rights of the law-abiding citizens and steer those of us who strayed off the path back on it— gently at first, firmly if necessary.

We have been through extremes on both sides of the criminal law issue and, hopefully, the pendulum is swinging back to the center. But as I noted earlier, it is rapidly swinging in the wrong direction for contract and tort law today.

Very few people would disagree that the let-the-buyer-beware philosophy was not well balanced and often the public would get cheated or injured with little or no recourse. But when the mind set of an entire nation is to sue for every injury or loss to the maximum possible, no industry can survive long. Eventually industry and jobs migrate to a friendlier climate and the whole economy declines. As the economy erodes (as ours has), the frenzy to sue grows.

If we allow this to continue, any business that has any degree of risk will either shut down or hide behind all the legal defenses it can muster. As stated earlier, litigation is usually the big companies' tool as the small companies get wiped out. The big corporations can use their financial resources to utilize the legal system and wear down possible litigants through delays, depositions, and appeals. The few big cases that result in huge awards do so at the expense of those who are looking for just compensation.

I have a close friend, Terry Taylor, who experienced this first hand in the construction business. He operated a company that specialized in government construction projects. His company had an impeccable reputation and was known for its quality and honesty. As any subcontractor will tell you, there are a lot of construction companies known for just the opposite, particularly when it comes to dealing honestly with their subs.

Several years ago, Terry bid on and won a large military job in Texas. During the course of the job one of his subcontractors, a grading company, delayed the project because of financial problems within his own company. Several of the other subs, whose work was dependent on the grading work being finished, missed their deadlines and incurred penalties due to the delays.

Eventually the delinquent grading contractor was removed from the job, another was brought in, and the grading work was finished— but well behind schedule. Terry paid the losses of the other subcontractors since it was clearly not their fault, and then he filed claims against the grading contractor's bonding company to recover his losses.

The insurance company that provided the bond simply refused to pay. They had a variety of excuses, but basically they saw that the commercial building boom of the eighties was over and Terry's company would soon be out of work. In short, they saw the possibility of avoiding their obligation through litigation. They knew that Terry had exhausted his resources to pay the other contractors and felt he could not sustain a lengthy legal case.

Terry sued for damages and the case dragged on for several months, with the insurance company lawyers requesting and getting continuance after continuance. All the while Terry had to pay his attorneys to take depositions, to travel, and to do the necessary legal research.

Anyone who has ever been involved in a lawsuit understands the enormous costs that can be incurred. Lawyers have their "time clock" running every time they open a book to do research or answer a phone call, and at $100 to $300 an hour, the tab can run into the tens of thousands of dollars very quickly.

By the end of the second year after his suit was filed, Terry was out of money and out of hope that the system would protect his rights. He had invested nearly a million dollars in legal fees and the case had still not gone to court. At that point his attorneys suggested that he settle for what the insurance company would pay—about $100,000. Obviously aghast, he refused, and by the grace of God and the ethics of the law firm's general partner, he was able to get the firm to continue his case on a contingency basis. But still Terry had to pay their out-of-pocket expenses for travel and legal assistance in Texas, so he went deeply into debt to continue the suit.

The case went to court in 1992 and Terry won on virtually every count. But did he collect the money due him? Not until the insurance company's attorneys filed an appeal, which wound its way through the halls of justice. The system works all too well for those who know how to use it. We will soon have a justice system that serves only the greedy, the guilty, and the wealthy.

As I read and collect data on each area of our economy daily, I get some sense of the long-term direction of our country. Basic industries, such as automobiles, computers, aircraft manufacturing, appliances, and the like, are consolidating and cutting back. Consolidation and cost cutting are not always bad. Every business needs to take a look at systems and overhead periodically, especially after a long run of prosperity, such as we had in the eighties.

But although many industries have gone through consolidations in the past it was always with an eye toward future expansion and better efficiency when the economy improved. Not so this time. The jobs that are being eliminated in many industries will not return—at least not to American workers.

Most Americans seem to believe that the government has a magical solution that, at the last moment, will stop any financial crisis and protect their way of life. I assure you, it does not! With the current attitude toward spending more, taxing more, and avoiding dealing with the real problems, this situation can get a *lot* worse— quickly.

Our president, his advisors, and many in the Congress seem more concerned with assigning the blame than they are in tackling the real issues.

After all, what can be done with a $4 trillion debt, a $350 billion annual deficit, and special interest groups on every side clamoring for more government largess? In reality, quite a lot, but the impetus must come from the *people*, not the politicians. There are many men and women in Washington who understand the problems well and would like to deal with them; but they're too few and generally of the wrong political party.

There are economic "watch" groups in Washington that publish the names and addresses of those in Congress (both Democrats and Republicans) who speak out on the side of responsible fiscal policy. I heartily encourage you to write them and let them know you support their efforts. It's a lonely life in Washington for those who see the real problems and attempt to deal with them, only to be accused of being heartless bigots because somebody's "ox" is being gored by spending cuts.

I am by no means an expert on Washington, D.C.; nor do I ever intend to be. That would require spending a lot of time in Washington, which I have no desire to do. But after spending some time there with some good friends in Congress, especially Representatives Dan Burton of Indiana, and Frank Wolf of Virginia, I can tell you I don't envy them their jobs.

Each time I have been there they were up and going long before I was (and I'm an early riser). With little or no success, they spend countless hours trying to convince their colleagues to cut spending and operate the government on a sound financial basis.

I can tell you also that their message, like that of many others who share their concerns, is not popular in the political capitol of our nation. They have made themselves very unpopular by pointing out a lot of "pork" flowing through the system.

We cannot place all the blame on the politicians. They're only responding to what they know the voters want.

Pork barrel spending alone is not the cause of our nation's financial problems; in reality it is but a symptom of the bigger problem. If you totaled all the "pork" in a given year it would probably amount to no more than $20 billion out of a total deficit of nearly $400 billion. But it is the attitude created by a little bit of pork for each district that leads politicians to spend a little more on each program.

It is the same attitude that I saw in government programs at the Space Center back in the sixties: If one person can do the job, hire two; if you don't spend your entire budget each year, the next year your budget is cut, so spend it all and then some; if members of the House or Senate appropriations committee came to the center they were treated like royalty. During any congressional visit, excess personnel were shuffled out of sight and everything was made to look like maximum efficiency. Anyone who dared to complain was dismissed at the first possible opportunity.

I can also tell you that federal employees who complain about government waste quickly find out their bosses don't appreciate "whistle blowers" either. They take it as an affront to their leadership. So eventually most of those who care end up quitting, and the government is left with the "team players."

The system is out of control and I'm not at all sure it is possible to put it back under control; at least not until the whole thing falls apart. Americans say they're willing to suffer to help resolve the problems, but that lasts only until the special project in their area is scheduled to be phased out.

To be fair, we cannot place all the blame on the politicians. They're only responding to what they know the voters want. We might wish that more of them would do what is right—regardless of the personal sacrifices. A few do and then they have to fight for their political lives during the next election when a liberal spender runs against them.

As I said, when a courageous group of politicians attempted to deal with our long-term Social Security and Medicare problems back in the eighties and simply asked retirees to take a cost-of-living adjustment based on the actual inflation rate of the economy, they were sent packing.

Then in 1988, when the Congress passed the Medicare Catastrophic Coverage Act, requiring that the more well-to-do retirees pay a greater portion of their extended health care benefits, the howl was heard all the way to Washington. If you will recall from our evaluation of future health care costs, Medicare and Medicaid have the ability (by themselves) to destroy our economy. But the elderly revolted, and by November of 1989 the law was repealed.

These lessons are not forgotten in Washington. That's why we hear almost no discussion today on real Medicare reform. In the long run, such an intractable position pits the wants of the elderly against the needs of the younger generation. That will not be an enviable position to be in if this economy implodes. Those who are in a survival mode tend to make rules that suit themselves.

At the outset I described at least seven major problems facing our country and our economy that can destroy what once was called the American Dream: debt, government regulations, litigation, a declining population base, health care costs, declining savings, and declining industry.

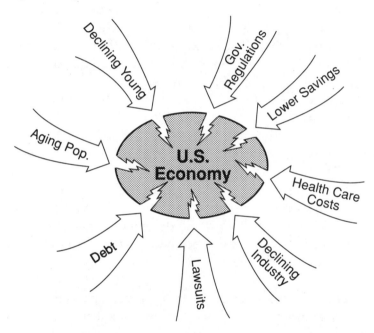

Some of these problems simply are not correctable. We *are* going to have a shortage of taxpayers to support a bulging number of retirees. That cannot be corrected (even by the Immigration Solution).

We *are* going to have a massive health care costs to fund, regardless of the national health care plan. As the chart below shows, if we don't get health care costs under control, we'll end up working for nothing but taxes and medical care.

The other factors are theoretically within our means to correct but only if real, constructive actions are taken now. And I don't mean that nonsense about more taxes solving the deficit problem. Anyone with reasonably good sense knows that tax increases retard economic growth.

U.S. Health Care Spending as Share of Gross Domestic Product

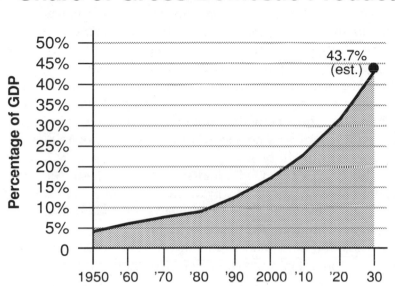

This chart is reprinted from *Health Affairs,* Winter 1992, by permission of the publisher: *Health Affairs,* 7500 Old Georgetown Road, Suite 600, Bethesda, MD 20814.

In 1977 President Carter asked us to "trust him" and the deficit would decline in three or four years. Instead, we had a recession, inflation, interest rate hikes . . . and a higher deficit. Twice in the eighties the Congress raised taxes and passed laws *mandating* spending cuts; neither time did spending go down. In fact, under the Gramm-Rudman-Hollings Act the actual rate of spending went up, along with the deficits.

Then in 1990 President George Bush agreed to a compromise tax bill that raised income and other taxes and *guaranteed* spending cuts to match every additional dollar raised in new taxes. That tax hike led to a recession and cost George Bush his job. Taxes went up, spending went up even more, and the deficit skyrocketed. For every new dollar in taxes raised, the government spent about $1.57.

Perhaps it is not possible to deal with the real problems in our political climate today. The time to have stopped the so-called "entitlements" programs was before they began. We need a lot of Davy Crocketts in the Congress and a Grover Cleveland in the White House. But we have to deal with what is, not what should be.

We should *never* have allowed the federal government to establish the degree of control it has over the economy; the more the bureaucrats meddle, the worse the problems get.

We were warned consistently by the founders of our nation not to become dependent on the government or allow the banking system to slip under the control of the central government or give politicians the ability to control our private lives, but again, here we are.

Now the question is: "What can we do about it?"

I would like to spend the remainder of this book discussing what we *can* do. I am a total realist about most things. I absolutely believe that God is the final authority in all things. I believe God can and will provide for those who serve Him if we first commit ourselves unconditionally to His plan.

I also believe that God commands us to be *participants* in His plan, not observers who sit idly by on the side lines. As Proverbs 16:9 tells us: *The mind of man plans his way, but the Lord directs his steps.* In other words, man plans and God directs.

As Edmund Burke once commented: "The only thing necessary for the triumph of evil is for good men to do nothing."

CHAPTER SIXTEEN
How Bad
Can It Get?

I want to discuss solutions, and I will, but first I would like to deviate slightly and take a look at some of the potential problems we are facing.

I am often asked *when* the great financial crisis will occur and how bad it will be. The answer to either or both of these questions is: Nobody really knows. However, I think it is possible to draw some logical conclusions and some worst-case scenarios.

The impact of any financial crisis is relative to how much it affects you personally. Ross Perot could lose half of his total net worth and still live quite comfortably, but to a widow with $100,000 in savings, even a small loss could be devastating.

I recall the first college course I took in critical thinking. It was one of the few courses in psychology that seemed to be particularly useful for anything.

The professor was a retired businessman who had made his living in the business world before entering the teaching field. His comment about trying to predict timing was, "A fool speaks confidently about things that cannot be defined." I have heard it described another way about economists, "often wrong, never in doubt."

Critical thinking usually implies considering the worst-case scenario and working backward. If you can plan well enough to survive the worst case, then anything less will be simple. However, quite often it takes too much time, effort, and money to prepare for the absolute worst; so you pick the worst case you can handle "realistically." Let me illustrate.

Perhaps the absolute worst financial disaster that could befall our economy would be if the dollar collapsed, the majority of banks failed, and half of all businesses failed. If this happened, there would be political chaos and riots in our cities. In this scenario, you would want a large ratio of your assets invested outside the U.S., and it would be wise to own a hideout in the Caribbean.

However, that's unrealistic and impossible for most of us, and it's probably not God's plan anyway. So what each of us has to decide is how much *can* I plan for, and how much *should* I plan for? Tough questions!

As I implied in an earlier chapter, timing is everything. Each time I think I have the timing for our economy narrowed down, it changes. Our government and its many manipulators are superb at pulling new "rabbits" out of their collective hats. In all honesty, during the late seventies I did not think our economy could survive beyond the mid–eighties. We had an inflation rate of nearly 18 percent, interest rates were 20 percent, the debt curve looked exponential, and we had a Democratic president who was totally estranged from his own Congress.

Laying all rhetoric aside and trying to look at the problems realistically, we are accelerating the crisis in our economy.

But then along came Ronald Reagan who, by the sheer power of his personality, gave *hope* to the average American, and we went on the greatest productivity increase (and credit binge) since World War II. Outside of a wartime economy, there has never been anything to match the economic growth of the eighties in the history of our country.

Unfortunately President Reagan listened to his economic advisors, who convinced him to separate his tax and spending cuts when new legislation was introduced in Congress. Perhaps he could have enacted some real spending cuts in the first year of his office, but once the Congress got the "feel" of his administration, they blocked every attempt at spending reduction. In fact, they increased the overall spending to match every new dollar of tax revenue—and then some.

Federal Receipts, Outlays, and Debt
(in Billions of Dollars)

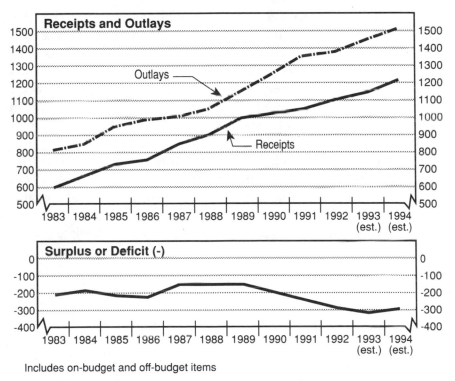

Includes on-budget and off-budget items

Sources: Department of the Treasury, Office of Management and Budget, and Congressional Budget Office (for 1993 and 1994 estimates)

As the graph demonstrates, revenue was not the problem, irrespective of what the Democrats said during the '92 elections. While Reagan was in office, the net income to our government increased by nearly 80 percent. But for every new dollar of taxes generated during those years, the government spent $1.52! In other words, actual spending increased to about 50 percent more than revenues. And regardless of whether our politicians remember it or not, according to our Constitution *all* spending bills are originated in the House of Representatives, not the White House.

President Bush was no Ronald Reagan when it came to domestic policy, and spending accelerated under his administration as Congress simply ignored him to a large degree. They sent spending bill after spending bill to the White House, many of which President Bush vetoed. But those that got through were quite sufficient to expand the debt by a trillion more dollars in three years. And, as I said before, under President Bush, the government got back into the regulation business in a big way.

At the current rate, government spending will exceed the economy's ability to fund its deficits sometime in the next five to six years. However, I will repeat: There are still ways the government can "enhance" its revenues, such as boosting gasoline taxes, legalizing drugs, initiating a national lottery, broadening the income base for Social Security taxes, increasing inheritance taxes, taxing non-profit organizations, disallowing home mortgage exemptions, adopting a national sales tax, and on and on.

Obviously the net effect of any or all of these will be economic deterioration; and they become a catch-22. Laying all rhetoric aside and trying to look at the problems realistically, we are accelerating the crisis in our economy.

During Ronald Reagan's administration we accumulated an additional $2.5 trillion in debt in 8 years, even with a dynamic economy that created nearly 15 million new jobs. Under George Bush we accumulated another trillion dollars in debt, in just four years, and suffered a recession for two years because he opted to increase taxes—believing the Congress would cut spending as promised.

Now that Bill Clinton is president, we are increasing both taxes and spending without any *realistic* plan for how to reduce the deficits. And remember, President Clinton started out with a $4 trillion debt and annual deficits of more than $350 billion; he has virtually no "flex." How long can we continue down this path? I don't know. But it won't be forever!

Most presidents generally have one shot at change. Once the public loses interest (or trust), the president's ability to implement changes

is basically eliminated. Unfortunately, the philosophy that has existed in Washington for a long time is: Leave it to the next group.

The ultimate financial crisis will occur when the government
can't generate enough income to operate another day. This can be
postponed by borrowing and taxing more; perhaps even some spending cuts. But in the meantime, the essential infrastructure of our
economy is being eroded constantly.

At some point the threshold is crossed and the changes are so
painful and severe that no politician dares to risk suggesting them.
Perhaps we have already reached that point—specifically in the case
of Medicare/Medicaid. As our government institutes a national health
care program, these costs will go up exponentially, and we will have
crossed over that line.

Economic erosion can already be seen in nearly every corner
of America as businesses fail because of excessive regulations, lawsuits, and simply not enough capital with which to operate in hard
times.

Tracking along with this stagnation of our economy is the increased social spending by our government, created by structural
(permanent) unemployment. To be sure, there are going to be some
bright economic spots along the way as new technologies are discovered and some jobs are created. But most of the new technologies require fewer workers with greater skills. These technologies
offer some hope for the younger workers entering the work force,
but they will be of little help to the millions of older workers who
are being displaced from manufacturing industries and are only
semi-skilled.

There is an economic truism: "The difference between a recession and a depression is whether or not you are employed." For several million American workers (perhaps 15 to 20 million), there will be
a depression. For the rest, hyperinflation is their biggest threat.

I would like to leave myself an "out" by saying again that it is
always *possible* that the Congress, with a Democratic president in office at least through 1996, will decide to reform its spending ways,
drastically reduce the regulations strangling our economy, and also
face up to the reality of runaway entitlements programs.

Personally, I do not believe that will happen. Too many of
those in politics enjoy the power that spending taxpayers' money
gives them. To be sure, the liberal spenders in Congress will blame
everybody else when the economy unravels, including their own

Democratic president, if he is in office. But the big spenders won't change their habits until it's too late to do anything constructive, or until they are removed from office—en masse.

I have several good friends in the Congress, both Republicans and Democrats, who struggle every day to help heal our economic wounds, and I would sincerely hate to see them leave. But I believe any one of them would agree willingly to leave the government they have served so admirably if they believed that, by doing so, the economy and the country could be salvaged. That, my friends, is called *statesmanship*—something that is woefully lacking in Washington today.

Without some form of constitutionally mandated term limits, too much power migrates to too few people in Congress. I support the idea of term limits because those who make the laws would have to go back home and live by them.

The one logical argument against term limits is that the non-elected federal bureaucracy (civil service) would eventually control the government. The solution then is to reform the civil service system at the same time and make it possible for each new Congress to get rid of the "deadwood."

I believe the scenario of economic disaster I described in *The Coming Economic Earthquake* has not changed appreciably. As the inevitable draws near, we will be able to see the picture more clearly.

If we had no significant amount of debt to contend with and the federal budget was coming down with a realistic expectation of seeing it balanced in the next five to six years, we would still have problems that could easily overwhelm us. As I said previously, there is virtually nothing that can be done in time about our declining base of trained workers.

The Immigration Solution may help the census numbers in terms of overall population (perhaps even a gain in our population), but common sense says these workers will add little to our net economic base because they will be at the bottom income tier. In fact their overall effect could easily be negative if they add to the entitlements problem.

It is simply more profitable for inner city (and suburb) teens to trade in drugs, stolen merchandise, and armed assault than it is to work at minimum wage jobs. Compounding this problem is the growing tendency not to punish criminal offenders. In an article entitled, "Crime Still Pays," the NCPA reports the average punishment in America for various crimes:[1]

Crime	Sentence
murder	1.8 years in prison
rape	60 days
robbery	23 days
arson	6.7 days
assault	6.4 days
dealing drugs	24 days

The American Dream of living a full life and not being confronted by violent crime is fading as quickly as the economic dream. As the following graph demonstrates, the future for law abiding citizens looks pretty grim if we have a major economic crisis in our country.

Crime and Punishment

* Median sentence for all serious crimes. Figures for 1991 were unavailable.

Source: National Center for Policy Analysis

The American way of life should revolve around the stability of our families. Instead, Americans think, live, and breath materialism. We have more assets than almost any other people on Earth, and yet we live in constant fear of the future. Tranquilizers are almost unheard of in places like Somalia, Bangladesh, and other Third World countries. The anxiety and fear of the future that we internalize is practically nonexistent in countries where *daily survival* is the paramount concern. There seems to be less stress over getting enough food to eat in the Third World than there is about how well our pension plans will perform in our country.

I have to confess that I have mixed feelings about the coming economic problems. The best way to get the attention of most Americans is through their pocketbooks. Our greatest concern is not necessarily the economy. If we can pare down the government, control deficit spending, and stop politicians from trying to micro-manage businesses, the economy can recover. The greater concern has to be the accelerating moral decline of our country. Given the moral decay in our nation, a major economic problem could spark major civil disorder.

At this point, the economic future of our cities is very much in doubt. There are too few jobs being created, and those that are carry lower wages. Unfortunately, there is little reason to believe the trend will change through government programs.

So-called "infrastructure" programs sound good during political campaigns but, in reality, they do practically nothing to help the inner cities. By the time the money is filtered through several levels of bureaucracy, there is little left for those for whom it was meant.

When the basic family unit is restored in the inner city and people strive to work for themselves, then businesses and jobs will return. The trillions we have spent on a failed welfare system could have funded millions of free enterprize jobs.

Fundamentally, nothing in our economy indicates any significant long-term growth. Normally either housing, automobiles, agriculture, or technology leads the way for long-term growth. Unfortunately, both businesses and consumers are still struggling with sizeable amounts of debt built up over the last decade, not to mention that of our government. The government has very little room to flex in terms of fiscal policy (long-term tax cuts, investment incentives, and so on) and monetary policy (interest rate reductions). In spite of their best efforts government policy makers have not enhanced business or enticed consumers to spend a lot more.

We have developed what must be called a "stumbling" economy, with real growth in the 2 to 3 percent range. I don't think we're going to see much more real growth unless some substantial economic policy changes are made. This is not likely, given the ever-increasing influence of the bigger-government advocates in Washington.

It is my opinion that, as the debt grows and the economy shrinks, we will see a period of deflation, with businesses, banks, insurance companies, and pension plans failing. Sometime prior to the end of this decade, perhaps by 1996 or 1997, this will deteriorate into a growing depression.

Remember that the Great Depression of 1929 didn't really materialize until well into the thirties. Many things were tried to restart the economy, including a federal banking system, federal deposit insurance, government work programs, and taxing the rich up to 90 percent of their incomes. Nothing worked except World War II.

When our government can no longer fund its day-to-day operations, either by increased taxation or increased borrowing, there will be no real choice but to monetize the debt (print new money to pay the bills), just as Germany, China, Russia, Argentina, Brazil, Uruguay, Romania, Bulgaria, and our Continental Congress did. The results were always the same: hyperinflation and worthless currency.

*A*ny bank panic will put an even greater strain on already overextended government resources. The government simply cannot afford to let the FDIC fail.

The laws already exist to allow the printing of new money by the Federal Reserve system. Actually, since the U.S. dollar was removed from the gold and silver standard, there have been no constraints on the printing of new money except common sense and the threat of hyperinflation. I would assume that all other options will be exhausted before such a drastic and foolish move would be made. However, as the debt cycle is allowed to expand, other possibilities, such as new taxes and even severe cuts in the entitlements programs, will be too little too late.

What I project (*not* prophesy) is a period of rapid devaluation of property and fixed assets, in which the real incomes of Americans will decline due to higher taxes (many of them hidden in regulations, tort, energy taxes, sales taxes, and the elimination of deductions). As average income families are forced to conserve and shrink their life-styles, the impact on small businesses will be enormous, leading to a rapidly deteriorating economy and more over-priced vacant commer-cial property.

This in turn can lead to more problems in our already shaky banking system, and we may see bank failures on the same scale we saw in the savings and loans. Several of the largest banks already are holding unsalable commercial properties as collateral on marginal loans and will have to do so for years to come. With large banks teetering on the brink of disaster already, any additional capital ero-sion will certainly sink several of them.

An article in the *USA Today* newspaper listed 464 troubled banks. Fortunately, the reduction in interest rates during 1992–1993 helped the entire banking system. Banks have been able to build re-serves by taking advantage of the spread between interest paid and interest earned.

The greatest danger to the national banking system is not the collateral being held, either overvalued or undervalued. It is the po-tential of future inflation that puts both borrowers and depositors at risk. Unfortunately, in an inflationary cycle, we end up in one of those catch-22s again.

By printing money the government creates inflation. Inflation then destroys the savings of depositors and makes it difficult for bor-rowers to repay their debts as well. This puts many banks in jeopardy and creates a strain on the underfunded FDIC insurance system.[2]

Any bank panic will put an even greater strain on already over-extended government resources. The government simply cannot af-ford to let the FDIC fail or it risks losing the entire banking system and any hope of a future recovery. So then what are the choices? Few, except to raise taxes, borrow more, and print money to cover the short fall.

As companies, properties, and banks fail, next in line are the pension plans, many of which are woefully underfunded—especially the public plans (including Social Security).

Government Pension Benefit Guaranty Corp. Deficit

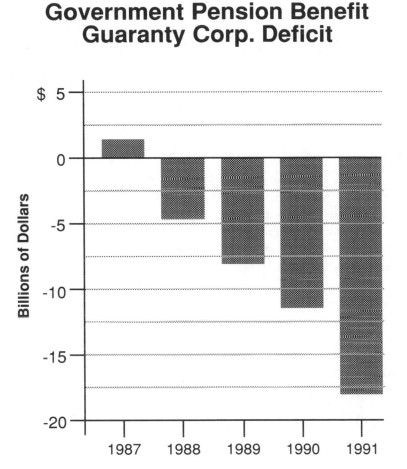

Source: PBGC

The burden to fund private failing pension plans is thrown back on the government through the Pension Benefit Guarantee Corporation. As of early 1993, some plans PBGC insures were underfunded by some $50 billion. Under depression conditions, the PBGC could just as easily be required to pick up another $100 billion or more. Where will those funds come from? More debt!

Unless you lived through the Great Depression or have talked with someone who lived through the collapse of the economies of Russia, Brazil, or Argentina, it is difficult to believe that such things can actually happen. The tendency is to write them off as either "alarmist mentality" or to assume that such things cannot happen in America. After all we have "controls" in place to solve these problems.

If you really believe that, then do nothing. Certainly you'll be more content, at least in the short run, and if indeed nothing happens you will enjoy the next few years a lot more than the "alarmists."

One thing we can all be certain of is that this crisis will not just jump up and bite us one day without warning. The economy won't collapse in six months or even twelve. And, long before anyone is foolish enough to monetize debt (print money), our politicians and their economic advisors will have tried every other alternative available.

So all you have to do is look for the signs as I have tried to outline them. Of course, if you wait until several of the signs converge, the time to do anything constructive will be past. So, rather than wait for all the economic signs, just look for some of the more obvious ones, such as decreased productivity, more restrictive regulations, a litigation explosion, higher taxes and more debt to support the national health care system, entitlements expansion (especially Medicare/Medicaid), and an acceleration of the deficit over the next four years.

Conversely, if instead we see the government reduce the annual deficits substantially, control the growth of entitlements, deregulate private business, encourage higher savings through tax breaks to create new investment capital, and reform health care through higher deductibles for users, then we can take heart in the direction our country is going economically.

Even these changes won't fix all the problems, but at least they will give our economy a fighting chance. Without such reforms, I must conclude the best we can do is to string out the inevitable a little longer. In reality, the longer the better, under any circumstances. It's not likely that a delay will make the inevitable a lot worse. If we don't deal with the real problems, I don't think the eventual collapse can get much worse than I have outlined.

This entire discussion has been a prelude to answering the real question: What can you do to prepare? It is not one thing; it is a series of things, based on where you are financially and what you feel God wants you to do.

I am not about to presume God's will for someone else. I believe I know what God wants us to do in preparation as a family, and it is not all the things that could be done. I could buy dehydrated foods, store some gold, hide some money, and prepare a mountain cabin to hide out in. Perhaps the Lord would have us do those things. But I sincerely doubt it.

Some of my friends are preparing to withdraw from the big cities in which they live. If I lived in Los Angeles or New York, I might be tempted to do the same. The crime rate is already approaching meltdown in a relatively good economy, with plenty of money still flowing. It's hard to imagine how bad it might be if a real crisis hits.

The media have convinced a whole generation that somehow society owes them a living and they have been oppressed by the "wealthy." This much I am sure of: The media will fan the flames even higher in the midst of crisis. After all, in their value systems it's ratings that count, not responsibility.

Each time I hear a Christian discuss the idea of escaping to the "wilderness," I'm reminded of the Lord's admonition: *"Who then is the faithful and sensible slave whom his master put in charge of his household to give them their food at the proper time? Blessed is that slave whom his master finds so doing when he comes"* (Matthew 24:45–46).

Personally, I'm praying for a revival in America, no matter what it takes. Christians must be in the midst of the unsaved if they are to share Christ's message. I believe we should prepare, but not withdraw.

I am reminded of a dear Christian lady who remained in the South Central Los Angeles area during the 1992 riots. She runs a shelter for homeless boys right in the middle of the worst gang-inhabited area. During the riots every building but hers was either burned to the ground or heavily damaged. Her building remained untouched.

Several years ago I heard a missionary speak about his service in Africa. He was ministering in an area where all of the other missionaries who had come before him either were murdered or run off by the natives. He and his family slept in tents outside a village where the head witch doctor lived. Over a two-year period, he led many of the tribe to the Lord and, eventually, led the witch doctor to Christ.

Later, when the missionary asked the witch doctor why the natives had not killed him as they had the other missionaries before him, he replied, "Because of the men in white who surrounded your camp every night. We went there to kill you many times, but these men held flaming swords ready to defend you."

Sometimes we lose sight of the fact that God is in *absolute* control of all human events. He not only allows crises to occur, but will sometimes orchestrate them to strip away the veneer of materialism.

In the next chapter I would like to share a brief fictitious scenario of what *may* happen in our economy, assuming our direction is not altered significantly.

I fully realize the risk I run: that someone mistakenly may see this as prophetic. It is not. It is a *possibility*, not a prophecy. This is how I see it. Others see the future differently. I offer the scenario in hopes that it will motivate some people to act; but I sincerely pray that no such calamity will actually ever occur.

After presenting this fictionalized scenario, we'll look at some specific things that each of us can do to prepare. When Christ first sent His disciples out to minister, He instructed them to take no provisions. They were to live with those to whom they were ministering. Apparently the Lord wanted them to know that God had already provided what they would need. (See Luke 9:1–4.)

Once the disciples understood that God could provide their needs, then they were instructed to carry provisions with them on the next journey. Preparation and provision are not forbidden biblically —unless they represent a lack of faith. (See Luke 22:35–36.)

All Christians (and non-Christians as well) need to constantly challenge their motives.

If your planning is motivated by fear, greed, and covetousness, it would be better to give all your money away. But if your motive is truly to be a good steward and be able to help others who don't have the ability to prepare, God will bless it. Jesus is Lord of the Gentile and the Jew, the saved and the unsaved. God wants everyone to come to salvation through His Son because He loves us all.

CHAPTER SEVENTEEN
A View of the Future

The scenario presented here is fictitious. As with any fiction, there is always an element of truth in it. This scenario is based on what "could" happen. It is presented as a possibility, not as prophecy.

* * * *

"Martin, what's wrong?" Angie asked her husband as he sat on the side of the bed. It was Monday, the day he had dreaded all weekend.

"Oh nothing, honey. I guess it's all the mess on TV. That's all."

But Martin Walker was not telling his wife everything, and she knew it. Virtually everyone in America knew about the riots in San Francisco, Los Angeles, New York, Chicago, and more than a dozen other big cities.

Riots have never been uncommon in America since the sixties, but these riots, triggered by soaring interest rates and inflation, were spreading like wild fire. The latest study showed an inflation rate of 25 percent per month! That meant that every four months a family's buying power, their savings, and their incomes were cut in half. Americans were angry—mostly with Washington but also with anyone who had more than they did.

Martin Walker and his wife Angie were pretty average people. They lived in a nice home with a 100 percent, 50 year mortgage, made possible by a low-interest, fixed rate loan from the bank where Martin worked. They wanted children, but knew there was no way their budget could handle such an expense.

Martin worked for the Burnet Banking Systems and had recently been promoted to senior vice president in charge of commercial loans. As with most banks, the title was in lieu of income, and Martin only made $46,000 a year. With the current cost of living being what it was, that salary barely qualified them as lower middle income. Buying a home was possible only because the bank offered their officers a non-inflation adjusted loan.

Martin showered and dressed with a feeling of dread he'd never felt before. Today was the day, he knew. Still ringing in his ears was the pastor's sermon on honesty and integrity—the cost of being a Christian, he had said. He wondered what his pastor would say if he knew just how much being honest would cost—not only him but the whole country. Martin knew that most of the businesses in their city were in financial trouble of one kind or another. But after today, there would be a lot more added to the list . . . his own bank included.

In the early nineties the banking regulators had insisted that all commercial banks re-evaluate all of their loans' collateral. If the value of the loan's collateral dropped, the loan was devalued proportionately. Non-performing loans had to be written off as bad debts. A lot of banks had failed and, in the process, took a lot of businesses with them.

By the mid–nineties, as the nation's money crisis expanded, the regulations had been "reinterpreted" to allow "slow-pay" loans to be carried on the books at their original value. Later the slow-pay exceptions were expanded to include "no pays." The government was desperate to keep more banks from failing.

If it weren't for that, Martin told himself many times after his discovery, *there wouldn't be a business or a bank left in town. But problem-shifting, instead of problem-solving only goes so far,* he reminded himself as he kissed Angie and headed out the door; *and the law is the law!*

Martin had been both flattered and excited when he was appointed a senior vice president after only three years at the bank. The other cadre of twenty or so junior vice presidents had ribbed him a lot about being a child prodigy. But within a few weeks, it was clear to him why he had been selected for promotion.

The board needed a young and inexperienced non-accountant to put in charge of commercial loans. Martin, being a marketing graduate, fit the role perfectly. He later assumed the same probably was true in the residential and small loans department. The bank needed patsies, not policy makers.

What the board could not have known was how seriously Martin took his job—any job. He studied day and night to learn all he could about commercial lending regulations. The first time he realized why he had been promoted was during a discussion with Andrew Warren, the president and CEO of Burnet banks, about what he had found in the loan file.

"Mr. Warren, we're in technical violation of the banking regulations," Martin said with as much confidence as he could muster. Here he was, lecturing a thirty year banker and co-founder of the second largest banking chain in the state. He knew this man was the epitome of success and, without a doubt, held Martin's job in his hands.

> *T*he bank had virtually no reserves since the Fed had lowered the reserve requirements to make more loans available to the government.

"How do you figure that, Martin? Which regulations?" Andrew Warren asked smoothly. Inwardly he was not nearly as calm as he appeared to be. He had known that eventually one of the new "kids" would see through their sham, and had said as much to his counterpart on the Federal Reserve banking committee. But neither he nor anyone else thought any of the inexperienced staff they had selected would know enough to spot the deception this quickly. They desperately needed time; the whole country needed time.

"The Omnibus banking regulations, sir," Martin answered, as he swallowed hard. We're still carrying loans that are in default on our asset base."

"I don't think so, Martin," the older man said with an authority garnered by many years of bluffing politicians. "Can I see your proof?"

"I don't really have any verification yet, sir. But I just know from a small survey that maybe 70 percent of my loans aren't performing. That alone would lower our asset ratio below federal standards."

"Like I said, Martin, I'll be glad to discuss it if, and when, you have some hard evidence."

What the older man couldn't know was that Martin Walker had already taken steps to secure the data from the bank's computer file. Andrew Warren would put a security block on all records that day, but it would be one day too late.

That conversation had taken place on Friday, the same day the system technician had delivered two full boxes of commercial loans data to Martin's office. Martin spent until late Friday evening pouring over the records. But he knew within the first hour that the situation was far worse than he had expected.

Over 80 percent of the bank's commercial loans were in technical default. No payments had been made on 50 percent of the loans for more than three months; and yet, they were carried on the books at original value, plus accumulated interest.

Martin had spent a fretful weekend trying to decide what he should do. By Sunday evening he had made up his mind: He would confront Mr. Warren first and then, if necessary, he would make his findings public.

He suspected it would do no good to go to the banking commission. *If Andrew Warren is in on the deception*, he thought, *the commission probably is too. No, I'll take my evidence to the media. It will certainly cost me my job and very likely will destroy the bank as well.*

If Martin's hunch was right, it just might endanger the whole banking system! That concept was beyond his comprehension. All he knew was that he could not allow the sham to continue.

He kissed Angie goodbye and tried not to notice the worried look on her face. He arrived at the bank at exactly 7 A.M. and noticed that Andrew Warren was already in his office. Clearly he was expecting Martin's visit.

Andrew Warren allowed his mind to drift back to the meeting of the banking committee several months earlier. He had just reported the status of his banking group's loan portfolio. His bank's best customers barely had the ability to keep the interest current on their outstanding loans. Even worse, the bank had virtually no reserves since the Fed had lowered the reserve requirements to make more loans available to the government.

"For Pete's sake!" Andrew Warren had shouted at his old friend who groused about so many bad loans. "What do you expect? Interest rates are nearly 20 percent since you guys changed the law again. Most of my customers could barely keep up the interest payments at 12 percent, and then you indexed them."

"I told you we would allow you to carry the loans at face value on your books, Warren," James Reading shouted back in mock anger.

The other members of the board sat in stunned silence as they listened to the conversation unfolding. They each had thought the Fed's private letter had been directed at their district only. Now they realized that probably every bank in the country was carrying bad loans on their books.

"I don't care what you allow me to carry on the books," Warren said with a shrug. "The fact is, we're running out of options. The Congress was stupid to allow the banking laws to be changed like they did. To index all loans to the inflation rate is insane. No business in the country will survive if this inflation keeps going up."

"Just what alternatives would you suggest, Andrew?" James Reading asked in exasperation.

Actually he agreed with his long-time friend. It really was insanity. *But whoever said politicians were particularly sane anyway?* he thought to himself. *The government needs money, lots of money, to feed it's insatiable appetite. They were already taking 95 percent of all the money in the market. Now it's 100 percent.*

Unbelievable! he thought to himself. *The government is paying nearly 20 percent on more than $8 trillion worth of debt. But "paying" is a very liberal interpretation of what's going on,* he reminded himself with a sigh. *They just roll the debt over every six months. At this rate the debt will be $10 trillion next year; then $12 trillion six months later. . . .*

"Maybe you could convince some of our 'fine-feathered' friends in Washington that Americans can't pay 60 percent in taxes, 20 percent interest rates, and survive a 300 percent inflation rate as well," Warren said with a scowl on his face. He knew Reading always referred to the Congress as a bunch of turkeys who would drown from looking up if it rained. There were some sane voices in Washington, but they were too few and too late.

"We are where we are, Andrew," his friend said matter-of-factly. "I would suggest that we look at the situation as objectively as possible. The Senate banking committee has written a private letter to the Fed allowing all federal reserve banks to disregard both the reserve requirements and asset ratio requirements."

"In other words," Warren interrupted, "we are to create new loans out of thin air to cover the old loans that are non-performing. Right?"

"Essentially that is correct," Reading said with an involuntary shudder that he hoped no one else noticed. He continued, "The Congress and the president don't think it is in the best interest of the country for the Fed to print any more money just now."

"I can see why they would think that," Warren said sarcastically, "especially since inflation just topped 300 percent a year with the last batch they printed. But I can tell you this, Jim. I'm not going down with the ship like the S&L guys did. You either get me some authorization or the government can print its own money."

"We'll have an executive order in a day or two," the exasperated banker told his longtime friend. But in the meantime, you'd better shop around for some young talent to head up your commercial division; and the rest of you had better do the same. The last thing we need is someone blowing the whistle in the middle of this project. Our credit wouldn't be worth a dime."

That meeting had taken place more than six months earlier—just two weeks before Martin Walker was promoted to senior vice president in charge of commercial loans.

Martin had really dug into his work. Not only had he taken a crash course on federal lending regulations, in the last week he had also done an evaluation of 10 of his biggest accounts. What he discovered had shaken him to the very core. . . . The bank was insolvent.

In conversations with some of the other department heads, Martin realized that every one of them had been selected in the last few months, and none had previous experience in asset management. He suspected that an audit of their accounts would show a high percentage of non-performing loans too.

What Martin found most peculiar was that the FDIC hadn't asked to review any of the bank's case files in more than six months. *That's very strange, given the state of the banking system*, he thought as he had headed down the hall to Mr. Warren's office the Friday before.

But now it was Monday and here he was, confronting his boss again.

"I have the proof, Mr. Warren," Martin said politely but firmly.

"No doubt you do, Martin," Warren sighed softly. "No doubt you do."

When Andrew Warren agreed with Martin's statement, it set him back. He had a ready response for every answer except that one.

"But . . . but . . . ," Martin stammered. "If you knew we were in violation, why did you let it happen? Am I going to be the bank's fall guy?"

"Hold it, Martin! Before we go any farther I need to say something." Warren leaned forward and looked the younger man directly in the eyes.

"I apologize for dragging you into the middle of all this. I can only tell you that I had no real choice either. I know that doesn't justify not telling you the truth earlier, but I hope you'll see why. You're obviously a bright young man, and you caught onto our mad scheme faster than anyone expected. Frankly, I'm glad you did. But now I also have to emphasize to you to proceed cautiously. This thing is bigger than you can imagine."

"You ma . . . may be . . . right, Mr. Warren," Martin said, still stammering a bit. "But how can we justify breaking the law?"

"I'm going to show you something, Martin, because you deserve to know the whole truth."

With that, the older man pulled a single envelope from his desk drawer. Removing the contents, he handed Martin the letter with the great seal of the United States on it. The letter was signed by the president of the United States, with a short personal thank you to Andrew Warren at the bottom.

After staring at the executive order for several minutes Martin said, "Can he really do this?"

"I'm not absolutely sure myself," Warren said with a sigh as he eased his frail frame back in the big chair. "But since we're part of the Fed, I suspect he can."

"Mr. Warren," Martin said less timidly now, "do you really think this will work?"

"Absolutely not. In fact I believe it will bring down the whole banking system, along with the Reserve; and I said so."

"Then why go along?"

"Because, as a good friend of mine said when I asked the same questions: 'What other choice do we have?'," Warren answered.

"We could call the local TV station and tell them that the president has ordered us to create new money for the government since it can't pay its bills any longer. And we might also mention that, if we continue to do this, eventually the assets of this bank and all others will be dissipated in bad loans to the government," Martin suggested.

"To put it bluntly, my boy, the minute you do that, the cork is out of the bottle. The boys in Washington won't take it kindly that we blew the whistle on them," said Warren.

"But you have the executive order from the president. Won't that . . ."

Andrew Warren interrupted, "The Fed's lawyers will read it a thousand different ways, and none will be to our benefit. This letter was meant to keep us out of jail if the whole system failed. It was not meant to give me the authority to bring the Federal Reserve to its knees. These are desperate times, Martin. We'll be lucky to survive the inevitable collapse under the best of conditions but, alone, the wolves will have us for lunch. Think of your own family."

"I have, sir. And I have also thought about the thousands of people who trust us who will lose everything if we keep doing this. Maybe they already have. I just know I have to tell the truth. As a Christian I am committed to it."

---

*T*he president's advisors warned that any attempt to raise taxes at all probably would result in a taxpayers' revolt.

Andrew Warren just sat silently in his chair for several minutes. Finally he had made up his mind. He thought, *I could fire this young upstart, lock him out of the building, and deny all his wild accusations. With the resources of the government aligned against him, Martin Walker would quickly find himself fighting for his freedom instead of his integrity. He's totally vulnerable as the executive in charge. It would be Martin against the world . . . and the federal bank examiners. After all, how could the bank have known about his loose activities with his customers anyway?*

Fortunately for Martin, Andrew Warren was an honorable man, and he knew Martin was right. He said, "Do what you have to do."

"I just want to do what's right," Martin said respectfully. "Will you help?"

"I can't do that, son," the older man said softly. "I promised a friend that I would cooperate. But I never said I would force someone else to join in our deception. I would suggest that you put the bank's records back in the files. But I'll understand if you make a copy to take home."

"Yes, sir," Martin replied, clearly relieved. He knew that the older man probably had just signed his own resignation."

The country really had been in turmoil for months prior to the Fed's decision to "relax" the banking rules. As the government began to run out of money, it had tapped every nook and cranny for new revenues. Personal income taxes and payroll taxes took nearly 40 percent of most families' incomes. Those in the upper 10 percent had seen their taxes go from just over 40 percent to nearly 90 percent. Sure, everyone was sacrificing to help meet the debt payments, but that was small consolation to many who were doing without basic necessities.

The attempts at welfare reform were little more than a joke. The minute the Congress passed the Welfare Reform Bill, the liberal defense groups filed suit in federal court and found a judge who ruled it unconstitutional. And with the other special interest groups lining up in Washington, Congress simply lacked the courage to take them on.

But it was the national health care bill that really sunk the economy. Probably the government would have run out of money anyway, but the health care bill greatly accelerated the process. Within three years of passing the Health Care Reform Act, guaranteeing health care benefits to all non-insured Americans, the annual cost went from $100 billion to $600 billion.

The government had not anticipated that all the big corporations would choose to pay the 10 percent payroll tax rather than continue their own health insurance. So the government had to pick up another 40 million employee's health care costs too. For the companies, it was a great deal because their costs dropped by nearly 50 percent. For the government, it was the final straw.

Americans griped and complained about the high federal taxes and even more so when the states started levying higher taxes to cover their lost revenues too. By 1995 there was a national energy tax, a national sales tax, a national lottery, a tax on foreign corporations, a tax on tax-exempt bonds, and any other tax the politicians could dream up. Spending at the federal level accelerated even while tens of thousands of businesses failed for lack of capital and declining profits.

But it was the 1995 Budget Act that ignited the fury of the taxpayers. The president and the Congress teamed up to eliminate almost all the deductions for working families. The Budget Act eliminated the tax exemption for all religious organizations, and authorized a capital gains tax on all appreciated assets. Americans found themselves paying taxes on the appreciated value of their homes and cars—even their retirement accounts. In 1996 the voters overwhelmingly chose a new president—one who would straighten this mess out, the media declared.

Unfortunately the new president found himself on a sinking ship without so much as a life vest. The government had tapped virtually every source of new taxes and the president's advisors warned that any attempt to raise taxes at all probably would result in a taxpayers' revolt.

Already various groups from the Retirees Revolution to Taxpayer's Anonymous had been recommending that their constituents stop paying any taxes until the government lowered the rates. A collective shudder went through Washington at the thought of a taxpayers' strike. It would cripple the government overnight.

So, in early 1996, the new president, under the authority of the 1976 Omnibus Banking Act, authorized the Treasury to print government bonds to be sold to the Federal Reserve—nearly $300 billion worth.

By June the international monetary community had devalued the U.S. dollar by nearly 50 percent. That meant that, in the U.S., prices on all imports rose by 50 percent.

At first the American Manufacturers Association hailed the action as a boon to American business because, almost immediately, American goods became more competitive.

But such fortunes are not long lasting in a global business environment, and quickly the cost of imported raw materials, such as steel, plastics, electronics, and textiles, doubled. Even more damaging, as far as the government was concerned, foreign investors simply stopped lending to the United States for fear inflation would erode their funds.

In 1993 the government had adopted a policy of issuing short-term bonds to capitalize on the low interest rates. But now that policy backfired on them as the short-term interest rates went to 15 and then to 20 percent. Even worse, much of the government's debt issue went unsold and the Fed had to buy even more of it themselves.

The government printed another $400 billion to compensate for inflation, and both interest rates and inflation soared again. By early 1997 inflation had reached nearly 25 percent per month! A futile attempt was made to impose price controls, but every special interest group in Washington quickly got their products exempted under the congressional "hardship" rule that had been pressed into law.

It seemed as if everyone except the American consumer had a "friend" in Washington. It became impossible for average Americans to make ends meet. In the cities, protest riots became so common the media hardly gave them air time—that is, until the shootings began in Washington.

First it was the drive-by shootings in front of the Capitol building, where tourists normally congregate, hoping to get a glimpse of the president as he comes and goes. It took an army of nearly 1,000 D.C. police to make Pennsylvania Avenue safe enough to get out of a cab. The crowds had long since faded from sight.

Then the snipers began their reign of terror. Virtually anyone was a target as angry ex-government employees and gang members alike took to the roofs and overpasses to vent their anger. Once it started in earnest, it was quickly out of control. Ordinary citizens armed themselves in an attempt to protect their families, and it took the Army to reestablish any semblance of control in the nation's capital.

Washington, D.C. had become an armed camp, and no member of the government was safe outside of the tunnels connecting the various office buildings. Even worse, with the media focusing on the violence, it was quickly spreading to other cities.

It was in that environment the new president grappled with the escalating economic problems. The problems were many, the solutions few. It was this economic chaos that forced the new president to issue an executive order directing that all civil liberties be suspended in the major cities of America. Martial law was declared, and the National Guard was mobilized and sent in to establish order. Tanks and armed personnel carriers were poised to combat rioters.

The secretary of the Treasury felt a chill go over his body as he heard the chairman of the Federal Reserve tell the president that to fund the government's shortfall would require another issue of $600 billion in new money, with an estimated inflation factor of at least another 10 percent per month. And the new supply of money would only last two months, three at the best.

In truth, nobody really knew what was happening anymore. Each time new money was printed, the inflation rate went up but never by a calculable figure. It really depended on the consumer confidence factor, which was near zero. It was clear the economy, the government, and the country were out of control; and, step by step, the diminutive billionaire president was being forced to take direct control.

At first he resisted the intrusion into civil liberties, but then his lifetime training in assuming authority began to surface and he relished the idea of total control; he could straighten this mess out.

Martin Walker didn't cause the problems. In fact, he did what others should have done years earlier: He told the truth.

At the office of the local CBS affiliate, business reporter Kathy Moore could scarcely believe what she was hearing. Actually, if Martin had not brought the bank records verifying his accusations, she probably would not have believed it.

The second largest banking system in the state was totally insolvent. What was worse, it was so far beyond the legal lending limits that less than 5 percent of the stated assets were of any real value. And the Federal Reserve bank had not only known about it but had actively pursued deception with the approval of the White House.

Kathy almost jumped out of her chair. *If even half of this is true,* she thought, *it will be as big as Watergate . . . bigger.*

She spent the better part of an hour talking with Martin before she decided that he knew what he was talking about and had the facts to back it up.

"Wait here," she said excitedly as she got up from her desk. "I need to get my editor in here."

She rushed out of her office and into the office of Alex Loren, senior news editor at the station.

Clutching the bank reports in her hands, she said, "Alex, you need to look at this right away!"

Alex Loren barely glanced up from the computer terminal he was using. He had long since learned to ignore the ranting of his television "personalities." They thought every story they found was going to be a Pulitzer winner.

Finally he looked up from his terminal into the flushed face of his morning news desk host. "Yeah, okay, Kathy. Let's see what you've got."

Kathy flipped the file open to the White House executive order. That definitely got her boss's attention. He sat upright in his chair, flipped his ever-present bifocals down from the top of his head where they resided when not in use, and carefully read through the entire file.

"Is the guy that brought this still here?" the burley news editor asked enthusiastically.

"Yes, sir. He's in my office," Kathy replied in an unaccustomed burst of courtesy. She knew she didn't want to get into one of their philosophical arguments about partisan politics, which she so often accused her boss of practicing. With a non-politician now in the White House she always assumed the news chief was soft on him.

That day the noon news carried the story: "Burnet Banks Broke!" And each hour on the hour the story was expanded as bank officials were interviewed. Andrew Warren refused all interviews, and several of the lesser board members quickly tried to distance themselves from the widening scandal.

By 6 P.M. the story had spread to the networks and was quickly widening to include virtually every Federal Reserve bank in the nation. It was clear that the whole national banking system was in jeopardy. The only thing that saved the system was the fact that most banks were already closed. But on the west coast the banks that were still open saw something that would chill the heart of the strongest banker: thousands and tens of thousands of depositors lining up to demand their money. The American banking system was poised for a total meltdown Tuesday morning.

At the White House an emergency meeting was being held with the president, the chairman of the Federal Reserve, the attorney general, and the White House chief of staff.

"Mr. President, reports are coming in from all over the country of open fighting between the army troops and armed citizens in the big cities; and the White House switchboard has been jammed for the last four hours. You have to do it," the attorney general urged.

"He's right Mr. President," the Fed chairman agreed. "If you don't, the whole banking system will go down the tubes tomorrow."

"And the cities will go up in flames," the attorney general added somberly. "Once the people learn that they can't get their money

back, they'll join the rioters, I'm afraid we'll have anarchy throughout the country."

"If I understand correctly, you want me to declare a national
emergency and invoke martial law for the whole country. Right?"

The president had already made up his mind. He knew he'd
have to assume absolute control if he were ever to get this country
straight again. After all, hadn't he often said the Constitution was
outdated? *Besides, that whole bunch in Congress is a bunch of worthless
wimps*, he thought.

"A national emergency is what we need, Mr. President," the
Fed chairman answered as the president tuned back into the conversation. "You can shut down the banks for as long as necessary and
reorganize the monetary system in the interim."

"But how will people get food and other necessities if they can't
get to their money?" the attorney general asked.

"We'll issue credit vouchers," the Fed chief replied with irritation in his voice. He knew what had to be done, and he didn't need
another lawyer telling him how to save the economy.

"I've already decided to do it," the president said sharply. "I
didn't create this mess, and the Congress has had its chance."

"You'll need to sell the public on the program, sir," the chief of
staff offered. "Tell them the truth: that otherwise the rioters will take
over and the whole economy may collapse."

"It's really not as bad as it looks right now," the Fed chairman
chimed in.

"Well, it looks about as bad as it can be," the president said
angrily. "I never thought your idea with the banks would work for
long. It didn't even last six months. That kid at Burnet did what you
should have done six months ago and what the previous administration should have done three years ago: leveled with the American
people."

"Perhaps you're right, sir," the chairman replied defensively.
"But it's too late to worry about that now. All we can do is salvage
what we can. If the banks go we won't be able to recover the economy. You could lose control of the country."

"I know that!" the president said, slamming his clenched fist on
the big desk top. "I want the attorney general's office to prepare the
legal notification." Then he looked toward the Treasury secretary
and said, "We need the cashless plan. Right?"

"It's the only way, Mr. President. No one will trust the dollar
again. It's lost too much value. And as long as we have to deal with

this banking crisis, we might as well kill the dollar and go cashless. Then at least we can control how much credit is in circulation, and we can set some absolute price controls. No one can buy or sell anything outside the parameters we set. It should help bring order to the inner cities."

"Yes, and you can shut down the drug trade too," the attorney general added as he watched the president sign the executive order declaring a state of national emergency. "We're in charge now," he declared jubilantly."

"You mean *I'm* in charge, don't you?" the president asked.

* * * * *

The story is fictitious. The possibility is not. We have a $4 trillion debt and it's growing. Unless it is brought under control, the government will eventually consume all the available money in the credit system. There will come a time when the debt cannot be funded through additional taxes, debt, or promises.

CHAPTER EIGHTEEN
National Solutions

I t's always a good idea to look back and see what lessons we can learn from those who make the same mistakes we're making to-day. This process doesn't necessarily guarantee any better deci-sions though, because each generation always thinks they're smarter than those who came before them.

Perhaps the single greatest exception to this rule can be found with the Jews. They will not soon forget the lessons learned from the holocaust. Each successive generation reminds their offspring that Jews can and will be persecuted again if they aren't vigilant. This attitude is clearly reflected in the militancy of the nation of Israel today. They won't wait to be attacked, as their forefathers were in Germany.

Americans could benefit by adopting the same attitude when it comes to the current attack on morality. Just look back at the nations that allowed the morals of their society to degrade to basic passions. They faded into oblivion.

The Greeks degraded into a nation of idle talkers who were easily overrun by the Romans.

The Romans degraded into a nation of welfare recipients who were easily overrun by the barbarians. The Romans' affluence provided them so much idle time that it took greater and greater thrills to satisfy the lusts of the aristocrats. This lust peaked in about A.D. 200 with the bloodthirsty games in the Colosseum.

The barbarians (Germans) developed into a highly productive society and then degraded into a nation of few morals, fewer values, and no respect for any ethnic group.

The Germans suffered through a decade-long depression after World War I, ultimately voting in the Nazi party on the promise that Hitler would solve all their economic woes. He did so at a very high price: World War II. I pray we will not repeat these errors in judgment. The best way to avoid that possibility is to wrest our government and our economy from the hands of inept politicians who cater to special interest groups.

THE BOOK OF AMERICANS

I once heard pastor Charles Swindoll refer to the book of Romans as the "Book of Californians." Borrowing that appropriate analogy, I believe we could also refer to portions of the Book of the Revelation as the "Book of Americans." Most assuredly we could find an analogy between the church in America and the church in Laodicea described in Revelation 3:14–22 and not be far off the mark; today we are lukewarm.

Americans, including many of God's people, have become so indulgent and comfortable that they no longer rely on the Lord. Christians in America are, in great part, neither hot nor cold. The very fact that evil can prosper so well in the midst of a nation where 80 percent of the people profess to believe in God and some 20 percent claim Jesus Christ as Lord of their lives is testimony to lukewarmness.

For a long time I have believed that most of the statistics about Christianity in America were unduly "evangelistic." I heard pastor John MacArthur say that he thought 50 percent of regular churchgoers were not actually Christians. I am inclined to agree with that assessment. Of course almost everyone in church believes they're among the "born-again."

If we care to accept it, the Lord gave us some pretty convicting evidence of salvation in His Word—not the least of which is obedience to His Word. In Matthew 7:21 Jesus said, *"Not everyone who* says to me, 'Lord, Lord,' will enter the kingdom of heaven; but he who does the will of My Father who is in heaven."

He also speaks of serving God, not money, and of keeping God ahead of all others—including mother, father, wife, husband, and children.

Sometimes when we read these words we tend to brush over them, but they are templates for salvation—not for the works they yield, but for what they imply: total surrender to our Lord and Savior.

I do not say these things to condemn anyone but to advise those who may think they are Christians but, in reality, are not. Salvation does not come as a result of conviction. Many people are convicted of their sins, and many die with that conviction. It is through confession and surrender that we are saved. As Paul said in Romans 10:9: "If you confess with your mouth Jesus as Lord, and believe in your heart that God raised Him from the dead, you shall be saved."

What does this have to do with the American Dream? I believe the time is coming (in the near future) when it will not be popular to be called a Christian. In fact, if may be downright costly.

There are many people now in positions of great influence who would consider the abolition of all religion in America beneficial to society and the imprisonment of practicing Christians a moral act. We represent the single organized group that opposes their assumed right to sodomy, the murder of the unborn, pornography, free sex, and eventually their "right" to dispose of the unwanted elderly.

In our society we have several examples of the wrath of the liberals against Christianity. Just look at the treatment of abortion protestors compared to that of environmental protestors. The pro-life protestors are hauled off to jail with dislocated shoulders and broken bones as a result of their treatment. The environmentalists are treated like civil rights protestors.

For true believers the suffering is worthwhile when compared to eternity. But for those who are not, it is a terrible waste to suffer now and not have the rewards later either. It's certainly better to be sure you are a Christian and accumulate some rewards for all the lumps you're taking.

I absolutely believe that God can and will provide for His followers, even in the midst of the worst times imaginable. That doesn't mean we won't suffer—even the apostles did. But I do believe God will work through those who take an *absolute* stand for His way as a witness to others.

The one certainty is that God promises wisdom and peace to those who will follow Him; and we're going to need all the wisdom we can muster in the years ahead.

As I have said repeatedly, it is my opinion that we're not going to solve the economic or moral problems facing our nation. To do so would require a moral fiber that is virtually non-existent in politics (and society) today. The combination of welfare, government handouts, and a steady barrage of "situational ethics" training in the public schools makes real reform all but impossible, barring a true spiritual revival.

---

*V*irtually anything we see in the area of finances is little more than an external reflection of the internal spiritual condition.

Government "entitlements" programs, along with over-regulation, are sucking the life's blood out of the economy and making more and more Americans dependent on Washington. It is amazing to me to listen to public debates in which young Americans actually believe that more government spending can solve our economic problems.

We have created a situation in which solutions are theoretically possible but politically impossible. Without immediate reform, even "theoretical" remedies soon will become impossible. Eventually economic chaos will dictate a solution. When the concern over riots and disorder overshadows the concern about diminishing lifestyles, the voters may seek out a political "savior."

It is very possible that, when the crisis gets serious enough, a majority of Americans will vote away a large portion of their individual freedoms in order to restore some vestige of social order. This has been the pattern of previous societies that faced similar problems with far less to lose.

Usually those who are willing to risk everything are those who hold to absolute convictions. Few Americans today have absolute convictions, with the exception of the core of Christianity and the left-wing radicals.

You do have to respect the dedication of the radicals and activists; they are willing to risk all they have to accomplish their aims. The question is: Are the rest of us willing to do the same? If not, then we very possibly will lose this nation.

Perhaps the very decline of our society will spark the Christians to action and we'll turn the country around—but not necessarily financially. We need a moral turnaround or all we'll be doing is sticking our finger in the leaking dike. Our society is feeding off the fruits of sin today and is suffering the consequences. And anyone who has ever practiced sin will tell you it's a lot of fun—but only in the short term.

I want to emphasize that the real problem is *spiritual*, not financial. Virtually anything we see in the area of finances is little more than an external reflection of the internal spiritual condition. That's true of an individual or a nation. I have done enough counseling to realize that you can easily get diverted into treating symptoms instead of problems.

The classic example of this can be seen when parents continually bail out their grown children who overspend. Usually the parents, who may be far more financially conservative than the children, believe they are helping. But if the spending is the result of wrong basic attitudes about money, the parents won't help the problem. In fact, they usually will make it worse.

Very often, when parents finally decide to stop feeding their children more money, the reaction on the part of the children is resentment rather than appreciation for what has already been given. Once someone has adjusted to receiving a handout, it becomes a "right." The same is certainly true on a national scale as well. Try to stop the money to any special interest group and watch the reaction!

Periodically I have been accused of proposing secular solutions for spiritual problems. I can assure you that is not true. But we do live in a physical, material world that demands real-life solutions.

Clearly, the Lord and His disciples understood that the remedies to a society's ills are spiritual, but they also provided a great deal of practical advice about how to solve everyday problems. There are some 900 direct references in the Bible about how to handle finances. Certainly they could all be lumped under the category of "trust God." But the references also discuss things such as how to deal with creditors, husband-wife communications, tithing, lending, investing, saving, and so on.

The point I am making is that God wants His people to be wise in the practical aspects of everyday life. So the advice offered from this point on, about how to help solve our problems in a practical way, is offered without compromise to our greater responsibility to share Christ with a lost world.

DEBT CONTROL

The generation of Americans below the age of 60 cannot totally comprehend the realities of a worldwide financial crisis, except in books, movies, or by word of mouth, which are not the equivalent of real life experiences. To have lived through the Great Depression of the thirties is to appreciate the magnitude of a global financial crisis. The recessions we have experienced since that time have been what a popgun is to a cannon—irrelevant.

We are brewing up a financial crisis on a scale that may make the Great Depression look like a "popgun" in comparison. Never in the history of economics has a nation as wealthy and as influential as ours attempted to live so far beyond its means, while simultaneously doing everything politically possible to strangle the economy.

Earlier in this book I examined a lot of evidence that shows our business base (which supports everything else) being burdened to the point that new enterprises are difficult or impossible to start successfully. Even established businesses are having a hard time coping with all the rules and regulations.

As noted earlier, 40 years ago there were few other places for these entrepreneurs to go; today any number of countries will offer them unlimited capital, lower taxes, and fewer regulations to entice them to their economy. Therefore, it should be no surprise that hundreds of companies have migrated out of the U.S., and more will follow in the next few years unless we can change the climate in America. How can we do that?

APPRECIATE SUCCESS

When the economy dips, as it did in 1991 and 1992, much of the available funds for running our social "experiments" dry up. When this happens the tendency is to look with resentment at those who have money and think they aren't doing their fair share. Instead, the attitude should be to appreciate their efforts and *encourage* them to invest even more of their surplus capital in private enterprise to create jobs—not tax them as a punishment for success.

In other words, our policy should be to reward success and encourage others to achieve. That may sound capitalistic, and it is. A capitalistic system (which we are) only operates when a surplus of capital is made available to start new businesses and expand existing ones. The poor don't invest; they consume. Only the "wealthy" have the surpluses to invest. The Communists successfully eliminated the wealthy class by making everyone poor. Is that really what we want?

Effect of Federal Budget Deficit on National Savings

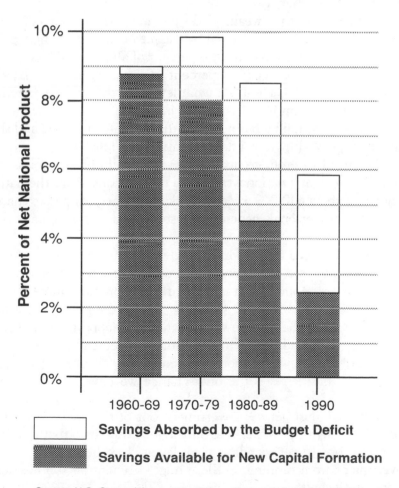

Source: U.S. General Accounting Office, "Budget Policy," June 1992

Today the federal government consumes nearly 60 percent of all the available capital in our economy. That only leaves 40 percent of the available capital for business, and that amount declines every year.[1]

Business must have access to reasonably priced capital to expand and compete successfully. The cost of capital, not labor, is what hurts American businesses the most. Remember, although you may not see jobs disappearing because American businesses cannot raise the capital they need, they are. The banking regulations passed by the 102nd Congress make it even harder for banks to lend to private enterprise. We do need the special programs to help inner city programs, but the real job factor is not a government program. It is small business. If we lose the free enterprise system, there will be no money for new jobs, government or otherwise.

Incidentally, the "wealthy" do pay more than their fair share. Don't believe the hype promoted by the media and tax-hungry politicians. In 1980 approximately 48.6 percent of all personal income taxes were paid by the upper 10 percent of wage earners. Today that figure is close to 55 percent. At what level will the average American think the tax system is "fair?" In the interest of what politicians call fairness, we're stripping businesses of their supply of capital and shipping it off to Washington. I don't think that's "fair."

We need to promote tax reforms that will encourage less consumption, such as a national tax on all transactions above the national norm of about $10,000 a year (excluding homes); and in exchange, eliminate the personal income tax system; this will encourage thrift and investment.

Then we need to build in incentives to ensure the money is put into productive enterprises and not more government programs. We all need to write our legislators regularly and promote more free enterprise and less government spending. Unless the politicians believe this is a program the average wage earner will support, there is not a chance it will be addressed in Washington. Remember, we have to begin thinking long-term about the good of our children. More capital in small businesses is the only chance we have of creating new jobs.

First we must get the government out of the credit business to the highest degree possible. The only logical way to do that is to force the politicians to cut spending at all levels. In other words, stop the government from running up these huge deficits that rob businesses of operating capital.

I am not here to propose a detailed plan to reduce the deficits and begin paying back what we already owe. However, after many years of doing financial counseling with families, I can tell you that you don't need a complicated program, and you absolutely don't need more taxes. Virtually every family I ever counseled said they needed more money—from those making $10,000 a year to those making $200,000 a year. But until they learned to live on what they had (and less if they were in debt) any additional money was wasted.

---

*U*nder this plan it would take about five years to eliminate . . . the deficits through a combination of spending cuts, spending controls, and economic growth.

I would propose the following plan to reduce and control our federal deficits.

1. Establish each year's budget based on the previous year's budget, less 5 percent for 5 successive years. The Congress could make the necessary spending cuts anywhere they decided, but *all* programs except Social Security (which is self-funded) would have to be included in the cuts.

   I certainly would not do any planning based on estimates by the Congressional Budget Office (CBO) or the Office of Management and Budget (OMB); neither has been within a trillion dollars of actual income and expenses for any five-year period.

2. Estimate the income of the government based on the previous year's income plus 3 percent for inflation—and no more! Any additional income would be used exclusively to retire debt.

3. Authorize a national transaction tax of one-half percent on every dollar that goes in and out of the banking system and all other depositories, such as credit unions, S&Ls, and so on. For instance, if you deposited $1,000 in a bank, the gov-

ernment would get $5. This tax system would generate $1.5 trillion a year, and there would be no need for the IRS, tax accountants, or tax attorneys.[2]

All tax or spending increases for any reason other than a declared war should require a two-thirds vote of Congress and would be temporary until approved by voters in a general election. That will put the spending process squarely back under the control of those who pay the taxes.

4. Establish an independent committee, much like the Grace Commission under President Reagan, and review all government regulations for cost and achieved benefits. Any that were found to be too costly to the economy would then be subject to voter approval.

   Also re-establish the economic review process so that every new regulation is reviewed for economic impact and the results published at least six weeks prior to any vote in Congress. If Americans know the facts clearly, they will let the politicians know how they feel.

5. Adopt a balanced budget amendment and send it to the states — one that has enough teeth to force a balanced budget in Washington *forever*. (Since this process might take several years, the other budget controls are necessary in the short-run).

6. Establish term limitations for all political offices. I would also suggest making all laws passed by Congress applicable to the Congress and do away with all federal retirement plans by merging them into the Social Security system. In other words, let's do away with the imperial Congress.

There are plenty of other changes that could theoretically be made, but if just these changes were implemented we could salvage our economy and get it growing again. Under this plan it would take about five years to eliminate most, if not all, the deficits through a combination of spending cuts, spending controls, and economic growth.

Can we do these things? Absolutely.

Will we do these things? There's hardly a chance.

It is abysmally clear that the United States government lacks the collective will to make the necessary changes under the existing political conditions.

Ignoring all the rhetoric about existing laws being adequate to force the budget cuts, a constitutional amendment is probably the only realistic chance we have of bringing the budget under control. I can't even imagine the Congress self-imposing the kind of spending constraints I outlined.

If we don't succeed in forcing some quick changes within a very few years, the government will exhaust all of the available money in our economy. I gave the details of this in a previous book, *The Coming Economic Earthquake*, so I don't want to repeat them here.

But for those who didn't read that book I would like to present some of the statistical information in graph format. If you can read the following charts and come to any other conclusions, I would sincerely like to hear from you.

Deficit Growth Under Gramm-Rudman Acts

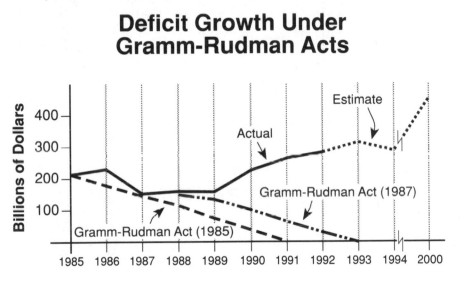

Source: Congressional Quarterly, U.S. Department of the Treasury, and Congressional Budget Office

Even if the president had the resolve to balance the budget, he lacks the constitutional authority to do so. Those in government who derive their support base by spending other peoples' money won't stop until (and unless) they have no other choice.

It's simple enough to get a list of which senators and congressmen and women consistently vote to spend more every year. All you have to do is join any of the taxpayer's groups listed in the Appendix and ask for information. Look for the politicians who voted for the most spending bills in each session of Congress and against any reform moves, such as the Balanced Budget Amendment.

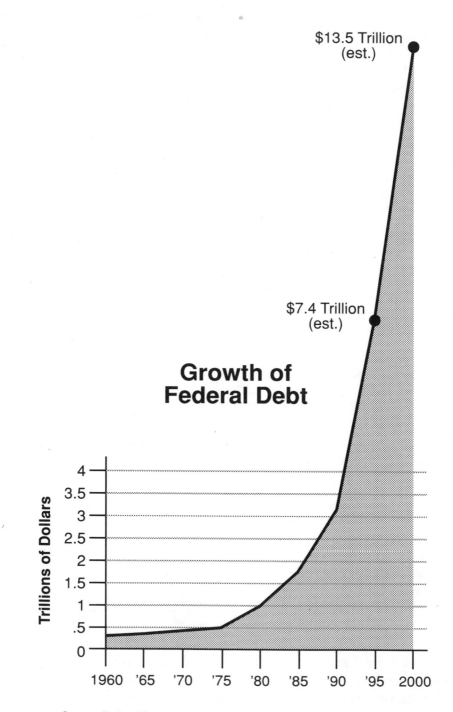

$13.5 Trillion
(est.)

$7.4 Trillion
(est.)

**Growth of
Federal Debt**

Trillions of Dollars

4
3.5
3
2.5
2
1.5
1
.5
0

1960   '65   '70   '75   '80   '85   '90   '95   2000

Source: Federal Reserve, Grace Commission

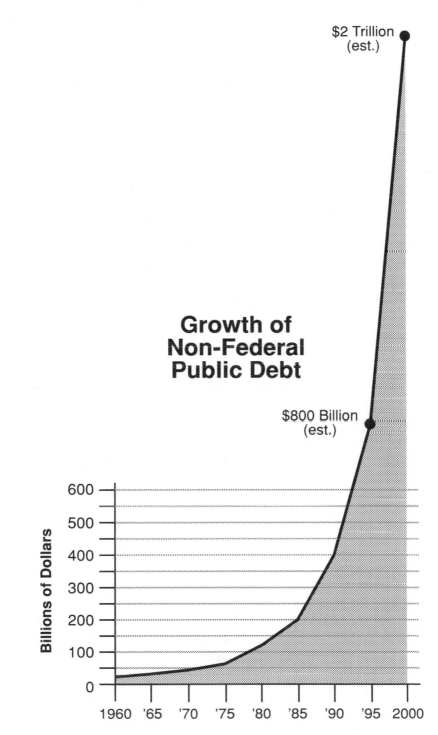

**Growth of
Non-Federal
Public Debt**

$2 Trillion
(est.)

$800 Billion
(est.)

Billions of Dollars

600

500

400

300

200

100

0

1960 '65 '70 '75 '80 '85 '90 '95 2000

Source: Federal Reserve, Grace Commission

Remember that those in the Congress who refused to support even a watered-down version of a Balanced Budget Amendment in 1992 said, "We don't need an amendment to make us do what is right. We already have the mandate from the voters to do so." Well, where are the changes? The potential collapse of our economy is no longer decades away. It's down to years now.

Most assuredly the supporters of good fiscal policy in the government will introduce other balanced budget amendments in Congress. When they do, you need to start a grass roots campaign in your community to get tens of thousands of people to write and support it; maybe the liberal spenders will get the message. If we don't stop this runaway deficit spending and begin to deregulate our economy, we will lose more than just our economic comforts.

To assist in maintaining regular correspondence with your legislators, if you have a computer I would recommend a computer program called *Write Your Congressman*. This program will draft the letters, provide the correct staff member to write, and supply the correct address. It is not absolutely necessary, but it will make the writing process so simple more people will do it. Perhaps you can discuss this need with others in your church and purchase one program for the church office that can be utilized by several people. Information on this program is provided in the Appendix.

If you can't afford a computer to keep up a dialogue with your representatives, you can get their names and addresses from your local library. Tape them to your refrigerator door as a reminder to write *regularly*.

I don't know of anything I can stress that will be more effective for change at the national level than to *write* your elected officials, including the president. So few people actually take the time to write and express their opinions that a few letters make a big impact. These politicians are being confronted by special interest groups' lobbyists every day in Washington. Unless you get active, it is their agenda that will be implemented, which is why we are where we are today.

There are no quick fixes for our problems in the area of government deficits, and there is no substitute for educated voters who will speak up. We have allowed this mess to envelop our nation because of apathy and ignorance. Now is the time to speak up.

REGULATORY REFORM

I heard Representative Tom DeLay (R–TX) say recently, "You can either have jobs or regulations, but both cannot exist together." I totally concur, and we need to do something about it. Congressman DeLay is one of the leaders in Washington trying to roll back the tide of excessive and abusive regulations. But his is a lonely task in a city where regulations evolve into power and politics. You need to become knowledgeable about these regulations and their cost to our economy.

I hope I have provided at least enough information to cause you to question most of what you hear from the media and the liberal extremists. However, you must spend the time necessary to become thoroughly knowledgeable yourself.

Your public library should have the majority of the resource books listed in the Appendix. If not, usually they can be ordered from other libraries.

There is no alternative except to launch an all out attack on abusive government regulations and make each and every agency prove the real worth of these constraints on economic growth. Certainly this will not be an easy task. Those who helped to pass this legislation will fight to the death to maintain and even tighten their strangle hold. The only answer is to take the same route they did in gaining control.

You must first understand and believe the problem exists; then you have to *write* and voice your opinion. Remember that there are many good people in Washington who will vote for what is right if we can just convince them. The evidence is on our side; we just need to get them to read it and listen to the voice of reason.

USE THE LOCAL MEDIA

You should provide accurate data on environmental issues to your local newspaper and radio and television stations. Studies show that the national media are very liberal and biased, but quite often the local media are not. But it is important that you be able to provide documented proof to combat the ignorance that surrounds the environmental issues. Also remember that all of these people are not our enemies; most of them are simply ignorant about the facts. They too have listened to the extremists and have believed what they heard.

Too often average citizens don't get involved because they do not think they are capable. This country belongs to "the people"—not to the politicians or the extremists. Get involved!

When you read about things like the spotted owl groups shutting down all logging in the Northwest or environmental groups trying to ban all ranching from federal lands, you need to write the newspaper and voice your opinion, and state your facts clearly.

There are any number of excellent resource groups that will provide factual data. I have listed some of these in the Appendix. If the cost is too high for one family, get several in your church to divide the cost and share the information. After all, how much is freedom worth?

Once you have accurate data, write your representative in Congress, your senators, the president, the secretary of the interior, the head of the EPA, the secretary of the interior, and anyone else involved. If you'll do this and organize others in your community to do the same, you *can* make a difference.

When it comes time for elections in your area, find out where your representatives stand on these issues. If you agree with their stand, work for them and contribute to their campaigns. But if you disagree, then do the same thing for those who oppose them. You may not win the first time, but the lesson will not be lost on the politicians, I assure you. That is precisely why the extremists win: They don't forget at the polls, and they vote with their money.

LITIGATION REFORM

I would be extremely naive if I suggested that we can change the legal system easily or quickly. We have allowed the courts to slip out of our control. Once appointed to office, federal judges are insulated from any real control except from a higher court; but the laws they are bound by are not. Laws are drafted and passed through the legislative process and it is there that we must focus our efforts.

There are several countries that have adopted limits on lawsuits that jeopardize businesses in their countries (Canada is a good example). Tort suits are permitted in these countries, but the maximum awards are limited. The general principle is to protect the greater needs of society rather than let a few individuals collect so much they destroy the economic base of a whole nation. That sounds like a pretty rational approach to me.

In the Appendix there is a list of senators and members of Congress who are the most influential in the area of litigation reform. I would encourage you to write and clearly voice your opinion. Again, let me assure you that the activists stay in constant contact with this group of legislators.

MEDICARE REFORM

It is important to provide adequate health care for our elderly citizens and all others. But the health care system, both private and public, must be reformed. At the time of this writing our new president has not put forth his own health care bill. If it establishes control over the automatic cost-of-living increases built into the present Medicare system and contains a realistic way to pay for health care without taxing businesses out of existence (the play-or-pay plan), we should strongly support the effort. But if it does not put realistic caps on the COLAs, health care costs alone will destroy the future of the next generation of American workers.

If you are a current retiree, *you* need to support reform. If you don't, most assuredly one day you will be facing a hostile group of younger workers who may decide they won't pay anymore.

The most logical approach to elderly health care is to offer several different plans, with the bottom line being a very basic program similar to a major medical plan that pays only for catastrophic losses. This type of coverage should be available to everyone. After all, no one should have his or her life savings jeopardized because of medical problems. But any coverage above that minimum should be an option, and should be paid for by the users.

Health care insurance should never be first-dollar coverage (in my opinion). Insurance should only be used to cover risks that are catastrophic in nature.

This same basic concept must ultimately apply to all aspects of Social Security, including retirement benefits. Those who don't really need the benefits should not receive them. I know the argument that "those who paid into the system deserve the benefits," but that is impossible beyond the next 20 years or so.

It is time to adopt a survival attitude about all entitlement programs, including Social Security, federal pensions, military retirement, and so on. The financial crisis we're facing is so enormous that unless we all pull together our economy will fail. It is certainly not beyond the realm of possibility that even if we do all the right things quickly it will not be enough. Unfortunately there is no one person (or group) in the Congress leading the reform of the system. As I stated earlier, those who attempt it are usually voted out.

By no means is Medicare our only problem in the health care area; but it is the driving force. According to a recent study, it is government spending in the health care area that is driving up costs the most. For every dollar spent by the government on health care services, the patients receive approximately 48 cents worth of actual care. And that ratio seems to stay constant, no matter how much is spent.

This should not come as any great surprise to anyone. It merely reflects the inefficiencies of government-subsidized *anything*.[3]

With medical services going up at more than three times the Consumer Price Index rate, it is clear that overall reform is necessary. Unless the medical profession is willing to police itself (which is highly unlikely), our government will attempt to do so for them, and neither they nor we will like the results.

Doctors who practice medicine primarily for the money it can generate are doing as much to destroy the American Dream for the next generation as the attorneys are who destroy businesses through abusive litigation.

When doctors invest in referral resources such as radiation therapy clinics, imaging clinics, laboratories, and such, and then refer patients to their own facilities, they are clearly operating in their own self-interest rather than that of their patients. I see little difference between self-referral in medical clinics and financial planners who steer clients into investments where they make substantial commissions without disclosing it. Many physicians have had this happen to them personally and they resent it. There is no doubt that many of their patients feel the same way.

It is a sad indictment of the medical profession today that many physicians have adopted an attitude of "get it while it's still available." These are the practitioners who are raising their fees and doing questionable procedures to glean as much money from the system as they can before it's regulated. Christians who are guilty of this need to heed the apostle Paul's admonition in Philippians 2:3: *"Do nothing from selfishness or empty conceit, but with humility of mind let each of you regard one another as more important than himself."*

We can certainly use a good dose of that kind of ethic today. As Proverbs 22:1 says: *"A good name is to be more desired than great riches, favor is better than silver and gold."*

CHAPTER NINETEEN
Local Solutions

Not only have we allowed the spending of the federal government to get out of control, we have lost control of our local governments as well. At first glance, that might not seem significant. After all, most states must balance their budgets (according to their state constitutions). Mandated balanced budgets are important, but there also must be some controls over spending, even with a balanced budget.

Any government, state or local, has the ability to tax us right out of our homes and shut down businesses. State ad valorem taxes, income taxes, and sales taxes now equal more than one-half of all federal taxes.

Even more ominous over the long run are the local and state regulations that affect businesses and, consequently, jobs. Forcing more regulatory laws through the Congress is not as easy as it once was because the economic conservatives have gotten better organized. Groups such as the Heritage Foundation in Washington, the National Center for Policy Analysis, the National Taxpayers' Union, Citizens Against Government Waste, and United We Stand now provide accurate factual data on the impact of new taxes and regulations that help defeat some of these measures—if the information gets adequate circulation.

But few such organizations exist at the local and state level. There are some groups, such as the Georgia Public Policy Foundation (in my home state) that are linked with other conservative groups throughout the country. But again, these are limited in scope and funding.

It's important to support and help fund these groups. A partial list of conservative groups at the state level is provided in the Appendix. Often, for no more than the cost of a soft drink a week, you can help maintain a voice of sanity in the area of regulations and taxes. With virtually no accountability, state and local governments can shut down businesses just as effectively as the EPA or OSHA.

This lack of accountability has not been lost on the activist groups, environmental and otherwise. The state legislatures are easily manipulated where social and economic liberals have been entrenched for a long while (as in my state). So the activists have been able to get progressively more restrictive legislation passed at the state and local level.

In Florida, for instance, some environmental standards are harsher than those of the EPA, or at least they were until the head of Florida's environmental office, Carol Browner, was appointed to head the EPA in Washington.

One of the single most important objectives is to get control of the state and local tax structure.

In many local areas it is virtually impossible to have any significant business growth because the restrictions on housing development preclude new businesses coming into the community. If workers can't find adequate housing, the companies won't survive long term. The restrictions may come in the form of complicated building codes but, more often, they are an outgrowth of land-use restrictions imposed by the environmentalists. It is relatively simple to shut down community growth by restricting the use of available water supplies. Without water and sewage development, growth stops.

There is no simple way to recapture our local governments except to get involved. In the first place, the majority of Christians and other conservative people don't vote very often, while the liberals on the left do. And second, I doubt that the majority of conservative voters even know who is running for office at the local level or what they really stand for. We need to get involved and get educated. We need a plan of action and people to implement it.

I have a friend in Atlanta who helped to take back the local politics in his area with the help of a few others who were concerned about saving this nation for the next generation. They were able to replace two very liberal state representatives—a U.S. congressman and a senator—just by organizing and getting the facts out to all the eligible voters they could reach.

The strategy he used has been organized and distributed by the Christian Coalition from Virginia (address provided in the Appendix). It involves just a few people in each polling district who will dedicate a few hours a week to every election.

The most productive effort in any campaign involves reviewing the voting records of every incumbent and presenting information to churches and civic groups to distribute prior to the election. This strategy has been proved in hundreds of areas throughout the United States. Voters will respond properly once they have accurate information available to them.

During the 1992 elections, a group in central Florida utilized the precinct-by-precinct approach to get many conservative candidates elected. These men and women who were elected now represent a formidable barrier to any new anti-family social agenda in the local communities, as well as in the state legislature. They also have helped to oppose much of the new anti-business environmental legislation.

In California the results were even more dramatic during the 1992 elections. Through the dedicated efforts of a small group of conservatives, the previous majority party of liberals in the state legislature was turned out of office and a much more conservative cadre of men and women was elected. If it can be done in California it can be done anywhere. All it takes is people who know the facts, are willing to get involved, and have a strategy.

One of the single most important objectives is to get control of the state and local tax structure. Many voter groups have been able to bring this issue to the voters of their state and local communities through referendums. Perhaps the most well known was the 1978 Proposition 13 in California which, among other things, froze real estate taxes for landowners. Many other states have passed similar legislation to limit all taxes, unless approved by the voters.

Voters have shown that they will approve legitimate tax increases once the runaway spending has been brought under control. But when countless billions are spent without regard for those who pay the bills, and the services provided decline, it is time for reform.

I don't want to take the time and space to define this strategy here because others have done a good job of organizing and detailing it. In the Appendix I have included the names of at least two groups who have the strategies well documented and are willing to help others organize their communities.

It is always easier to stand on the sidelines and think that someone else will do the work and change the system. That attitude on the part of God's people is exactly why we are where we are today. You need to believe that no one else will do it if you don't. This is not an academic exercise in civics. We are in a struggle for the very survival of our republic and our spiritual heritage, as well as the economic futures of our children and grandchildren.

We have already allowed the extremists to gain a significant foothold because of our apathy. Unless we act now we won't be wondering how to turn this ship around in the near future; we'll be looking for a life boat as the ship goes down.

Look around and decide if things are getting better or worse with the leadership you have had in your state and local government. If your elected officials are doing a good job, support them at every opportunity; but if not, do everything in your power to get them removed from office. And remember, in the political arena it takes money to defeat an incumbent, so support the candidates of your choice. I can assure you the activists do . . . and will.

USING THE CHURCH

It continually amazes me how Christians and other conservatives have bought into the misinformation promoted by the liberal left. Not only have many Christians swallowed the line about saving our "endangered" environment at all costs, but they also accept the notion that the church should be totally divorced from all political activity—the ignominious "separation" theory. Naturally the liberal activists want us to believe that nonsense. It helps their agenda considerably.

Those who espouse the philosophy of separation of the church from politics have little knowledge either of the church or the religious heritage of our nation. Earlier I recommended a book by Peter Marshall, *The Light and the Glory*, which documents much of our early Christian political heritage. There are several other excellent works listed in the Appendix. I heartily recommend that you read some of these and then read them to your children. The public education system under the tutelage of the National Education Association (NEA) has done a thorough job of eliminating all reference to America's Christian heritage. Literally they have rewritten the history books.

On June 25, 1962 the Supreme Court decided to overthrow nearly 200 years of constitutional history and ban all reference to God in classrooms throughout the United States. Most of the justices didn't live long enough to see the full impact of their decision: kids on drugs; violence so bad that teachers in many schools are afraid to flunk students for fear of their lives; rampant sex, even at the elementary levels, with its accompanying venereal diseases; and an epidemic of teen suicides. And we call this progress.

Don't allow anyone to take away the right of the church to be involved now, when it is most needed.

The legacy of the 1962 Court will carry us well into the twenty-first century as we graduate more and more kids with no moral foundation.

Senator Robert Byrd (D–WV) was so grieved by this decision that he took the Senate floor on June 27th and, in an eloquent speech, recounted the spiritual heritage of our nation. I don't want to take the space to present his entire speech, but I would like to share a portion of it.

Thomas Jefferson expressed the will of the American majority, in 1776, when he included in the Declaration of Independence the statement that "all men are endowed by their Creator with certain unalienable rights, that among these are life, liberty, and the pursuit of happiness."

Little could Mr. Jefferson suspect, when he penned that line, that the time would come when the Nation's highest court would rule that a nondenominational prayer to the Creator, if offered by school children in the public schools of America during class periods, is unconstitutional. . . .

Wherever one may go in this great National City, he is constantly reminded of the strong spiritual awareness of our forefathers who wrote the Federal Constitution, who built the schools and churches, who hewed the forests, dredged the rivers and the harbors, fought savages, and created a republic.

In no other place in the United States are there so many, and such varied official evidences of deep and abiding faith in God on the part of Government as there are in Washington. . . .

A visitor entering Washington by train sees the words of Christ prominently inscribed above the main arch leading into Union Station. Here at the very entrance to the seat of Government of the United States are the words: "The truth shall make you free" (John 8:32). . . .

A visitor to the Library of Congress may see a quotation from the Old Testament which reminds each American of his responsibility to his Maker. It reads: "What doth the Lord require of thee, but to do justly and love mercy and to walk humbly with God?" (Micah 6:8).

The Lincoln Memorial . . . pays homage to the greatness of a simple and heroic man whose very life was offered on the altar of liberty. . . . We can almost hear Lincoln speak the words which are cut into the wall by his side: "That this Nation, under God, shall have a new birth of freedom, and that government of the people, by the people, for the people, shall not perish from the earth." In his second inaugural address, the great president made use of the words "God," "Bible," "providence," "Almighty," and "divine attributes."

On the walls of the Jefferson Memorial . . . are inscribed Jefferson's words: "I have sworn upon the altar of God eternal hostility against every form of tyranny over the mind of men." . . .

Benjamin Franklin, at the Constitutional Convention in 1787, stood to his feet one day, the oldest man in that illustrious gathering, and addressed the chair, in which sat General George Washington. Franklin said: "Sir, I have lived a long time; and the longer I live, the more convincing proofs I see that God still governs in the affairs of men. If a sparrow cannot fall to the ground without our Father's notice, is it possible that we can build an empire without our Father's aid? I believe the Sacred Writings, which say that: Except the Lord build the house, they labor in vain that build it." . . .

Our country's truly great men—Lincoln, Jefferson, Washington, Franklin, Wilson, Robert E. Lee, and I need not name others—these gigantic pillars of strength in the structure of American history were men who believed in a Higher Power, and they had the courage to express that belief in their words, their writings, their deeds. . . .

Inasmuch as our greatest leaders have shown no doubt about God's proper place in the American birthright, can we in our day, dare to do less? . . .[1]

I trust you grasp the intent of what Senator Byrd is saying. Our nation has a Judeo-Christian heritage, whether the liberals like it or not. They can deny the past, but they cannot change it. The church has been intimately involved in politics since before this country was founded. Don't allow anyone to take away the right of the church to be involved now, when it is most needed.

As I have discussed the idea of taking political activity back into the churches of America with those who are actually doing it, I got an education on just how effective the left has been in promoting this separation of church and state nonsense . . . within Christian circles!

In the interest of separating Christianity from all political activity, the churches of America have also allowed the Church (God's people) to be separated from the morals of our society. It is vital to understand that you cannot separate government and values in any society or you leave a void that will quickly be filled by those who want no moral or social constraints. Once in control, they will spread their religion—humanism—and use our tax dollars to do it. That is exactly what we have allowed them to do while shouting separation of church (our church) and state.

Once the Church ceases to have an effective voice in politics and the values candidates stand for, Christians become accustomed to getting their information from the secular media, just like everyone else.

With the exception of a few Christian radio and television programs, our primary means of communicating with one another is the network of thousands of local churches throughout America and the world. We need to defend the right of the established church to speak out on *all* issues—politics included.

The liberal activists are very intelligent in their strategies, and they have been extremely successful in controlling the political activities of religious non-profit organizations outside the churches. The IRS regulations against political activity by non-profit (religious) organizations are clear and precise.

Religious non-profit organizations that engage in political activities to any degree (5 percent or greater) are subject to losing their tax-exempt status. This rule is enforced vigorously, I can assure you. Therefore, those organizations (ministries) that have access to the religious media (radio and television) are very restricted in what they can and cannot say.

Those who support the more liberal agenda, using their chief enforcement agency, the ACLU, would also have us believe the same restrictions apply to churches. Unfortunately, many denominations have bought into the lie and told their members the same restrictions do apply. They do not! Almost unanimously the several constitutional attorneys I spoke with agree that, according to the Constitution, the government has no authority over the churches whatsoever! The tax exemption of the church is not granted by the government; it is guaranteed by the Constitution to prohibit the government from controlling the church.

The history of the church and its leaders being involved in American political activity is a clear path leading all the way back to the first colony. History clearly demonstrates that the earliest discussion of American independence was debated in the colonial churches, without whose support the separationists knew they could not succeed.

The Reverend John Witherspoon was one of the earliest supporters and confidants of the founding fathers and later was a signatory to the Declaration of Independence. It was the stabilizing influence of the Christian foundation of America that encouraged the elder statesman, Benjamin Franklin, to believe that a Republican form of government might be able to succeed in our country.

On the walls of every monument in Washington, D.C. Scripture verses are inscribed in marble and stone—a lasting testimony to the fact that there was no separation of church and state in the founding and building of our nation. As Senator Byrd said, in the Jefferson memorial these words of Thomas Jefferson are inscribed, "I have sworn upon the altar of God eternal hostility against every form of tyranny over the mind of men."

It is the very flexibility of Christianity in accepting other religions without violence and individuals, regardless of their race or origin, that has made this republic succeed where others have not.

The church, like any organization, has had its share of abusers. But the moral integrity of what we call the American Dream can be traced back to this single source: Christianity. The "liberals" today would have Americans believe that the church is bigoted and narrow-minded. They either have forgotten, or choose not to remember that the churches of the eighteenth, nineteenth, and twentieth centuries spoke out against slavery, inequality, and oppression long before society in general did. Certainly we as Christians are opinionated and narrow-minded when it comes to the rights of the unborn, homosexuality, pornography, "free" sex, and euthanasia—without apology.

Christianity in American has been the tempering element of moral right and wrong that has kept each generation in line and not allowed the extremism so common to other countries—most notably Germany, Russia, China—to take over our society. If the liberal left, who want no constraint on their personal activities, and the extremists, who want to save "Mother Earth" by disinfecting her of the human virus, have their way, America won't be a very nice place in which to live in 20 or 30 more years. If we don't act *now*, the next generation will look back on this time as the "good ole days" (that's a sobering thought isn't it?).

General Omar Bradley (the GI's general of World War II), delivering his last speech at the U.S. Military Academy in West Point, New York said, "This country has many men of science, too few men of God. It has grasped the mystery of the atom, but rejected the Sermon on the Mount." As a lifetime soldier who has seen countless thousands of young Americans in uniform, he further observed: "This shocking apathy to the conditions of their schools and the sterility of the curriculum is responsible even today for the political immaturity, the economic ignorance, the philosophical indifference, and the spiritual insolvency of so many young men. . . ."[2]

We should not abuse the forum God has provided through the abundance of local churches throughout America but, also, we should not ignore it. There is no other organization where so many like-minded people meet regularly throughout our country. Political issues that directly affect morality and Christian liberties should be discussed in the churches.

I can assure you the usefulness of those who attend church on Sunday has not been lost on the liberals. They use the churches wherever they can to spread their agenda. But when the churches oppose that agenda, they vigorously oppose any political activity. If you don't believe it, just keep your eyes open during any major political campaign.

Those who feel that the regular worship services are not the right time and place to discuss political activities (including me) should ask the pastor and governing body to provide alternate times to present and discuss issues. Bring in both sides of these issues and allow open debate. One thing I believe about truth: It will always prevail over lies, if people can hear it.

Let me reiterate: There is no substitute for knowledge when it comes to defeating lies. If you are to get involved, be certain that you first understand the truth about basic moral issues from God's Word, the Bible. Then be certain that you have the scientific facts, presented clearly and simply, from knowledgeable, qualified authorities on the topics. The information is readily available.

If you will take the time to check out the resources listed in the Appendix and then use the materials they provide, you quickly will become a resident expert on virtually any topic you choose. Don't be intimidated by credentials (degrees) of the opposition. If you investigate the process by which credentials are given at many of the noted academic institutions, you will find out that they are often a flag for "political correctness"—not wisdom and knowledge.

To be sure, there are many bright, dedicated people on the side of the extremist groups, but that does not make them right.

"Let no man deceive himself. If any man among you thinks that he is wise in this age, let him become foolish that he may become wise" (1 Corinthians 3:18).

CHAPTER TWENTY

Preparing for the Worst

I have told you as much as I know about why the American Dream is disappearing. Spiritually there is no mystery; God's people simply have not been willing to pay the price to be the salt and light in our society. When Christians are inseparable from the world around them in what they do on a daily basis, it's very difficult to affect much change.

Usually Christians talk differently and even attend different organizations than non-believers. But, in truth, the level of commitment is not a lot different. In fact it would be great if the average Christian had as much commitment to God's work and causes as most Rotarians, Kiwanians, or Shriners do to their programs.

A good friend, Dr. Ted Baehr, who started an organization to help bring morality back into the media, has statistical evidence that as many kids of Christian parents attend R–rated movies as the average non-Christians' kids do. I know from personal experience that there is no discernable difference between the attitudes of most kids who attend Christian schools and those who attend public schools. This is most certainly an indictment of our faith today.

There is a cliché: "Those who are regularly exposed to small doses of watered-down religion become inoculated against Christianity." Unfortunately, that is true in much of Christian education today. Christian schools (and homes) need to teach Christian principles and Christian heritage—regardless of what the accreditation association says.

It's interesting that some large colleges and universities are not accredited schools, but they seem to do quite well anyway. We need to set accreditation standards that secular schools would strive to meet.

No set of rules, financial or otherwise, are going to solve our future problems. Unless our lives are committed to the Lord we have no more right to call upon God in our day of trouble than anyone else in our society does. In fact it may be that the average non-Christian is better off when it comes to future economic problems. I doubt there will be any directed persecution of non-Christians as the economy gets worse. I have no doubt that Christians will experience persecution, financial and otherwise, especially since we must take some unpopular stands against sins such as abortion and euthanasia.

The reality of economic survival will rewrite the rules of morality and ethics in America, as it has in other nations that have gone down this road. We have already seen the mentality of the abortionists who make millions from the misery of pregnant women and their unborn children. They have been more than willing to use laws written to control organized crime to prosecute anti-abortion protestors. Regardless of your attitude about the protestors, it is difficult to credibly argue that picketers and protestors are a part of organized crime in America.

Similarly, those who must eventually oppose the removal of people who are not "economically viable" will eventually feel the political impact of the activists. I personally believe that as the economic "pie" gets smaller there will be a "thinning" of people. If you sincerely disagree, you need to read some of the resource materials recommended in the Appendix.

WHAT CAN YOU DO?

The Bible is full of examples of people throughout history whom God warned to prepare for hard times—both spiritually and materially. Most notably were leaders such as Noah, Daniel, Joseph, and David, who were specifically warned about God's impending judgment.

Others, such as Elijah and Nehemiah, were dropped right in the middle of economic hardship with little or no preparation, and yet the Lord still provided for them.

I honestly don't know which, if either, example is applicable to our generation. I sincerely believe that we are headed for some very difficult economic times as a nation. Perhaps God is sending His judgment on us because we have allowed sin to become the norm in our society. Perhaps we are just in a normal economic cycle caused by our own greed and indulgence. In either case, we are guilty of abandoning God's principles—especially those dealing with finances.

The certainty is that we are supposed to be participants in God's plan, not simply idle *observers*. If you even think that the economy is going to experience the problems I have outlined in this book, you'd better do something! But what can be done?

Obviously we each have different needs and adapt to economic changes differently. My 84 year old mother has a different set of financial priorities than I do, and my 44 year old cardiologist friend has a different set of objectives from mine. But we all have at least one financial objective in common: to provide for ourselves and our families if and when this economy collapses. How we do this may vary, depending on our age, income, and even our emotional well-being at the time. But the certainty is: We all need to do something.

GETTING DEBT FREE

I stressed the concept of getting debt free in *The Coming Economic Earthquake*, and I will probably do so in everything else I write, even if Bill Clinton and the Congress solve all of our financial woes, which I sincerely doubt.

Often the point is made that it would be better to be deeply in debt if hyperinflation hits our economy in the future. The theory is that you can repay the loans with cheaper dollars. Unfortunately, the fact is that most people don't have the money to pay off their loans during a hyperinflationary period. It takes virtually all they make just to live.

I talked with several people who lived through the hyperinflation periods in Argentina, Brazil, and Mexico. Without exception, they all related stories of middle income families who were destitute within a few months after the inflation cycle struck. Their incomes never kept pace with inflation, and eventually it took all they made just to buy enough food for the next meal.

Obviously there were people who prospered during these periods, but generally they were the black marketers or the super wealthy who moved their money to another country—usually the United States.

If I could give one single piece of counsel to the majority of people (especially retirees) it would be to pay off your home mortgage if at all possible. In some instances it is even worth having to pay the taxes to withdraw funds from a retirement account to eliminate your home mortgage; although, for those under age 59½, this may not be the wisest thing to do—because of penalties.

I would rather pay the taxes and have access to my own funds . . . than see them eroded in a government security.

I fully realize that even suggesting that someone close out a retirement account to pay off a home mortgage is controversial, especially with financial planners. Many financial planners have told me that they would recommend *The Coming Economic Earthquake* to their clients if it were not for this issue. I also realize that often this does not make the best economic sense. It really boils down to whether you believe an economic crisis is really coming. I *do*.

Perhaps I have been so close to this problem over the last few years that I have lost any objectivity. Nearly everything I read coming out of Washington looks bad, and since the 1992 election it would appear the process is being accelerated.

I can only tell it like I see it. Again I emphasize that I am not a prophet of the Lord. I have a sense of dread about the moral direction of our country, as any Christian should have. But I also have a sense of urgency about the financial direction we're headed.

It's truly hard to see how we will be able to sustain an $8 or $10 trillion debt and deficits that exceed the government's ability to tax or borrow—especially since the economic base of our country is being steadily eroded through taxes, regulations, and litigation.

But again, all I can do is present the facts, make some recommendations, and leave the decisions up to you.

RETAINING PENSION PLANS

It is a remarkable coincidence that the available surplus funds in public and private retirement accounts nearly match the potential deficit in the Social Security system from about the year 2010 to 2040 (excluding the "trust" fund). As the existing tax system is bled of every available dollar to feed the health and income needs of future retirees, I personally believe the attraction of these pension funds will be irresistible to politicians with few other options.

As I said earlier, I do not believe the funds will be stolen or confiscated—at least in the literal sense. Instead, the American public, in my opinion, will be sold a concept similar to that involving the Social Security trust funds today.

At present the government substitutes zero coupon bonds (bonds on which the interest is paid upon maturity) for the actual cash surplus in the Social Security trust account. As I mentioned previously, this effectively substitutes a government IOU for the cash, which is then spent in the general budget.

Does the government actually steal the money? Not in a literal sense. After all, a U.S. government note is securing the assets. But the government already owes more than $4 trillion, and continues to spend $300 to $400 billion a year more than it collects in revenue. So what makes anyone believe they will be able to repay the "loans" when the money is needed?

The same "substitution logic" will work with private retirement accounts as well. In fact, it is altogether possible that, with a good sales job, the government could convince the average American that such a substitution of collateral is in his or her best interest.

One could arguably state that U.S. government securities are the safest investment in the world. Therefore substituting U.S. bonds for mutual funds, annuities, and even bank CDs would help to protect the retirement accounts (sounds good doesn't it?). But the simple truth is, inflation can erode the value of such fixed income assets in short fashion. And how will the government pay when the pension plan holders want to retire? With highly inflated dollars most likely.

If you have an incentive to invest in a tax-deferred account, such as a company pension plan where your employer supplements your contribution, it may make short-term sense to do so. But if you see the economic events that I have outlined falling into place, it would be prudent to stop putting more money into retirement accounts. Personally, I would rather pay the taxes and have access to my own funds to invest than see them eroded in a government security.

An article in *The Wall Street Journal* in 1993 gave me the first hint of government interest in private or public pension accounts. The article said that members of the Clinton economic team were studying the feasibility of requiring some pension money to be made available for inner city development. This is a worthy cause that would be hard to confront without sounding like a heartless bigot— just the thing to "open the door."

If the economy recovers, the national debt is controlled, regulations are brought back into reason, and business begins to boom again (and pigs learn to fly), then there will be no motive for the government to absorb retirement funds. Otherwise, I believe it is a good idea to pay your taxes and invest your own money—or at least a portion of what you plan to use in retirement.

INVESTING

I am always caught between the proverbial "rock and a hard place" when it comes to giving advice about investments for the future. Since this is not a book on how and where to invest, I certainly will not take the space to elaborate on every kind of investment. If you would like to be better informed about investments, especially in our volatile economy, I would recommend any of the books on investing listed in the Appendix.

Ultimately, however, it boils down to whether you believe the economy is going to grow in a fashion similar to that of the previous three to four decades or whether we will see declining economic growth and bigger deficits. Perhaps it actually will be a mix of good and bad economics over the next few years.

All I can tell you is what I gleaned from the materials I reviewed and the conclusions I have drawn. One thing about it though: If you are debt free and reasonably well diversified in your investments, you probably won't fare too badly, irrespective of the economy.

I believe diversification is the key to retaining your assets, and diversity has to extend beyond the borders of the United States. There will be companies in the U.S. that will perform very well over the next decade, while others will fail. As our buying patterns shift, so will the good and bad investments.

A classic example of this shift can be seen in companies such as the Home Depot Corporation. As the patterns of remodeling and home construction have changed, Home Depot has adapted and succeeded in a very competitive business. Investing in innovative companies like this can help compensate for both *deflation*, when families are forced to do many of their own home repairs, and *inflation*, when the company's stock appreciates.

Another example of adaptation and change is the Wal-Mart Corporation. At a time when Americans have become very cost conscious, Wal-Mart has capitalized on the "fast food" mentality in merchandizing. Where other discount retailers were unable to survive in smaller towns, Wal-Mart carved out a very profitable niche.

Unfortunately, companies like Home Depot and Wal-Mart don't create many high-paying jobs, which is a part of the overall problem, but they do generate profits for their investors. The same could have been said of Sears Roebuck and J.C. Penney in the sixties and seventies. But trends change, and the growth companies of one economic era become the casualties of the next.

This perspective is critical when looking at the next six to ten years, especially for those with substantial assets in a single industry (or company). What worked in the seventies may be totally wrong for the nineties and even more so in the twenty-first century.

If you are not particularly adept at evaluating individual stocks, I would suggest diversifying into mutual funds. However, just buying a mutual fund does not guarantee diversification any more than it guarantees profits. You must select the funds with great care and a lot of preparation.

If I were to suggest one source of useful information on the subject of mutual funds it would be my good friend Austin Pryor's book, *Sound Mind Investing*. This book is essential reading for anyone seeking to diversify through mutual funds.

FOREIGN INVESTMENTS

In my opinion, anyone who wants to preserve assets beyond the looming financial collapse in America would do well to seek investments that are not solely in American enterprises or in countries that are very dependent on the American economy (such as Japan, Canada, and Mexico).

Finding such investments is not simple. If it were, virtually everyone would be doing it. You must seek good financial advisors who can help find these investments. Realistically, if you don't have at least $50,000 to invest in foreign investments, the cost will be too high to justify it, except through diversified mutual funds.

In the Appendix I have listed a few financial newsletters that offer counsel in this area. I would always give this caveat: Any advisor can and will be wrong from time to time. If you can't afford to lose the money, don't take the risk!

INSURANCE INVESTMENTS

Perhaps one of the most commonly overlooked areas of investing today is insurance. In past years, prior to the mutual fund revolution, most insurance products were nominal investments at best. But with the growth of mutual funds and the increased competition for investment funds, insurance companies have greatly improved their investment return on both cash value policies and annuities.

Since this is not a book on investing and since this subject has been covered thoroughly in other books, I would encourage you to check the Appendix and get one or more of the books listed.

When looking at insurance products as safe havens for assets in a time of crisis, it is critical to select the companies with great care. Often the companies that offer the highest rates of return are also the riskiest. As I have said in previous books on this topic, the higher the rate of return, usually the higher the risk.

There are some excellent mutual fund and insurance company rating services available (see the Appendix). Before investing either in mutual funds or insurance products, ask the salesperson you're dealing with to show you where the company is rated. I would never accept a company with less than an A+ rating.

Also recheck the rating of the companies you select from time to time. Often it is the investments they hold that affect their ratings. The difference between one percent of interest earned may well jeopardize your savings in a bad economy.

WHAT ABOUT GOLD AND SILVER?

Traditionally precious metals (particularly gold) have been a safe haven in times of economic turmoil. I honestly don't know if this will be true when the U.S. economy faces its biggest crisis, but there is no reason to think otherwise.

There are actually very few investments that can stand the test of both deflation and hyperinflation; gold is one of those (or at least it always has been so in the past). That in no way means I encourage anyone to cash out their stocks and bonds and invest heavily in gold and silver. I don't. But for those with assets in excess of $100,000 it would seem entirely prudent to place some money in precious metals—but not for speculation.

Speculation means that you're buying and selling to make a short-term profit. That works well for a few people, but as I said in *Investing for the Future*, the only people I know who consistently have made money buying and selling precious metals for speculation are the salespeople.

I suggest that if you decide to buy precious metals as a hedge against the future, buy; and then store them in a safe location known only to you and your immediate family. In the thirties the government made the ownership of gold illegal (except for jewelry). It is possible they could do so again if the need arises due to a monetary crisis. However, I don't consider that a high probability, since so few people actually own gold today—unlike the thirties when it was commonly used as currency. Plus, the government now has the legal authority to print fiat money (which they didn't have in the thirties).

We have tremendous resources within Christianity, but they are not being utilized very well right now.

Gold coins, such as the South African Krugerrand, the Canadian Maple Leaf, and the American Eagle would be my choices for holding gold. If worse comes to worst economically, minted coins will have a daily traded value that can be translated into actual purchases.

How much should you hold? That is almost impossible to answer, but certainly no more than 5 to 10 percent of your liquid assets—probably less in most instances. Remember that my suggestion is based purely on the assumption that we will have a severe financial crisis (probably a collapse), and precious metals would be used as a temporary substitute for the rapidly devaluing dollar.

CASH

The question is often asked in conferences, "Should I have cash stashed somewhere for emergencies in case the banks fail?" Again there is no simple way to answer that question for everyone, so the best I can do is give an honest opinion.

If I had the assets to do so, I would have a small amount of cash (not stocks and bonds) stored in a very safe location. In reality, the only situation under which this cash would be needed would be if we have massive bank failures and there were a period of time when cash was not accessible. In reality, most bank cards would probably still be honored and no cash shortage would exist.

But, if the banking system itself fails, due to the lack of consumer confidence (such as happened during the Great Depression), currency could be in short supply. Remember that bank credit cards are only as good as the banks that honor them. The probability of your credit cards not being useable is relatively low; but who really knows in a major crisis?

The loss of a small amount of interest to have some cash available is worth it, in my opinion. Perhaps my thinking in this area is somewhat clouded by all the information I have read about the Great Depression and the banking collapse of the thirties. During that time it was nearly impossible to get cash, even to pay utility bills or buy food. Most banking authorities assure us that can never happen again, but the same thing was assured just prior to the Great Depression also. You simply will have to make this judgment for yourself.

LEAVE THE COUNTRY?

Several Christians I know well already have purchased homes or condominiums outside the U.S., in anticipation of a major financial and social upheaval. That is totally impractical for the vast majority of people, and I would not do so, even if it were financially possible.

I believe that God has placed us here specifically for this time. We need to use wisdom and prepare, but I don't believe we need to run. If we do run, the enemy has won the battle without a fight. (Remember, one guy who ran away from God's plan ended up in the belly of a fish.)

I encourage you to stay and fight, using God's weapons: prayer and planning. There will be many people in need if this economy collapses. We can recapture a lot of the ground we have lost by sharing and helping during this time. Remember what Christ said about our witness: they shall know us by our love. *"A new commandment I give to you, that you love one another, even as I have loved you, that you also love one another. By this all men will know that you are My disciples, if you have love for one another"* (John 13:34–35).

But also remember that it is very difficult to help someone else if you're a part of the problem yourself. Get debt free, do some good sound financial planning now, diversify as much as possible, and get involved at every level now!

If your church doesn't have a working benevolence plan, start one! If your church has never taken a resource survey to determine who can share in a time of real need, you need to do that too. We have tremendous resources within Christianity, but they are not being utilized very well right now. You can't wait until the crisis comes to get prepared. The greater the crisis, the greater the turmoil we will experience.

I honestly pray that none of what I have discussed in this book or *The Coming Economic Earthquake* will ever happen. I pray that the president and the Congress will do what's right to salvage our economy, not what's expedient. But others with stronger convictions have tried and failed. It is my considered opinion that we are too far down the road to economic socialism to turn our economy around. There are simply too many special interest groups eating off the "system" to expect any real changes, and the extremists would rather lose it all than compromise their agenda.

I expect we will simply keep on doing the same old things, hoping for a miracle that will allow us to spend more than we make and blaming someone else for our problems.

God can certainly do a miracle and turn this economy around; after all, He built it in the first place. But, unfortunately, we are going the way of Sodom and Gomorrah—not Nineveh. The economic mess we have created is nothing more than an external indicator of our spiritual condition. As Deuteronomy 28:43–45 says: *"The alien who is among you shall rise above you higher and higher, but you shall go down lower and lower. He shall lend to you, but you shall not lend to him; he shall be the head, and you shall be the tail. So all these curses shall come on you and pursue you and overtake you until you are destroyed, because you would not obey the Lord your God by keeping His commandments and His statues which He commanded you."*

I would willingly suffer through an economic collapse if I thought it would help to restore America's spiritual integrity. God alone knows whether or not a financial disaster will turn this nation around or turn us more toward humanism. Without a change in our economic policies, ultimately the basic laws of economics that God has established in His word will take over and the system will fail.

There is simply no way we can continue down the road of debt and indulgence without paying the price. I just pray that God's people will decide to be a part of the solution, irrespective of what form the correction takes.

The American Dream has not died. It simply is being smothered under a blanket of greed, selfishness, sin, and ignorance. Unless and until you and I decide to get involved and risk everything we have to turn this nation around, it will continue to degrade until, ultimately, the dream *will* disappear. Remember, when the American Dream dies, our children and grandchildren will be the losers.

If this book has helped you to see God's plan a little more clearly, please share it with someone else. Perhaps a copy to your state and national leaders will awaken some of them to the crisis as well.

Truly, we are in a battle for the spiritual and economic future of America. Don't stand by and let this happen. Get involved!

I'll leave you with this story someone sent me right after *The Coming Economic Earthquake* was released.

* * * * *

Many years ago, a drove of wild hogs lived in a big bend of the Ocmulgee River in Georgia. They had survived floods and fires and freezes and hunters and droughts. Hunters bragged when their dogs fought the hogs and returned alive. Finally, one gallant man came by the country store on the river road and asked how he could find the wild hogs.

Several months later the hog-hunting stranger came back to the same store and asked for help to bring out the hogs, which he said he had in a pen out in the swamp. And, people came from miles around to see the captive hogs that all the natives knew couldn't be captured.

"It's very simple," droned the successful stranger. "First I put out some corn. For three weeks, they wouldn't eat it. Then some of the young ones grabbed an ear here and there, and scampered to the underbrush. Soon they were all eating it. They knew that if they didn't, one of the others would.

So then I began building a pen around the corn, a little higher each day. Before long I noticed they were all waiting for me to bring the corn and had stopped grabbing for acorns and roots. I built a trap door. Naturally, they raised Cain when they'd seen I had 'em. But, I can pen any animal on the face of the Earth if I can first get him to depend on me for a free handout."—Tom Anderson (1963)[1]

"Beware, and be on you guard against every form of greed; for not even when one has an abundance does his life consist of his possessions" (Luke 12:15).

Notes

Chapter 3

1. Peter Marshall and David Manuel, *The Light and the Glory*, pp. 106-121.
2. Ibid.
3. Ibid.
4. Eduard Eggleston, *Beginners of a Nation*.

Chapter 4

1. The Tax Foundation.
2. Michael Fumento, "Will New Taxes Erase Red Ink?" *Investor's Business Daily*, 2/10/93.
3. John Merline, "Is OSHA Really Protecting Us?" Ibid., 8/6/92.
4. Robert Genetski, "The True Cost of Government," *The Wall Street Journal*, 2/19/92.
5. David Chilton, "A Bureaucratic Publicity Stunt," *World* (magazine), 1/9/93.

Chapter 5

1. *McCullouch v. Maryland* (1819).
2. *Bob Jones University v. United States*, 461 U.S. at 604 (1983).

Chapter 6

1. Robert W. Lee, "A New OSHA Assault," *The New American*, pp. 21-24.
2. Ibid., p. 19-26.
3. Ibid., p. 23.
4. Ibid., p. 22.
5. "Is OSHA Really Protecting Us?" *Investor's Business Daily*, 8/6/92.
6. Robert W. Lee, "A New OSHA Assault," *The New American*, 12/28/92, p. 23.
7. Jonathan Weil, "Federal Regulations to Prevent Infection of Health Care Workers Will Be Costly," *The Wall Street Journal*, 7/2/92, pp. B1, B5.
8. Ibid.
9. Robert W. Lee, "A New OSHA Assault," *The New American*, 12/28/92, p. 20.
10. *Accident Facts*, National Safety Council (annual).
11. Jay H. Lehr, Editor, "Minerals and Health: The Asbestos Problem," *Rational Readings on Environmental Concerns*, p. 101.
12. Ibid.
13. Ibid.
14. Jonathan H. Adler, "The Consequences of EPA Regulations," The Indianapolis Star, 8/5/92.

Chapter 7

1. Joseph C. Maurer, "Superfund, Super Fraud," *The New American*, 6/1/92, p. 25.
2. Ibid.
3. Neland D. Nobel, "Costs Are Climbing," Ibid., p. 18.
4. "Agreement a Victory for Conservationists," *USA Today*, 10/24/92.
5. Randy Fitzgerald, "Dispatch from the Spotted Owl Front," *Washington Times*, 10/24/92.
6. Joe Wrabek, "They're After Your Property," *The New American*, 6/1/92, pp. 23-24.

Chapter 8

1. Robert Genetski, "The True Cost of Government," *The Wall Street Journal*, 2/19/92.
2. Keith E. Idso, "Greening of the Planet, *The New American*, 6/1/92, p. 10.
3. Hugh W. Ellsaesser, "The Great Greenhouse Debate," *Rational Readings on Environmental Concerns*, p. 408.
4. Ibid., p. 410.
5. Michael Fumento, "Is CO_2 Buildup Really a Crisis?" *Investor's Business Daily*, 6/3/92.
6. P.R. Zimmerman, "Termites: A Potentially Large Source of Atmospheric Methene, Carbon Dioxide, and Molecular Hydrogen," *Science*, 11/5/82, pp. 563-565.
7. Robert W. Lee, "Fury of Mother Nature," *The New American*, 6/1/92, p. 5.
8. Sherwood B. Idso, "Carbon Dioxide and Global Change: End of Nature or Rebirth of the Biosphere?" *Rational Readings on Environmental Concerns*, pp. 419, 422.
9. S. Fred Singer, "Global Climate Change: Facts and Fiction," Ibid., p. 393.
10. Ibid.

Chapter 9

1. S. Fred Singer, "My Adventures in the Ozone Layer," *Rational Readings on Environmental Concerns*, pp. 535-536.
2. Robert W. Lee, "The Evidence Is Thin," *The New American*, 6/1/92, p. 12.
3. *Facts on File*, 12/3/92.
4. Ibid.
5. Ibid.
6. Rogelio A. Maduro and Ralf Schauerhammer, *The Holes in the Ozone Scare*.
7. *Facts on File*, 12/3/92.
8. Robert W. Lee, "The Evidence Is Thin," *The New American*, 6/1/92, p. 12.
9. Julian L. Simon, "Disappearing Species, Deforestation and Data," *Rational Readings on Environmental Concerns*, p. 744.
10. Robert W. Lee, "Lungs of the Earth," *The New American*, 6/1/92, p. 13.

Chapter 10

1. "Sierra Club Pressures California Legislators to Mandate Limits for Family Size," *Christian Home Education News*, Oct/Nov 1992.
2. George G. Reisman, "The Toxicity of Environmentalism," *Rational Readings on Environmental Concerns*, pp. 819-828.
3. Gordon Edwards, "DDT Effects on Bird Abundance and Reproduction," Ibid., p. 195.
4. Ibid.
5. Ibid., p. 197.
6. Ibid., p. 200.
7. Ibid., p. 198.
8. Ibid., p. 203.
9. Richard S. Fawcett, "Pesticides in Ground Water—Solving the Right Problem," Ibid., p. 73-78.
10. J. Gordon Edwards, "The Myth of Food-Chain Biomagnification," Ibid., pp. 125-131.
11. Leonard T. Flynn, "Pesticides: Helpful or Harmful?" Ibid., pp. 61-71.
12. Ibid., p. 65.
13. Ibid., p. 64.
14. Robert M. Devlin, "Regulatory Harassment of U.S. Agriculture," Ibid., p. 80.

Chapter 11

1. Michael Fumento, *Investor's Business Daily*, 7/23/92.
2. Ibid.
3. Ibid.
4. Ibid.
5. Ibid.
6. "Wilson Calls for End to 'Regulatory Quagmire,'" UPI, 2/16/93.
7. David S. Broder, "Letter from California: Chaos in Streets Mirrors State's Economic Ills," *Washington Post*, 2/17/93.

8. Ibid.
9. Charles E. Rice, "Net Loss of Freedom," *The New American*, 6/1/92, p. 29.
10. Ibid.
11. William F. Jasper, "Eco-Villains?" *The New American*, 2/8/93.
12. Ibid.
13. Warren Brookes, "The Strange Case of the Glancing Geese," *Forbes*, 9/2/91.
14. Ibid.
15. Rick Henderson, "The Swamp Thing," *Rational Readings on Environmental Concerns*, p. 796.

Chapter 12

1. Glenn W. Bailey, "Litigation Abuse Is Destroying My Company," *The Wall Street Journal*, 7/15/92, p. A13.
2. Ibid.
3. Peter Huber, *Liability: The Legal Revolution and Its Consequences*, p. 24.
4. Ibid, p. 19.

Chapter 13

1. Spencer Rich, "'Defensive Medicine' Changes Could Save Billions, Study Says," *Washington Post*, 2/3/92.
2. Peter Huber, *Liability: The Legal Revolution and Its Consequences*, p. 104.
3. Paul J. Grant, "Tort Reform in the 1990s," *Quality*, 1/91.
4. Ibid.
5. Ibid.

Chapter 14

1. Rogelio A. Maduro and Ralf Schauerhammer, *The Holes in the Ozone Scare*, pp. 265-266.
2. Jeanne A. Harris, "Planned Parenthood and the Myth of Population Control," *New Dimensions*, 9/10/91, p. 31.
3. John C. Goodman and Aldona Robbins, "The Immigration Solution," National Center for Policy Analysis, Report No. 172, 8/92.
4. Ibid.
5. USPA & IRA Newsletter, Winter, 1/92, p. 8.
6. Summary of the 1991 Annual Report of the Board of Trustees of the Federal Old-Age and Survivors Insurance and Disability Insurance Trust Funds, May 1991.
7. William Drozdiak, "Dutch Pass Euthanasia Measure," *Washington Post*, 2/10/93.
8. "Dutch House Approves Controlled Euthanasia," Reuter (news service), 2/2/93.
9. John C. Goodman and Aldona Robbins, "The Immigration Solution."
10. 1991 Social Security Report, p. 6.
11. Ibid., pp. 10-11.
12. Gary Robbins, Aldona Robbins, John C. Goodman, "How Our Health Care System Works," (Policy Report No. 177), 2/93.

Chapter 16

1. Morgan O. Reynolds, "Why Does Crime Pay?" National Center for Policy Analysis, 12/92.
2. "The USA's Most Troubled Banks," USA *Today*, 5/26/92.

Chapter 18

1. "Budget Policy: Prompt Action Necessary to Avert Long-Term Damage to the Economy," United States General Accounting Office, 6/92.
2. "A Cashless Society," *Arkansas Business*, 5/4/92.
3. "How Our Health Care System Works," National Center for Policy Analysis, 12/92.

Chapter 19

1. Congressional Record, 6/27/62, pp. 11839-11841.
2. Ibid.

Chapter 20

1. *The New American*, 11/6/92.

Appendix
Resources

BOOKS

Bankruptcy 1995: The Coming Collapse of America and How to Stop It, Harry E. Figgie, Jr. with Gerald J. Swanson, Ph.D., Little, Brown and Company, Boston, 1992.

Beginner's of a Nation: A History of the Source and Rise of the Earliest English Settlements in America, Eduard Eggleston, Johnson Reprint Corp., subsidiary of Harcourt Brace Jovanovich, 1970 reprint of 1896 edition. Book out of print.

The Bible's Influence on American History, Tim LaHaye, Master Books, a division of CLP, San Diego, CA.

The Coming Economic Earthquake, Larry Burkett, Moody Press, Chicago, IL, 1991.

The Complete Financial Guide for Couples, Larry Burkett, Victor Books, Wheaton, IL, 1989.

The Complete Financial Guide for Single Parents, Larry Burkett, Victor Books, Wheaton, IL, 1989.

Encyclopedia of Investments, 2nd Edition, Jack P. Friedman, Warren, Gorham & Lamont, Inc., 1991.

Environmental Overkill, Dixy Lee Ray, Regnery Gateway, Washington, D.C., 1993.

The Government Racket: Washington Waste from A to Z, Martin Gross, Bantam Books, 1992.

The Holes in the Ozone Scare: The Scientific Evidence That the Sky Isn't Falling, Rogelio A. Maduro/Ralf Schauerhammer, 21st Century Science Associates, Washington, D.C., 1992.

Investing for the Future, Larry Burkett, Victor Books, Wheaton, IL, 1992.

Liability: The Legal Revolution and Its Consequences, Peter W. Huber, Basic Books, NY, 1988.

The Light and the Glory, David Manuel/Peter Marshall, Fleming H. Revell Company, Old Tappan, NJ, 1977.

Preparing for Retirement, Larry Burkett, Moody Press, Chicago, IL, 1992.

Rational Readings on Environmental Concerns, Dr. Jay H. Lehr, editor, Van Nostrand Reinhold, NY, 1992.

Social Insecurity, Dorcas R. Hardy, Villard Books, a division of Random House, NY, 1991.

Sound Mind Investing, Austin Pryor, Moody Press, Chicago, IL, 1993.

The Thoughtful Christian's Guide to Investing, Gary D. Moore, Zondervan Books, Grand Rapids, MI, 1990.

Trashing the Planet, Dixy Lee Ray with Lou Guzzo, Regnery Gateway, Washington, D.C., 1990.

Your Finances in Changing Times, Larry Burkett, Moody Press, Chicago, IL, 1975.

What Has Government Done to Our Money?, Murry N. Rathbard, The Foundation for Economic Education, 1992.

NEWSLETTERS, FINANCIAL
(offering counsel in foreign investments)

Dessaur's Journal
PO Box 1718
Orleans, MA 02653
508/255-1651
(by subscription only)

Harry Brown Special Reports
PO Box 5586
Austin, TX 78763
800/531-5142
(by subscription only)

The International Harry Schultz Letter
Ferc PO Box 622
Ch-1001, Lausanne
Switzerland
(by subscription only)

NEWSLETTERS, ENERGY

Access to Energy
Box 2298
Boulder, CO 80306

COMPUTER PROGRAM

Write Your Congressman:
Contact Software Int'l Inc
1840 Hutton Dr #200
Carrollton, TX 75006
800/365-0606 or 214/919-9500
Fax 214/919-9760

RESOURCES – ORGANIZATIONS AND INDIVIDUALS

National Taxpayer's Union
325 Pennsylvania Ave SE
Washington, DC 20003
800/TAX-HALT

The Heritage Foundation
214 Massachusetts Ave NE
Washington, DC 20002
202/546-4400

Citizens Against
Government Waste
1301 Connecticut Ave NW Ste 400
Washington, DC 20036
800/USA-DEBT

National Center
for Policy Analysis
12655 N Central Expy Ste 720
Dallas, TX 75243
214/386-6272

Citizens for a Sound Economy
1250 H St NW Ste 700
Washington, DC 20005-3908
202/783-3870

United We Stand America Inc
PO Box 6
Dallas, TX 75221
214/960-9100

Christian Coalition
PO Box 1990
Chesapeake, VA 23327-1990
800/325-4746

Financial assistance for foreign investments:

Global Insights (Diego Veitia's)
International Assets Advisory Corp
201 W Canton Ave Ste 100
Winter Park, FL 32789
800/432-0000, ex. 114
in California 800/243-3355

Mutual Fund Forecaster
Institute of Econometric Research
3471 N Federal Hwy
Fort Lauderdale, FL 33306

Templeton Funds
700 Central Ave
St Petersburg, FL 33701-3628
800/354-9191

Huntington Investments, Inc.
251 S Lake Ave Ste 605
Pasadena, CA 91101
800/354-4111

For "Congressional Spending Study":

National Taxpayers Union (see address above)

Groups that help others organize their communities:

Christian Coalition (see address above)

Project America
16805 Peru Rd
Umatilla, FL 32784
904/669-1295
Contact: Pat Mahoney

Groups that provide factual data on environmental issues:

Science and Environmental
Policy Project (SEPP)
1015 18th St NE Ste 300
Washington, DC 20036

Society for Objective Science (SOS)
PO Box 579
Moorestown, NJ 08057
($50 annual dues)

Insurance company rating services:

A.M. Best Company
Ambest Rd
Oldwick, NJ 08858-9999

Moody's Investor Service Inc
99 Church St
New York, NY 10007-2787

Duff & Phelps Inc
55 E Monroe St Ste 3600
Chicago, IL 60603

Mutual fund services (fees charged for all materials):

Guide to Mutual Funds
(general–all types)
Investment Company Institute
1600 M St NW
Washington, DC 20036

Mutual Fund Values Newsletter
(general–all types)
Morningstar Inc
55 W Jackson Blvd
Chicago, IL 60604

Income and Safety
(income-oriented funds)
Institute of Econometric Research
3471 N Federal Hwy
Fort Lauderdale, FL 33306

No-Load Fund-X
(all types of no-load funds)
235 Montgomery St
San Francisco, CA 94104

Lynch Municipal Bond Advisory Inc
(tax-free fund)
PO Box 25114
Santa Fe, NM 87504

Sound Mind Investing Newsletter
(general–all types)
2337 Glen Eagle Drive
Louisville, KY 40222

Mutual Fund Education Alliance
(general–all types)
The Association of No-Load Funds
520 N Michigan Ave Ste 1632
Chicago, IL 60611

Utility Forecaster
(utility stocks and mutual funds)
1101 King St
Alexandria, VA 22314

Mutual Fund Forecaster
(growth mutual funds)
Institute of Econometric Research
3471 N Federal Hwy
Fort Lauderdale, FL 33306

Senators and members of Congress influential in litigation reform:

House
Rep. James M. Inhofe (OK)
Rep. John Kyl (AZ)
Rep. Jim Saxon (NJ)
Rep. Charles W. Stenholm (TX)

Senate
Sen. Jake Garn (UT)
Sen. Orrin Hatch (UT)
Sen. Strom Thurmond (SC)

State policy groups (listed alphabetically by state):
* Denotes member of the new State Policy Network, which all state groups have
been invited to join.

Mr. Michael Ciamarra, Exec. Dir.
* ALABAMA FAMILY ALLIANCE
PO Box 59468
Birmingham, AL 35259
205/870-9900

Mr. Michael Sanera, President
* ARIZONA INSTITUTE
FOR PUBLIC POLICY
2700 S Woodlands Village Blvd
#300-329
Flagstaff, AZ 86001
602/526-2597

Michael Block, President
* BARRY GOLDWATER
INSTITUTE FOR
PUBLIC POLICY RESEARCH
The Valley Bank Center–Concourse
201 N Central Ave
Phoenix, AZ 85004
602/256-7018

Mr. Lance Izumi,
Senior Policy Analyst
GOLDEN STATE CENTER FOR
PUBLIC POLICY
1211 H St #A
Sacramento, CA 95814
916/446-7924

Mr. John Andrews, Jr., President
* INDEPENDENCE INSTITUTE
14142 Denver W Pky #101
Golden, CO 80401
303/279-6536

Mr. Laurence Cohen, Director
YANKEE INSTITUTE FOR
PUBLIC POLICY STUDIES
117 New London Tpke
Glastonbury, CT 06033
203/633-8188

Mr. John H. Lopez, Exec. Dir.
DELAWARE PUBLIC
POLICY INSTITUTE
One Commerce Center #200
12th & Orange Sts
Wilmington, DE 19801
302/655-7221

Dr. John W. Cooper, President
* JAMES MADISON INSTITUTE
FOR PUBLIC POLICY STUDIES
PO Box 13894
Tallahassee, FL 32317-3894
904/386-3131

Mr. Matthew J. Glavin, President
* GEORGIA PUBLIC
POLICY FOUNDATION
2900 Chamblee-Tucker Rd Bldg 6
Atlanta, GA 30341-4128
404/455-7600

Mr. Michael Finch,
Executive Director
THE HEARTLAND INSTITUTE
IN ILLINOIS
634 S Wabash Second Fl
Chicago, IL 60605
312/427-3060

Mr. Michael R. Pence, President
* INDIANA POLICY REVIEW
Chamber Bldg Ste 615
320 N Meridian
Indianapolis, IN 46204
317/236-7360

Mr. David Tuerck, President
* BEACON HILL INSTITUTE FOR
PUBLIC POLICY RESEARCH
Suffolk University
8 Ashburton Pl
Boston, MA 02108-2770
617/573-8750

Ms. Virginia Straus, Director
PIONEER INSTITUTE
21 Custom House St #801
Boston, MA 02110
617/261-9755

Mr. Thomas Shull,
Executive Director
* HEARTLAND INSTITUTE
IN MICHIGAN
2525 Penobscot
Detroit, MI 48226
313/961-1950

Mr. Lawrence Reed, President
* THE MACKINAC CENTER
119 Ashman St
PO Box 568
Midland, MI 48640
517/631-0900

Mr. Mitchell B. Pearlstein, President
* CENTER OF THE
AMERICAN EXPERIMENT
2342 Plaza VII
45 S Seventh St
Minneapolis, MN 55402
612/338-3605

Mr. R. Emmett McAuliffe,
Executive Director
* HEARTLAND INSTITUTE
IN MISSOURI
2458 Old Dorsett Rd #230
Maryland Heights, MO 63043
314/344-1100

Mr. Steven Schlosstein, President
CENTER FOR THE NEW EAST
Box 425
Princeton, NJ 08542-0425
602/924-4290

Mr. Thomas W. Carroll, President
* EMPIRE FOUNDATION
FOR POLICY RESEARCH
301 Hamilton St
Albany, NY 12210
518/432-4444

Mr. Marc Rotterman, President
* THE JOHN LOCKE
FOUNDATION
3401 Gresham Lake Rd
Raleigh, NC 27615
919/847-2690; FAX 919/847-8371

Ms. Judith Brenneke, Vice-President
* HEARTLAND INSTITUTE
IN OHIO
3941 Orchard Rd
Hights, OH 44121
216/381-9250

Mr. Terry Allen, Executive Director
* RESOURCE INSTITUTE
OF OKLAHOMA
26 NW 7th St
Oklahoma, OK 73102
405/239-6700

Mr. Steve Buckstein, President
* CASCADE POLICY INSTITUTE
813 SW Alder Ste 707
Portland, OR 97205
503/242-0900

Mr. Don Eberly, President
* THE COMMONWEALTH
FOUNDATION FOR PUBLIC
POLICY ALTERNATIVES
600 N Second St #400
Harrisburg, PA 17101
717/231-4850

Mr. William C. Myers,
Executive Vice President
* SOUTH CAROLINA
POLICY COUNCIL
1518 Washington St
Columbia, SC 29201
803/779-5022

Mr. Fritz Steiger,
Executive Vice President
* TEXAS PUBLIC
POLICY FOUNDATION
8626 Tesoro Dr. #810
San Antonio, TX 78217
512/829-7138

Mr. Robert Williams, President
EVERGREEN
FREEDOM FOUNDATION
PO Box 552
Olympia, WA 98507
206/956-3482

Mr. John Carlson, President
WASHINGTON INSTITUTE
FOR POLICY STUDIES
223 105th St NE #202
Bellevue, WA 98004
206/454-3057

Mr. Kirby Brant, President
* HEARTLAND INSTITUTE
IN WISCONSIN
PO Box 53
Watertown, WI 53094
414/261-1430

Mr. James Miller, Exec. Dir.
WISCONSIN POLICY
RESEARCH INST.
3107 N Shepard Ave
Milwaukee, WI 53211
414/963-0600

Index

Abortion, 12, 181, 266
AIDS, 82
    effect on Social Security, 187
American Dream
    disappearing, 13, 27, 47, 81, 140, 213
    defined, 15, 23, 27
    goal of, 23
    how attorneys are destroying, 157, 254
    how doctors are destroying, 254
    how government is destroying, 73, 81
    in Colonial times, 46
    spiritual side of, 29, 37, 239, 241, 262, 276
Americans with Disabilities Act, (ADA), 61
Automotive industry, 141, 165

Baby boomers, 181, 184, 186

Balanced budget, 11, 17, 52
    amendment, 246
Bank failures, 208, 216
Bankruptcy, national, 49
Biomagnification, 130, 133
Bradley, General Omar, 263
Bradord, William, 42
Budget act, 54
Bush, George, 61, 82, 148, 205
    accumulated debt, 210
    domestic policy, 210
Business, small, 80, 146, 200
    free enterprise, 23, 46, 78, 244
    funding, 244
    migration, 143, 242
Byrd, Senator Robert
    speech, 259

Carter, Jimmy, 205
Cash, storing, 274

CERCLA (Superfund Law), 92
  EBA report, 95
Christians
  as scapegoats, 37, 266
  behavior, 265
  opposition to, 13, 239
  values, 12
Church
  benevolence plan, 275
Churchill, Winston, 28
Clean Air Act, 96, 109, 146
Clean Water Act, 96, 146
Cleveland, Grover, 21, 47, 205
Clinton, Bill, 24, 40, 61, 190, 194,
      267
  increased taxes and spending, 48,
      52, 210
Collapse, economic and social, 48
Communism, 48, 57, 243
Congress, term limits for, 212, 246
Congressional spending, 10, 209
Constitution, 20, 67, 70
Corporate structure, 80
Crockett, Davy, 21, 205

DDT, 122, 130
Debt, personal, 267, 275
  reduced spending, 54
Declaration of Independence, 44, 262
Deficit
  acceleration of, 218
  cutting spending, 54
  federal, 11
  monetizing, 215
  plan to reduce, 245
  private business sector, 54
  reduction program, 10
  repayment, 18
  runaway spending, 250
Deflation, 215, 271
Deforestation, 99, 123
Disabled, 61

Economic
  conservatives, 255
  crisis, 40, 213

disasters, 139, 182
down cycles, 242
erosion, 211
growth, 56, 65, 204, 251
growth stimulus, 55
recovery, 55
survival, 51, 266
Economy
  depression, 211
  deteriorating, 210
  potential problems, 18, 51, 204
  "stumbling", 215
  threats to, 51, 208
  what to do, 218, 250, 252, 264,
      267, 274
Education, 266
Endangered Species Act, 99
  California Delta smelt, 102
  spotted butterfly, 101
  spotted owl, 98, 101
Entitlement Programs, 216, 240
  controlled growth of, 205, 218
  danger of, 183, 211
  survival attitude, 253
Entitlements, 67, 211, 240
  economic reform, 211
Environmental
  bald eagle, 130
  deforestation, 99, 123
  Endangered Species Act, 99, 101
  issues, 56, 78, 91, 105, 130, 144,
      252
  myths, 110, 113
  spotted owl, 98, 101, 252
  PCBs, 130, 152
  peregrine falcon, 131
  personal rights, 263
  pollution, 57, 60, 108, 139, 144
  protection, 251
  regulations, 56, 84, 139, 144
Environmental Protection Agency,
      (EPA), 58, 77, 80, 90, 114,
      121, 142, 146, 152, 256
  asbestos regulations, 86, 158
  ban on DDT, 122, 130
  Clean Air Act, 96, 109, 146

Clean Water Act, 96, 146
superfund sites, 92
toxic waste, 93, 124
wetlands, 97, 147
Euthanasia, 185, 266
"carefulness requirements", 186
in the Netherlands, 185

FDA, 178
FDIC, 67, 216
Family values, 12, 20
Federal debt (see Deficit)
Federal regulations, 59, 69
environment control, 72, 96
EPA, 58, 77, 90
OSHA, 77
worker safety, 79, 81, 84
Federal Reserve, 69, 215
Franklin, Benjamin, 70, 260
Free enterprise system, 23, 41, 78
Freedom, threat to, 67
Future (fiction), a view of, 222

Get rich quick mentality, 169
GI Bill, 31, 69
Global market, 140, 142
Global warming, 58, 60, 105, 109, 142
God
in control, 219
provides needs, 220, 239
returning to, 239, 276
Government, federal
and industry, 17, 23
as our hope, 16
as provider, 20, 22, 72
banking control, 206
central, 65, 67
congressional spending, 10
consumes available capital, 242
control, 14, 56, 65, 72, 89, 206
employees, 247
empowered by Constitution, 72
excessive control, 65, 72
in a major collapse, 48
in conflict with business, 17

infrastructure programs, 53, 211, 214
intervention, 22
lower tax revenue, 54
monetize debt, 72
"political correctness", 74
regulating businesses, 23, 72
regulations, 56, 81, 84, 113, 204
regulatory control, 61, 141, 251
social spending, 211
spending, 210, 254
spending cuts, 52, 54
tax revenues, 53
trends, 65
ultimate financial crisis, 211
using retirement accounts, 192
Government, local and state, 255
balanced budgets, 11, 17, 52
controlling tax structure, 257
IRS regulations, 74, 77
leadership in, 257
regulatory laws, 61, 145
restrictions to churches, 73
taxes, 258
Grace Commission, 246
Gramm-Rudman, 52, 205, 247
Great Depression, 16, 66, 145, 215, 217, 242, 274
Great Society, 22
Greenhouse theory, 108

Health care
changes to, 174
costs, 170, 185, 204
economic reform, 218
financial burden of, 189
for older people, 185
for terminally ill, 185
government controlled, 189, 211
rate of inflation in, 173
Heritage
economic, 40
moral and social, 16
national, 16, 168
spiritual, 28, 259
The Pilgrim's Dream, 41

The Colonial Dream, 44
Housing development, 256
Hyperinflation, 16, 211, 215, 267

Immigration solution, 190, 204
    problems with, 212
Industrialization, 140, 204
Inflation, 216, 245, 271
Inflationary cycle, 216
Infrastructure, 53, 214
Inheritance, 23, 25
Insurance
    health-care, 185, 253
    investments, 272
    mentality, 185
Interdiction
    communism, 48
    Hitler, Adolf, 48
    Mao Tse-tung, 48
Investing
    diversification, 270
    foreign, 271
    insurance products, 272
    mutual funds, 271
    precious metals, 272
    speculative, 273

Jefferson, Thomas, 20, 47, 70, 193,
        260, 262
Johnson, Lyndon, 22

Lincoln, Abraham, 47, 193, 260
Litigation
    in health care, 170
    reform, 161, 165, 179, 252
    result of, 157, 170, 204
    tort, 155, 169, 177

Materialism
    American way of life, 214
Medicare/Medicaid, 211
    Catastrophic Coverage Act, 203
    impact of AIDS on, 82, 187
    reform, 24, 253
Money, printing, 72, 215
Morality, 14, 29, 241, 261, 266

National banking system
    greatest danger, 216
National Center for Policy Analysis
        (NCPA), 187
New Deal, 22, 66

Occupational Safety and Health
        Administration, (OSHA),
        77, 142, 152, 256
    employee safety, 79, 81, 84
    infectious disease regulations, 83
Ozone depletion, 60, 113

Pension plans
    failed, 216
    government interest in, 269
    retaining, 269
Perot, Ross, 10, 21, 207
Personal rights, 29, 146
Pesticides, 129
Pharmaceuticals, 176
Political correctness, 74, 264
Population control, 13, 129, 181, 191
Pork barrel economics
    spending, 202

Reagan, Ronald, 12, 24, 208
    accumulated debt, 210
    deregulations, 59
    Grace Commission, 246
    tax and spending cuts, 209
Regulations (also see "Environ-
        mental")
    activist's agenda, 113
    by litigation, 85, 165
    cost in jobs and living standards,
        60
    for business and personal conduct,
        73
    for handicapped, 57, 61
    IRS, 261
    local and state, 146, 256
    private enterprise, 23, 78, 85, 146
        244
    relating to world hunger, 127
    restrictive, 97, 113

Retirement
   accounts, 184, 270
   affected by baby boomers, 183, 190
   pension laws, 193
Roosevelt, Franklin, 66
   direct economic stimulus, 55
   economic policies, 69
   government intervention, 21
   public works programs, 67

Salvation, evidence of, 238
Scenario of future, 222
Separation of Church and State, 68,
      73, 258
Situational ethics, 184, 240
Social Security
   availability of, 183
   deficit in, 183, 269
   feeding deficits within, 184
   future of, 183, 187
   immigration solution, 190
   pooled fund solution, 191
   reducing, 203
   retirement benefits, 184
   spending trust funds, 184, 192
   trust accounts, 186, 191
Solutions
   local, 255
   national, 237
Spending cuts, 52, 54, 245
   government, 11, 20, 210, 211, 244
   personal, 54, 241
Spiritual
   heritage, 28, 259
   problems, 20
Superfund law (see CERCLA)
Superfund sites, 92
Supreme Court, 70, 259

Tax
   exemptions, 74

luxury, 54
   reform, 244
   shelters, 54
Taxes
   increasing, 53, 189, 194
   local and state, 255, 257
   to fund health care system, 189
Third World, 178
Time traveler story, 33
Tort litigation, 155, 169, 177
   explosion, 218
   reform, 178
   system, 157
Trends, economic, 65

Unemployment, 211

Values
   changing, 20
   situational ethics, 284, 240

War
   Civil, 16, 69, 176
   Korean, 31
   on pesticides, 129
   on world hunger, 127
   Revolutionary, 21, 69
   Vietnam, 31
   World War I, 11, 20, 69, 238
   World War II, 12, 28, 30, 48, 68,
      184, 208, 215, 238
Washington, George, 21, 44, 260
Welfare, 20, 22, 56, 181
Wetlands, 97, 147
What can be done, 218, 250, 252,
      264, 267, 274
World hunger, 127

Zero defects, 60, 78
   risk, 160

Editing:
Adeline Griffith
Christian Financial Concepts
Gainesville, Georgia

Jacket Design
Joe Ragont Studios
Rolling Meadows, Illinois

Printing and Binding:
Arcata Graphics Martinsburg
Martinsburg, West Virginia

Jacket Printing:
Phoenix Color Corporation
Long Island City, New York